High Probability
Trading
Strategies

Founded in 1807, John Wiley & Sons is the oldest independent publishing company in the United States. With offices in North America, Europe, Australia and Asia, Wiley is globally committed to developing and marketing print and electronic products and services for our customers' professional and personal knowledge and understanding.

The Wiley Trading series features books by traders who have survived the market's ever changing temperament and have prospered—some by reinventing systems, others by getting back to basics. Whether a novice trader, professional or somewhere in-between, these books will provide the advice and strategies needed to prosper today and well into the future.

For a list of available titles, please visit our Web site at www.WileyFinance.com.

High Probability Trading Strategies

Entry to Exit Tactics for the Forex, Futures, and Stock Markets

ROBERT C. MINER

WILEY

John Wiley & Sons, Inc.

Published by John Wiley & Sons, Inc., Hoboken, New Jersey.
Published simultaneously in Canada.

For general information on our other products and services or for technical support, please contact our Customer Care Department within the United States at (800) 762-2974, outside the United States at (317) 572-3993 or fax (317) 572-4002.

Wiley publishes in a variety of print and electronic formats and by print-on-demand. Some material included with standard print versions of this book may not be included in e-books or in print-on-demand. If this book refers to media such as a CD or DVD that is not included in the version you purchased, you may download this material at http://booksupport.wiley.com. For more information about Wiley products, visit www.wiley.com.

Library of Congress Cataloging-in-Publication Data:

Miner, Robert C.
    High probability trading strategies : entry to exit tactics for the Forex, futures,
and stock markets / Robert Miner.
        p. cm. – (Wiley trading series)
        Includes bibliographical references and index.
        ISBN 978-0-470-18166-9 (cloth); ISBN 978-1-118-02635-9 (ebk); ISBN 978-0-470-40339-6 (ebk);
ISBN 978-0-470-40340-2 (ebk)
        1. Speculation.   2. Futures.   3. Stocks.   4. Foreign exchange market.
        5. Investment analysis.   I. Title.
    HG6015.M56   2009
        332.64–dc22   2008017697

Printed in the United States of America

SKY10082523_082224

Contents

Foreword

I met Robert Miner not long after the market crash of October 1987. I reluctantly went to a trading conference in downtown Chicago where he was one of many speakers. I was reluctant to attend the conference because I had recently lost my cushy job at the Chicago Mercantile Exchange where I had been managing a floor trading operation, working with institutional clients in the financial futures markets. Fortunately, I decided to attend the conference, which ended up opening the door to whole new career in the trading industry.

I had heard about Fibonacci retracements before, but only as they were applied to the price axis of the market. I remember the exact area of the room where I sat when Bob gave his presentation and illustrated, among other things, a very simple example of Fibonacci applied to the *time* axis of the market. I swear it was just like the proverbial light bulb went on above my head, and part of me knew that this was the key to my future. It was an "aha" moment.

I was so fascinated by Bob's presentation, I made my way over to his booth in the expo hall and told him how much I enjoyed his presentation. This led to shooting a couple of games of pool over cocktails, and that was the beginning of our friendship that has lasted over the years.

When I started studying Bob's work, I was so fascinated that I would work on my paper charts with a pencil, calculator, and proportional divider every chance I got. I did not own a computer at the time. Through this almost daily ritual with my hand updated paper charts, I would prove to myself how powerful were the strategies he taught. I started sharing some of my results with some friends and clients. It worked so well, some of them started offering to pay me for my analysis. I studied everything Bob had to teach over the years and perfected my trade strategies. All this eventually led to opening my own market analysis and trade recommendation business, Synchronicity Market Timing.

Without Bob Miner, I would not be enjoying the very successful career I have today. Most of what I've learned about technical analysis and trade strategies, I learned from Bob. I am forever grateful for what he has taught me over the years as I can truly say I *love* my work, and they even pay me for doing it!

Thanks Bob!!
Carolyn Boroden
aka FibonacciQueen, www.fibonacciqueen.com

Preface

igh Probability Trading Strategies is one of the few trading books from which you can learn a complete trade management plan from entry to exit.

If you are a new trader or one who has not yet found consistent success in the business of trading futures, stocks, or forex, you will learn specific trade strategies, from how to identify high probability trade conditions, to the specific entry and stop price, through exit strategies that are designed to maximize the gain from any trend. If you are an experienced and successful trader, I know that you will recognize several key strategies to incorporate into your existing trade plan that should immediately increase your success.

I've been teaching these strategies for over 20 years to traders around the world. I've refined and simplified the strategies over the years to get to the core of the most important information a trader needs to make a trading decision and manage the trade. The combination of book and CD will provide more information in a better learning environment than I can offer in an expensive weekend workshop.

You will learn my unique approach to the four main factors of technical analysis, including Multiple Time Frame Momentum setups and the one main guideline to recognize the pattern structure of trends and corrections. Plus you will learn my Dynamic Price and Time Strategies to identify *in advance* the probable price and time targets for trends and corrections. You will learn two powerful and logical objective entry techniques and how to manage a trade for short- and intermediate-term gains through the trade exit in any market and any time frame. I've also devoted an entire chapter called "Real Traders, Real Time" (Chapter 8) with trade examples submitted by my past students, who show how they apply every day the strategies you learn in this book to markets from around the world.

The video CD takes the learning experience to a much higher level than any book is able to do on its own. In the video CD, you will see more examples of how to apply the *High Probability Trading Strategies* for many markets and time frames in bar-by-bar and step-by-step recordings. Be sure to read the book first, cover to cover, before

---

Publisher's note: Wiley publishes in a variety of print and electronic formats and by print-on-demand. If this book refers to media such as a CD or DVD that is not included in the version you purchased, you may download this material at http://booksupport.wiley.com. For more information about Wiley products, visit www.wiley.com.

watching the video CD. The CD material assumes you have learned the techniques and strategies taught in the book.

I'm sure *High Probability Trading Strategies* and the accompanying video CD will become one of your most important trading reference materials. It may even become the complete trading plan you have been looking for to manage trades from entry to exit for any market and any time frame.

PART ONE

High Probability Trading Strategies for Any Market and Any Time Frame

CHAPTER 1

High Probability Trade Strategies for Any Market and Any Time Frame

This book is unique. Unlike most trading books, it will teach you a complete trading plan from entry to exit. Not a few well-chosen examples of isolated trade setups and strategies, but exactly how to recognize optimal trade conditions, objective entry strategies with the exact entry and exit price, and how to manage the trade with stop-loss adjustments to the trade exit.

The majority of trading books focus on a few techniques and show a plethora of carefully chosen examples to support whatever is being taught. Some of the phrases often used are "You could have bought around here or taken profit around here"; "depending on whether you are a conservative or aggressive trader, you could do . . . (this or that)"; "markets usually fluctuate around the volatility band, which is a good place to buy or sell"; and lots more nonspecific statements.

Brokers don't take orders "around this or that price level." They only take specific price orders. There is no such thing as a conservative or aggressive trader. There are only traders who either follow a trading plan or don't. To maybe do this or that "around" a volatility band or any other indicator or chart position is not a trade strategy. A trade strategy is a specific action to take, including the specific buy and sell price. In other words, worthwhile instruction will teach you *exactly* what to do and how and when to do it.

While many trading books do teach some useful specific trading techniques or at least provide some ideas to explore, it is very unusual for a book or any other type of trading course to teach exactly what to do, from how to recognize a trading opportunity, to the exact entry and stop price, and how to manage the trade until it is closed out.

Publisher's note: Wiley publishes in a variety of print and electronic formats and by print-on-demand. If this book refers to media such as a CD or DVD that is not included in the version you purchased, you may download this material at http://booksupport.wiley.com. For more information about Wiley products, visit www.wiley.com.

That is what this book does. It will teach you a high probability trade plan with specific strategies from entry to exit. Most important, it will teach you how to think about the four key factors of momentum, pattern, price, and time; how to recognize what is useful and relevant market information that can be used to make a specific trade decision; and then how to execute the trade decisions from entry to exit.

A book is a static medium. It takes a lot of screen captures of charts to illustrate a trade campaign from entry to exit, no matter what market or time frame is used. Thus, this book has a lot of charts. I've taken care that the information on each chart should be quickly and easily understood. Most charts include text comments pointing out the most relevant information based on what I teach you throughout the book.

When John Wiley & Sons approached me regarding this book, I insisted I would do it only if it included an instructional CD where I could record additional examples, bar by bar, using trading software training mode. They agreed, and the addition of the CD trade examples makes this package a complete learning experience.

Don't rush to watch the CD. The book provides all the background for what is shown in the CD. In the CD recordings, I assume you have read the book, cover to cover. I assume you are familiar with all the terminology, trade strategies, and book examples. You will be lost watching the CD if you haven't first read the book. The CD is not a review or regurgitation of the material in the book. Rather, it provides the medium to be able to show more examples but in a bar-by-bar recording, so you can better see how the strategies taught in the book are put into practice day by day and bar by bar for many different markets and many different time frames.

I believe this book and CD combination provides a better learning experience than even most live workshops, because you can study all the material at your own pace and replay the recorded CD examples over and over.

ANY MARKET, ANY TIME FRAME

The trade strategies you will learn in this book may be used for any actively traded market and any time frame. Stocks, exchange-traded funds (ETFs), futures, and Forex examples are used. The same market structure is made day in and day out in all of these markets and in all time frames, from monthly to intraday data. If an example is not a market or time frame you typically trade, ignore the symbol and focus on what is to be learned. The strategy taught will apply to all markets and time frames.

CONDITIONS WITH A HIGH PROBABILITY OUTCOME

The objective of any trade strategy is to identify conditions with a high probability outcome and acceptable capital exposure. You will learn the four main factors of any market position and how to identify if each is in a position for a high probability outcome. When a market is set up for change from four different perspectives, the trader has an enormous edge, much more so than if only one or two of the factors are in the same position. To win in the business of trading, just as in any other business, you must have an edge. The edge you learn in this book is to recognize when a market is in a position to complete a correction or a trend so you can enter a trade at the end of a correction in the direction of the trend or in the very early stages of the new trend and sell in the very late stages (often within one or two bars of the low or high).

Just as a farmer must know the optimal time to plant and harvest a crop, the trader must know the optimal time to buy and sell a position. Buying or selling too early or too late can result in, at worst, unacceptable losses or, at best, not maximizing the return from a position. The trader must clearly understand the relevant information about the market position to recognize the optimal conditions to buy or sell.

Markets can seem very complex. The plethora of relatively inexpensive trading software available with hundreds of studies and indicators can overwhelm a trader with often conflicting information, making it difficult to focus on the relevant information needed to make a confident trade decision.

The high probability approach taught in this book recognizes four market perspectives: multiple time frame momentum, simple pattern recognition, price reversal targets, and time reversal targets. The information from any one of these four perspectives could be overwhelming. But in this book, you will learn how to focus on just those few bits of relevant information from each perspective that should quickly identify both the market position and whether a market is in a high probability position for a trade.

I rarely do live workshops, but when I do I present a special exercise at the end of the session. I tell the students that I can apply what I have taught them to any symbol, including stocks, ETFs, futures, or Forex, and it will take three minutes or less to process all of the information needed to identify whether the symbol is in a high probability position for a trade setup or what that particular market must do to become a high probability trade setup. I have the students write any symbol on a piece of note paper. We collect them in a hat and I draw them out one by one. In less than three minutes, I apply everything I have taught them and arrive at a conclusion what is the probable market position of the symbol and the specific trade strategies. You, too, will be able to do this after you have studied this book and viewed the CD examples.

If a trader focuses on just the limited, relevant information needed to make a high probability trade decision, the chance of success is great.

LEADING AND LAGGING INDICATORS

The vast majority of traders use only *lagging indicators* for their trade strategies. Every indicator or oscillator in every trading platform and charting program is a lagging indicator. A lagging indicator will show you how the current market position relates to past data for the lookback period, but has little predictive capabilities. A *momentum indicator* can be useful to help identify trend direction and trade execution if used with the unique multiple time frame momentum strategy you will learn in this book. But the momentum strategy is still only useful when it is part of a trading plan that includes leading indicators.

A *leading indicator* will prepare you in advance for probable trade conditions. Using my unique approach to dynamic time and price strategies, developed over the past 20 years, you will learn how to identify *in advance* the probable price and time target zones not just for support and resistance, but, more importantly, for trend reversal. We call these price and time strategies leading indicators because they identify *in advance* conditions with a high probability outcome. If a market fulfills those conditions, a trade setup is made. I know they will become a very important part of your trading plan when you learn the power of being prepared in advance for specific price and time targets for trend reversal.

WHAT YOU WILL LEARN IN THIS BOOK AND VIDEO CD

In this book, you will first learn the four dimensions of market position: multiple time frame momentum, pattern, price, and time. Each factor provides an important piece of information you will use to make a trading decision. A trading plan that does not include these four market dimensions is missing a big piece of the market puzzle and is much less effective than one that includes all four dimensions.

Most readers are familiar with momentum studies, also called *indicators* or *oscillators*. A momentum indicator by itself is not of much practical use to the trader. All momentum studies are lagging indicators. They are great for showing you the current market position relative to the past, but are not of much help in pointing to the probable trend position in the future—unless you use them in the unique way you will learn in Chapter 2. Chapter 2 presents a momentum strategy used by few traders that will teach you how to use the lagging momentum indicators as a powerful technique as a filter for trade direction and execution setups. This multiple time frame momentum strategy will become the most useful and practical momentum application you can add to your trading plan.

Elliott wave pattern analysis has been so overcomplicated and misinterpreted over the years that many traders avoid it like the plague. I don't blame them. In Chapter 3, you will learn the simple guidelines based on Elliott wave structures to identify three frequent patterns for all markets and all time frames. One simple guideline will instantly reveal if a market should be in a trend or countertrend. This simple guideline itself should make a big difference in your trading results. It is critical for the trader to recognize whether the current market condition is part of a correction or trend, and, more important, if the correction or trend is in a position to be complete. This information can be a very important part of your trading plan and help prepare you for market reversals of any time frame. After you have learned the pattern guidelines in Chapter 3, you will be able to quickly recognize the probable structure position of any market and any time frame.

Most traders are familiar with Fibonacci (Fib) price retracements. Like a single time frame momentum study, they are not of much practical use by themselves to make a trade decision. Chapter 4 teaches you how to identify *in advance* which retracement level is likely to complete a correction of any time frame. It also teaches you how to project the probable trend targets in advance to be prepared for the price level at which a trend should be complete. You will also learn some new ratios that are not a part of the Fib ratio series that are a key to correction and trend price targets. Once you learn my Dynamic Price Strategies in Chapter 4, you should be prepared not just for temporary support and resistance levels, but for the specific price levels for trend and countertrend reversals.

Market timing in its true sense—identifying specific time target zones for trend change in any time frame—is rarely used by most traders. W. D. Gann taught many years ago, "When time is up, change is inevitable." Chapter 5 teaches you my unique Dynamic Time Strategies I've developed over the past 20 years, which will allow you to project the probable minimum and maximum time targets for trend reversal. You will also learn how to project time bands in any time frame to target a relatively narrow time range with a high probability for trend change. Practical market timing should be an important part of every trader's plan.

After you have learned these four key factors of market position that will prepare you to recognize optimal trade conditions, Chapter 6 teaches you two completely objective entry strategies and how to quickly determine the maximum position size for any trade. The strategies you learn in Chapter 6 will completely eliminate any guesswork on what price you should enter a market and what should be the stop-loss price. Most important, you will learn what all successful traders know: The proper position size for any trade setup on any time frame is one of the most important keys to long-term success for the business of trading.

Earlier I promised that you would learn how to manage a trade from entry to exit. Chapter 7 is the heart of this book, as far as I'm concerned. This is where you learn to apply all of the practical strategies, from recognizing high probability trade setups, to the specific entry strategy, stop-loss adjustment, and exit strategy. In other words, Chapter 7 teaches you how to manage a trade from entry to exit. You will learn how to make confident and logical decisions throughout the trade process.

Chapter 8 gives trade examples from students of my live and online workshops, educational CD programs, and other educational trading material I've produced over the past 20 years. These examples by other real-world traders show you how what you learn in this book has been put into practice every day in many different markets and many different time frames.

Chapter 9 offers more insight into the business of trading, what it takes to be successful, and a whole lot more. A lot of misleading information and sometimes just plain misinformation has been published about the business of trading. You'll find in this chapter that I don't pull any punches. If you thought I was a bit opinionated as you read through the earlier chapters, wait until you get to Chapter 9. I want you to be successful, and Chapter 9 will help keep you on track on the road to a successful trading business.

The video CD included with this book is an important part of the learning experience. Again, do not play the CD until you have read the book cover to cover. It will be a valuable resource, but you will only get the full benefit if you have first familiarized yourself with all the background material in the book.

LET'S GET STARTED

It's time to get started and learn *High Probability Trading Strategies: From Entry to Exit for the Futures, Forex, and Stock Markets*. We begin with a unique approach to momentum strategies, the multiple time frame momentum strategy in Chapter 2.

CHAPTER 2

Multiple Time Frame Momentum Strategy

An Objective Filter to Identify High Probability Trade Setups

The Multiple Time Frame (MTF) Momentum Strategy is the most powerful approach I've discovered in over 20 years to filter any market and any time frame for trade direction and execution. The MTF Momentum Strategy is a key factor to the trade plan that identifies high probability trade setups with minimal capital exposure.

Just about every trading book or course will emphasize that you always want to "trade with the trend." It's great advice. If you are always trading with the trend, you should mount up some very impressive gains.

Two big questions are usually not clearly answered: "How do you objectively identify trend direction?" and "Is the trend in the early or late stages?"

In almost every trading book and course I've seen over the past 20 or more years, the trading educators show many after-the-fact examples of how their trend indicator identified the trend direction *long after the trend was established.* It is easy to show a trend on any chart long after the trend is established. But how do we identify trend direction in the early stages? How do we identify when an established trend is in the later stages and in a position to make a trend reversal? Without some approach to help identify where within the trend the market likely is, typical trend analysis will usually be too early or too late to be useful over time.

It is easy to fill a book with after-the-fact examples of trends. Trendlines, moving averages, channels, momentum indicators, and many other techniques can show the trend on historic data. Unfortunately, *none* of these techniques can reliably alert you to the beginning stages of a new trend or whether a trend is in its final stages. They can only identify an established trend, usually long after the trend is established and the optimum entry is long over.

I know, we could say that a trendline break indicates a trend is complete and a reversal has been made. For every trendline break that follows a trend reversal, I can show you a trendline break fake-out that is followed by a continuation of the prior trend. Moving average crossovers are notorious for false trend reversal signals.

9

In fact, most methods of identifying a price trend are doomed to failure for practical trade strategies with as many false reversal signals as confirmed ones. This is a bold statement, but I believe it is true. It's time to stop the madness and and deal with the reality of trend position. I defy any trading educator to provide evidence that his so-called trend indicator consistently provides an accurate signal of trend position and trend reversal in a *timely manner* that a trader can take advantage of.

How can I make this statement? Let's defy the crowd and think for ourselves in a logical manner. What does a trendline, channel lines, moving average, or other indicator represent? Every moving average, channel, or indicator is based on historic price data. It can only represent what has happened or what is the current market position relative to the lookback period. It has little predictive value in and of itself. It will *always* be a *lagging* indicator of the trend position, never a leading indicator of what is likely to happen in the future.

Why are some of these techniques promoted over and over again as "trend indicators" with value for making practical trade decisions? Because it is easy to find lots of chart examples that seem to illustrate how valuable are each of the author's price trend indicators. However, let me make you this promise and this challenge. Name a trend indicator and for any market or any time frame that you are given an example of how it defines the trend, I will show you two examples where it quickly failed.

Every one of these techniques, whether a trendline, volatility channel, moving average crossover, or momentum indicator, can be a useful part of a comprehensive trading plan, but none of them alone will be of much use in and of itself to identify the probable trend direction for a future period. Over and over again, you will find that price reversals do not coincide with the trend indicator reversals. As I mentioned earlier, for every after-the-fact, well-chosen example given, I will quickly find at least two where the trend indicator did not work to identify a trend reversal in a timely manner.

However, there is a way to use some of these indicators to identify high probability trade setups.

In this chapter, you will learn how to use just about any momentum indicator as a trend indicator for trade direction in a unique but very logical way that you have probably not been taught before. We are not concerned with identifying the exact price-swing high or low of a trend. Rather, we are concerned with identifying trades in the direction of the trend, including near the early stages of the trend and avoiding the later stages. The Multiple Time Frame Momentum Strategy that you are about to learn is the most powerful strategy to filter any market for trade direction and trade execution setups. Not only do I believe the Multiple Time Frame Momentum Strategy is the best use of an indicator for trading strategies, I believe it is the only practical indicator strategy for real-world trading.

The Multiple Time Frame Momentum Strategy is not a stand-alone trade system (although it is probably much better than most "systems" that sell for thousands of dollars), but when it is included as part of a trade plan with the time, price, and pattern strategies you will also learn in this book, you will have a powerful trade plan that will not only identify high probability trade setups with minimal capital exposure, but warn you when a trend is near the end and a major trend reversal is likely.

I use the term *capital exposure* to describe what many trade educators call *risk*. Risk is the probability of an event happening. Capital exposure is the amount of money (capital) that may be lost if a market moves against you. I have much more to say about capital exposure later in the book.

Let's begin with the concepts of trend and momentum before we even look at a chart or the dual time frame momentum strategy rules.

WHAT IS MOMENTUM?

In the world of trading, there are hundreds of momentum indicators (also called oscillators). Most of these indicators use the same information, the open-high-low-close of a price bar, and represent about the same thing, the *rate-of-change* of price. There is nothing mysterious, magical, or unique about this. All price indicators look back over a given period, called the *lookback period*, crunch the price data, and compare the recent price position with the price position of the lookback period. Different indicators manipulate and display the output differently, but all price-based indicators represent about the same thing: the rate-of-change or how fast the price trend is moving. The indicator reversals represent the change in momentum—the increase or decrease in the rate-of-change of the price trend. That is why you can use almost any price based indicator for the Multiple Time Frame Momentum Strategy you will learn in this chapter.

The first and most basic concept is this: *Momentum indicators do not represent price trends.* Momentum indicators represent *momentum trends.* This should be obvious, but I can't tell you how many new traders over the years expect a price reversal every time a momentum indicator reverses. It just doesn't work this way, because the indicator does not represent the price trend. If it did, this book would be about three pages long because all we would have to do is reverse our trade position each time a momentum indicator makes a reversal, and we would compound money faster than rabbits on Viagra can reproduce.

Unfortunately, it is not that easy. Price and momentum do not always trend together. For example, a momentum indicator may make a bearish reversal and decline while the price trend continues to advance. How can it do this? The *rate-of-change* of the price trend is decreasing even though price continues to advance. The bullish trend is just slowing down, so the momentum indicator is bearish even though the price trend continues to be bullish. The outcome: The price trend and momentum trend run opposite of each other.

Let me repeat this basic and very important concept about momentum indicators: *Momentum indicators represent momentum trends, not price trends.* Never expect price to reverse when the indicator makes a reversal. Often both price and momentum reverse together, but sometimes they will diverge because the price trend is only slowing down, forcing the indicator to reverse.

This point is important to clearly understand, and the vast majority of traders just don't get it. So let me repeat it one more time: *Momentum indicators represent momentum trends, not price trends.* Price and momentum may not trend in the same direction. Not every momentum reversal will coincide with a price reversal.

We can only make money on price trends, at least until someone comes up with a momentum contract to trade! Even though momentum and price trends often do not move in the same direction, you will soon learn how we can use momentum trends in a simple and practical way as the primary indicator of trade direction and trade execution setups. You will also learn how, by incorporating dual time frame momentum trends in a comprehensive trading plan that also includes the time, price, and pattern position of a market, you can identify whether the market is at or very near a price trend reversal.

MULTIPLE TIME FRAME MOMENTUM STRATEGIES

In over 20 years of trading and educating traders beginning in the mid-1980s, Multiple Time Frame Momentum Strategies have become the most powerful trade direction and execution approach I've added to my trading plan and taught my students.

For at least the first 10 years I traded, I never used an indicator. I was basically a pure chartist using time, price and pattern position to identify trade setups and targets. My strategy was based on Gann, Elliott, and Fibonacci. In 1989, I released what I believe was the first futures trading home study course, called the *W.D. Gann Home Study Trading Course*, based on Gann, Elliott, and Fibonacci trade strategies. This course is no longer available.

It wasn't until the late 1980s that I even had a computer with a charting program. I studied a lot about indicators and discovered I could always find an indicator or make a change in a lookback period or other setting for the indicator to confirm whatever price trend bias I had. There was never an indicator on my charts, simply because everything I read and tested on indicator strategies didn't seem to work out, and I just could not find a logical and practical application for indicators.

Around the mid-1990s, at the prompting of one of my students, I began to look at how a momentum indicator could help confirm the pattern and price position. It took a couple of years to work out practical strategies for a momentum indicator to be a part of a real-world trading plan. Then, several years ago, I started working with momentum strategies using multiple time frames and was blown away with how valuable they could be as part of the trading plan, to identify trade direction and trade execution and to confirm a potential price reversal at price or time targets. Like everything I teach in this book, these strategies can be used for any time frame and any market, from day to position trading.

THE BASIC DUAL TIME FRAME MOMENTUM STRATEGY

I first teach the concept and application of a momentum strategy using two time frames. Later I give examples of how to use more than two time frames, but two are all you need. You will learn how to integrate this strategy into your trade plan.

Let's get down to the basic strategy for the Dual Time Frame Momentum Reversal Strategy. It is so simple and logical, you're going to wonder why you haven't been using this strategy since your first trade!

DUAL TIME FRAME MOMENTUM STRATEGY

- Trade in the direction of the larger time frame momentum.
- Execute the trade following the smaller time frame momentum reversals.

It is that simple and logical. It doesn't matter what time frames you use. If you are a position trader looking for trades that last from several weeks to months, you will use weekly and daily momentum trends. If you are a swing trader looking for trades that last a few days, you will use daily and hourly data. Day traders will probably use 60-minute and 15-minute data or even smaller time frames.

Let's break down the Dual Time Frame Momentum Strategy into its parts to identify trade direction and trade execution setups.

Larger Time Frame Momentum Trend Identifies Trade Direction

We know the momentum trend will not always be in the direction of the price trend. But a good indicator with the right lookback period will usually trend in the direction of price and reverse within a very few bars of the price reversal. When price and momentum diverge, as in the case of a bullish price trend and bearish momentum trend, the larger time frame bearish momentum will keep us out of trades when the price trend is slowing down. The specific trade strategies you will learn in a later chapter will usually keep you out of a trade when the momentum trend is diverging with the price trend, which, at the least, will limit losses on losing trades. And remember, you *will* have losses, so a trade strategy that minimizes losses on losing trades is essential for trading success.

> *Dual Time Frame (DTF) Momentum Rule 1*: Only trade in the direction of the larger time frame momentum trend unless the momentum position is overbought or oversold.

I'll define the overbought and oversold exceptions soon.

The larger time frame momentum position identifies the trade direction. It does not signal that a trade should be executed; it only signals the *direction* of a possible trade, long or short. The smaller time frame momentum reversals are the specific signal that must be made before the trade is even considered. The smaller time frame momentum reversal does not execute the trade, but completes the conditions that must be in place before a trade execution may be considered.

Execute the Trade Following Smaller Time Frame Momentum Reversals

The key to momentum strategies is to use at least two time frames—a larger time frame to identify trade direction, and a smaller time frame for trade execution setups. We only want to take a trade if at least two time frames of momentum are moving in the same direction. That ups the odds big-time for the trade to be successful. This is such a simple and logical strategy that it should be a part of everyone's trade plan.

If a trader only considers the momentum position of one time frame, he is at a great disadvantage. Momentum may trend consistently without making any reversals, but during that momentum trend, price will usually make corrections, sometimes sizable ones, without the momentum making a reversal. Or the speed of the price trend will ebb and flow without causing a momentum reversal. Wouldn't it be best to be able to identify during the price trend when either a minor correction is likely to be complete or the speed of the trend might increase? That is what is accomplished by using the Dual Time Frame Momentum Strategy.

> DTF Momentum Rule 2: *A trade execution may be made following a smaller time frame momentum reversal in the direction of the larger time frame momentum trend.*

The initial conditions for trade entry are met when the smaller time frame momentum makes a reversal in the direction of the larger time frame momentum trend. That gives us the best shot for the price trend making the biggest moves with minimal capital exposure.

MOMENTUM REVERSALS

A *momentum reversal* is when the momentum indicator reverses from bullish to bearish or from bearish to bullish. A momentum indicator that has two lines, like a stochastic or a relative strength index, makes a momentum reversal when the fast line crosses above or below the slow line. The fast line in most two-line indicators is usually the raw data; the slow line is usually a moving average of the fast line. When the fast line crosses the slow line the momentum trend is likely reversing. A momentum crossover is similar to a moving average crossover except the momentum crossover is of the indicator values and not the price data itself. A momentum reversal for some indicators may be signaled by the momentum lines crossing above or below the oversold (OS) or overbought (OB) zones, if the indicator is the type with OS and OB zones.

Other indicators will have other conditions that reflect a reversal in momentum. With a moving average convergence divergence (MACD) indicator, when the bars become taller or shorter or cross the signal line, the momentum speed is changing. Each indicator will have different conditions that signal a momentum reversal but they all represent about the same thing: The price trend is either reversing, slowing, or speeding up. Later we'll see chart examples that show momentum reversals, but for now, you must thoroughly understand the concepts before looking at a single chart with indicators. Understanding the concepts first is the key to developing a specific trade strategy for any market and any time frame, under any market condition.

A smaller time frame momentum reversal into the direction of the larger time frame momentum is the *Dual Time Frame Momentum* setup for a trade. It is a precondition that must be met before a trade is even considered. A Dual Time Frame Momentum Strategy will be the best filter you have to identify optimum trades. It can be a stand-alone trade strategy, but we use it as part of a trading plan that also considers the price, pattern, and time position for high probability trade setups with acceptable capital exposure.

Trade in the direction of the larger time frame momentum. Execute following a smaller time frame momentum reversal. These are the setup conditions that must be met before a trade is considered.

Okay, it's time to look at some charts and illustrate what you've learned so far, so at any time you can bring up a chart of any market and any time frame and almost instantly identify if the market is in a high probability position to consider a trade.

MOST PRICE INDICATORS REPRESENT RATE-OF-CHANGE

Figure 2.1 shows three different indicators with the bar chart plus a simple rate-of-change (ROC). The three indicators are a stochastic (Stoch), relative strength index (RSI), and DT Oscillator (DTosc), which is a combination of RSI and Stoch. All four studies have an eight-period lookback.

The momentum trends are about the same in all three indicators. While it is a little difficult to see this in the black-and-white screen shots, the momentum reversals for each indicator where the fast line crosses the slow line are all within a bar or two of each other.

What's the point of this comparison? Most price-based indicators represent about the same thing, that momentum cycles act and react about the same time. The settings for any indicator, including the lookback period can be tweaked for different markets and different time frames for the most reliable signals. But, as you can see from Figure 2.1, even without tweaking the settings for each indicator they each still represented the momentum cycles about equally well. Later in this chapter you will learn how to choose the best settings for any indicator for any market and time frame.

Figure 2.2 is another screen shot with just two indicators, Stoch and DTosc, with less data so you can see the momentum cycles more clearly. I've drawn thick vertical lines in the indicator window at each bullish and bearish momentum reversal where the fast line crosses the slow line.

The momentum reversals in both indicators were made plus or minus one bar of each other. Either the Stoch or DTosc would be equally helpful to identify momentum reversals for this data. Don't let anyone sell you on some magical, mystical indicator for momentum trading! All momentum indicators represent the same momentum cycles, and

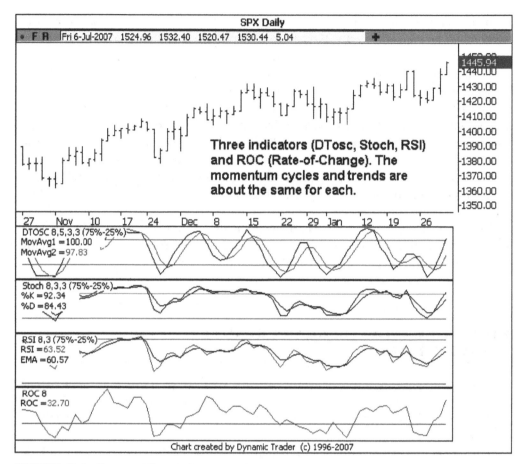

FIGURE 2.1 Compare Three Indicators and ROC

most make reversals about the same time. The black-box system scammers will claim they have a secret, foolproof indicator, but more than likely it is one you already have in your charting program.

There are only so many ways to crunch the open-high-low-close of price bars. Most variations come up with about the same result and can be equally useful.

MOMENTUM AND PRICE TRENDS OFTEN DIVERGE

Remember how I said earlier that price and momentum do not always trend together? If they did, this book would be almost complete. However, they don't. When a price trend slows down but doesn't reverse, the momentum trend will often make a reversal and trend in the opposite direction to price. Let's take a look at an example.

Figure 2.3 is 60-minute ES-0607 data. I've marked off a price-momentum divergence with the arrow lines.

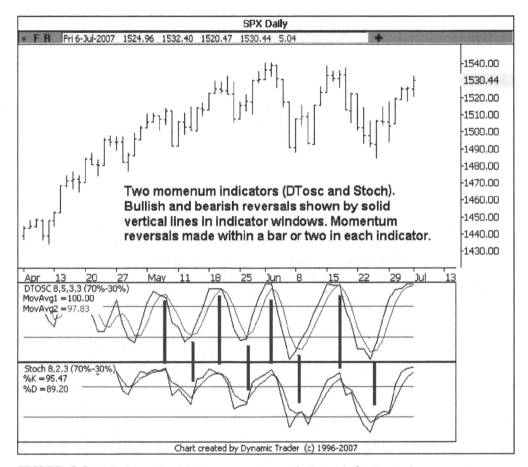

FIGURE 2.2   Bullish and Bearish Momentum Reversals Coincide for Two Indicators

Near the high point of this data, the price trend continued to a new high, but the momentum trend made a bearish reversal and declined as price continued higher. How can this happen? The rate of price advance slowed down even though the price continued higher. Most price-based momentum indicators represent the speed of the trend, and the speed of the trend slowed down here, so the momentum was bearish even while price made a new high.

Let's take a look at one more price-momentum divergence example.

Figure 2.4 is a 60-minute EUR/USD Forex chart. I've drawn the arrow lines to show a period when price and momentum diverged. Price continued higher, while momentum declined. Why? The *rate* of the advance slowed down even through price continued higher, which caused the momentum to be bearish for a while.

Every indicator will diverge with price now and then. This is why I challenge any of the indicator junkies to prove any trading system consistently profitable based on any single indicator for any market. I've done it again—put out another challenge, and here we are still near the beginning of the book. I can't help it, because I see and read so

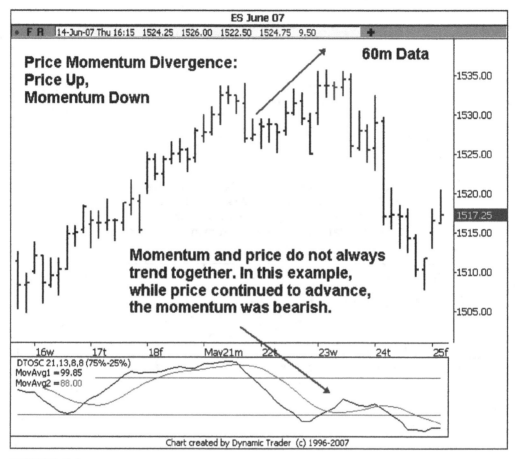

FIGURE 2.3 Price-Momentum Divergence

much nonsense in trading publications about so-called momentum systems that optimize settings for historic data and claim amazing results.

I've also seen entire trading plans based on price-momentum divergence strategies with many well-chosen examples. I've never seen one of these plans that actually made money, but the systems are sold to naïve traders who don't do their homework to prove to themselves how useful (or useless) the setups really are. For every price-momentum divergence example that resulted in a trend reversal, I can just about guarantee there were one or two and probably a lot more that did not result in a trend reversal on the same data. I don't know how many times I've read an article in a trading publication about a momentum divergence strategy where, on the same data on the chart the author used to illustrate price-momentum divergence setup and price reversal, there were other identical setups that would have resulted in losses that the author simply ignored!

But I digress from the important task at hand: how to use Dual Time Frame Momentum Strategies for trade setups.

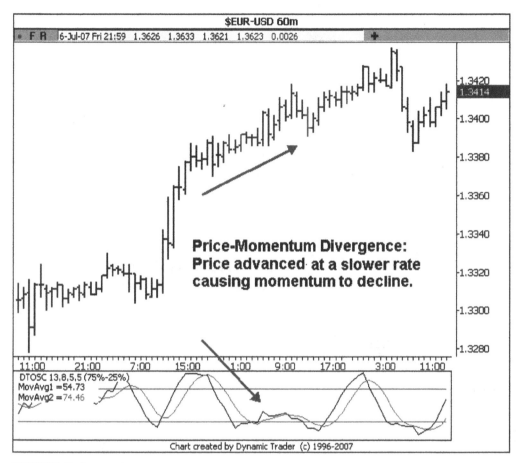

FIGURE 2.4 Price-Momentum Divergence on EUR/USD

HOW DUAL TIME FRAME MOMENTUM STRATEGIES WORK

The concept for Dual Time Frame Momentum Strategy trade setups is simple, practical, and logical: Trade in the direction of the larger time frame momentum; execute the trade following the smaller time frame momentum reversals in the direction of the larger time frame momentum. Let's take a look at a couple of charts and see how valuable this strategy will be. We'll use the SPX daily data for the higher time frame momentum and 60-minute data for the lower time frame momentum reversals for this example, but it works the same for any market and any two time frames.

Figure 2.5 includes about three months of daily SPX data with the DTosc momentum indicator. The dates of each momentum reversal are shown during this period. The dates across the top are bearish momentum reversals and the dates along the bottom are bullish momentum reversals.

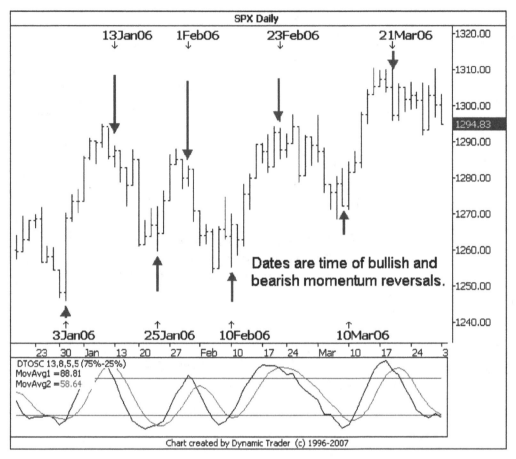

FIGURE 2.5 Bullish and Bearish Momentum Reversals

Most of the momentum reversals were made within a couple bars of the actual price high or low. Okay, I did cherry-pick this example somewhat so that I can clearly show the momentum reversals, but I want to be sure you get the idea. No matter what indicator or settings you use, all momentum reversals will not always be made this close to the actual price reversals, although most of the time they will. We'll have plenty of time to show you examples in the book and CD that are not so perfect, but first let's get the concept clearly down.

Figure 2.6 is the SPX 60-minute data for one of the periods shown on the previous chart when the daily momentum was bullish. The Dual Time Frame Momentum Strategy is to trade in the direction of the higher time frame momentum (daily in this case) and execute following a momentum reversal on the smaller time frame (60-minute in this case).

On the 60-minute (60m) chart, I've marked off a period when the daily momentum was bullish from February 10 to February 23 and drawn an arrow line between the closes of those two dates through the price bars. Before and after this arrowed line, the daily

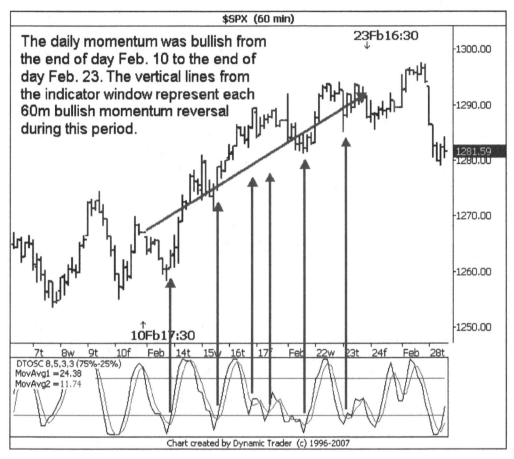

The daily momentum was bullish from the end of day Feb. 10 to the end of day Feb. 23. The vertical lines from the indicator window represent each 60m bullish momentum reversal during this period.

FIGURE 2.6 Smaller Time Frame Momentum Reversals

momentum was bearish, so we would not consider the smaller time frame bullish reversals as trade setups.

I've also drawn a vertical arrow line from each 60m momentum bullish reversal pointing up to the bar when the reversal was made. The momentum bullish reversal is when the fast line crosses above the slow line. Any one of these smaller time frame 60m momentum bullish reversals could be a setup for a long trade. Some were followed by sharp advances, some only modest advances. *All* were immediately followed by some advance. It only makes sense that advances should follow. If the larger time frame daily momentum is bullish, a smaller time frame 60m momentum bullish reversal puts two time frames of momentum in the same direction, which is a high probability setup for a continued advance.

Ponder this chart for a minute and consider when you think the most optimal times would be to take Dual Time Frame Momentum Strategy setup trades without considering any other rules, guidelines, or factors of your trading plan. How about soon after the higher time frame daily momentum makes its bullish reversal, like the first couple of smaller time frame bullish reversals? I know, this is only one example so far of Dual Time Frame Momentum Strategy trade setups, but think of the logic of making it a part of your trading plan to focus on setups soon after the higher time frame momentum reverses. We'll consider this more later in the chapter.

Let's take a look at another example, using 60m data for the higher time frame and 15m data for the lower time frame. Figure 2.7 shows the EUR/USD Forex 15m data for about a 24-hour period. The upward-sloping arrow through the bar data is a period when the higher time frame 60m momentum was bullish. The vertical arrows show the four lower time frame 15m momentum bullish reversals during the time when the higher time frame 60m momentum was bullish. I've labeled them 1 through 4.

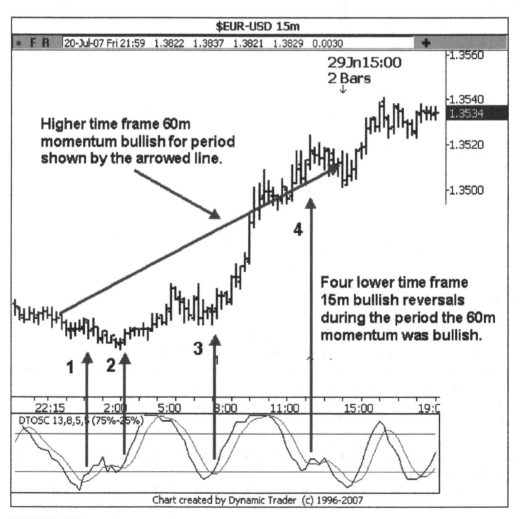

FIGURE 2.7 Smaller Time Frame Momentum Bullish Reversals

The first 15m momentum bullish reversal was followed by the EUR/USD continuing lower for a few bars. Would a long trade have been entered? We haven't talked about entry strategies yet so we will pass on this question for now. Remember, the smaller time frame momentum reversal in the direction of the larger time frame momentum is only the condition that must be met to consider a trade; it is not a trade execution strategy.

The second and third 15m momentum bullish reversals were followed by strong advances. The fourth reversal was followed by several sideways to down bars before the higher time frame 60m momentum made a bearish reversal where the arrowed line along the bars ends. Regardless of the specific trade execution strategy used, based only on the Dual Time Frame Momentum Strategy setups there were two set ups for clear-cut winners, and two no-trades or small losses.

The next example is bond weekly and daily data, which may be used to position-trade bond futures or a bond exchange-traded fund (ETF). Figure 2.8 shows the higher time frame bond weekly data. I've labeled the five weekly momentum trends for this 18-month period. I chose this period because it includes a fairly prolonged cycle of price-momentum divergence when the weekly momentum was bearish while bond prices continued sideways to up.

The five *momentum* trends during this period are labeled 1 through 5 in the indicator window below the bar chart. Period 1 is a bullish momentum trend that began in May and ended in August. For the next several months, the momentum trend was bearish (period 2), although bonds eventually went higher but ended the period with little net advance. How can there be a price bull trend with a momentum bear trend? You know the answer to this. The rate of advance slowed down compared to what it had been. The bond market became choppy with short swings up and down. This decreased rate-of-change and choppy market would force any price momentum indicator to become bearish.

It would be nice if we knew in advance when a market was going to go into a trading range or slow down a trend, but we can never know this in advance. We are always trading on the right-hand side of the chart after the last bar, which is the unknown side of the chart. We can only use the information available as of the last price bar to make a decision. I've actually read articles and chapters in books about "how to trade a trading range." *You can never know in advance if a market is going to begin a trading range—never.* If any trading instructor tries to teach you special strategies for trading ranges, run, don't walk. The strategies will all have worked great after the fact. But you will never know in advance when to use the so-called trading range strategies because you can never know *in advance* if a market is going to begin a trading range.

During periods 3, 4, and 5, the weekly momentum and price trended together. Let's take a look at the smaller time frame daily momentum trends and reversals for each of the five weekly momentum trends shown on this weekly chart.

The first daily bond chart (Figure 2.9) is for weekly period 1, when the weekly momentum was bullish from May through August. Bonds made two daily momentum bullish reversals *below the overbought zone* during this period. The overbought line is the 75% horizontal line near the top of the indicator window. One of the daily bullish reversals

FIGURE 2.8 Bull and Bear Momentum Trends

was made in the OB zone between the points I have labeled 1 and 2. The momentum bullish reversal made in the OB zone is not numbered. You will learn later why we ignore momentum bullish reversals in the overbought and momentum bearish reversals in the oversold zones.

Since the higher time frame weekly momentum is bullish for this period, only daily momentum bullish reversals would be potential long trade setups. The weekly momentum turned bullish the week ending May 21. The first daily momentum bullish reversal on June 10 was made almost three weeks after the weekly momentum bullish reversal. For this three-week period, bonds continued the bear trend. If a trader only looked at one time frame, in this case the weekly momentum, a bullish momentum setup would have been made although the bond market continued to decline.

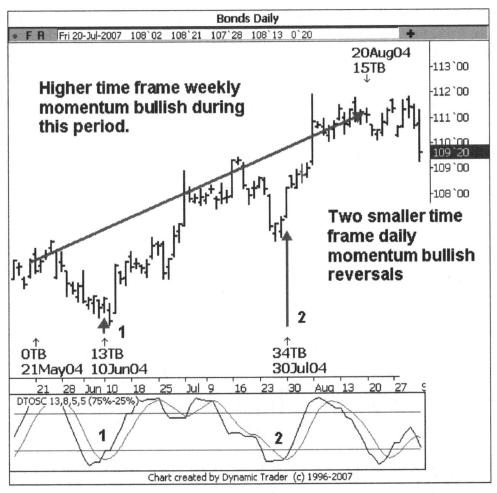

FIGURE 2.9 Smaller Time Frame Bullish Reversals in the Direction of the Larger Time Frame Momentum Trend

Waiting for the smaller time frame daily momentum bullish reversal before considering a long trade kept you out of a long trade immediately following the weekly momentum bullish reversal, when price continued to decline but made a great setup June 10 following the daily momentum bullish reversal. This is an excellent example of why you must always consider at least two time frames of momentum position before even considering a trade. Both smaller time frame daily momentum reversals were followed by a strong advance.

There was one additional bullish momentum reversal between points 1 and 2. Why is it not considered a setup? It was made in the OB zone. A smaller time frame momentum bullish reversal must be made below the OB zone to be a valid setup. If the momentum bullish reversal is in the OB zone, the upside should be very limited and you will want to avoid a long trade.

The next daily bond chart (Figure 2.10) is for weekly period 2. That was the period when the higher time frame weekly momentum was bearish, yet price was sideways to marginally up by the end of the period. If the higher time frame weekly momentum is bearish, only short trades would be considered following daily momentum bearish reversals.

The first daily momentum bearish reversal (point 1 on the daily chart) was made on a wide range down day which ended up being a swing low. Would this be a losing trade? I want to stress again, the Dual Time Frame Momentum Strategy setups are not about trade execution. They meet the minimum conditions to *consider* entering a trade. Specific trade entry and stop strategies will be taught in a later chapter. For now, consider that a low of a daily bar was not taken out following the daily momentum bearish

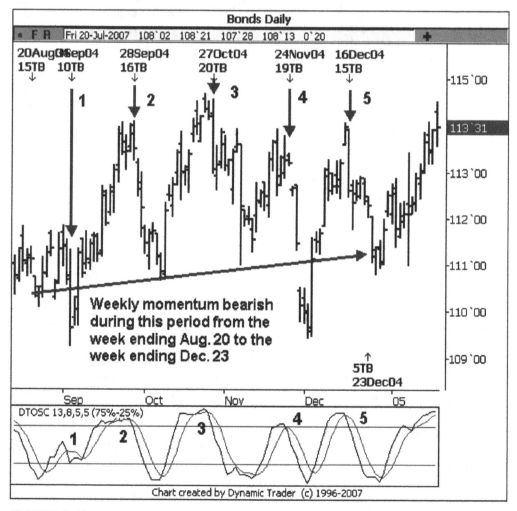

FIGURE 2.10   Smaller Time Frame Momentum Bearish Reversals, Weekly Period 2

reversal—a hint of trade strategies you will soon learn. Regardless of the time frame you trade, a trade is not entered until a bar high or low is taken out following the smaller time frame momentum reversal.

Daily bearish reversal 2 was made on the swing high bar followed by a sharp decline. Nice setup. Daily momentum reversals numbers 2, 3, 4, and 5 were all made within a bar or two of a swing high and followed by very tradable multiday declines.

Now I don't want you to think at this point that every Dual Time Frame Momentum Strategy setup will result in a profitable trade. Nothing could be further from the truth. A complete trading plan depends on more factors, including trade entry, stop-loss, exit strategy, multiple units, acceptable capital exposure per trade, and more. All I want you to learn at this point, until it becomes second nature to you, is that a trade setup is made following a smaller time frame momentum reversal in the direction of the larger time frame momentum. This is a completely objective, logical, and practical strategy for high probability, low capital exposure trade setups for any market and any time frame. Trade setups are not trade executions. Trade setups are simply conditions that must be met before a trade is considered.

During this bond weekly period, bonds were essentially in a trading range, making nice swings up as well as down. The daily momentum made bullish reversals within a bar or two of each price low. However, because the higher time frame weekly momentum was bearish during this period, only short setups would be considered. Wouldn't it have been nice to know in late August that bonds were going to make nice, clearly defined trading range swings for the next four months! We could make a ton of money with a trading range strategy. Wait a minute! We never know in advance when a trading range is going to begin or end, so we don't have a trading range strategy. Only academic authors with questionable trading experience have a trading range strategy, and we're not going to listen to their nonsense.

The third weekly momentum trend was bullish from the week ending December 23 through the week ending February 18 (Figure 2.11). During this higher time frame weekly bullish momentum period, the smaller time frame daily momentum made two bullish reversals. Each was followed by a strong move up.

Let's note a couple of important things at this point. First, I haven't changed the daily momentum settings for any of these examples to optimize the signals. You will learn how to choose the best settings for any indicator later in this chapter. Second, I also haven't talked about stop-loss or exit strategies, both of which are crucial to a sound and consistently profitable trading plan. Those also come later in the book. Right now I'm just focusing on identifying trade entry setups based on the dual time frame momentum position.

Let's look at the next period, when the higher time frame weekly momentum reversed to bearish (Figure 2.12). During this period between the weeks ending February 18 and April 8, the smaller time frame daily momentum made two bearish reversals.

The first daily momentum bearish reversal during this period was made about three weeks after the weekly momentum turned bearish. The market immediately made a minor corrective rally after the short setup. Any short trade strategy would have been a

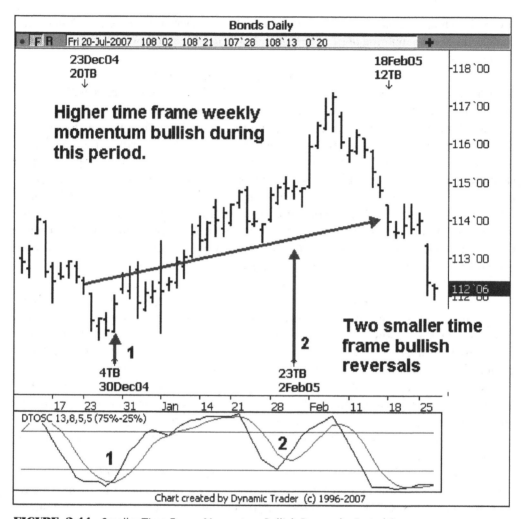

FIGURE 2.11 Smaller Time Frame Momentum Bullish Reversals, Period 3

small loss. The second daily momentum bearish reversal was made just one day after the swing low in March and would have also resulted in no trade or a loss, depending on the entry and initial protective stop strategy.

Wouldn't this have been aggravating, considering bonds made a consistent decline of almost five points following the weekly bearish reversal and bearish momentum trend! No matter what your trade strategy, this can happen. This is another reason I used this period to illustrate the Dual Time Frame Momentum Strategy setup. I could have picked a series of well-chosen examples that worked flawlessly every time, but I want you to learn the realities of trading. You never know what is going to happen on the right hand side of the chart. That's the side without the bars. That's the side you have to make decisions for. If you don't stick to your trading plan, you are doomed to failure, period. End of story.

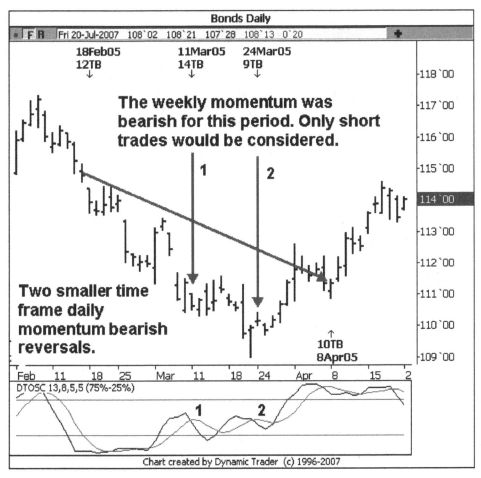

FIGURE 2.12 Smaller Time Frame Momentum Bearish Reversals, Period 4

Probably the primary reasons such a high percentage of traders blow out and quit within months are no trading plan and no consistency.

Now let's look at the fifth weekly momentum trend shown earlier on the weekly chart, the bullish momentum period from the week ending April 8 though the week ending June 17. The daily chart (Figure 2.13) shows three daily momentum bullish reversals during this period.

The first daily momentum bullish reversal was not made until about three weeks after the weekly bullish momentum reversal. The daily momentum was overbought through most of this period, which is a typical momentum position in a strong trend. The first smaller time frame daily momentum bullish reversal (point 1) was made just before a price high followed by a corrective decline that lasted several days. It would have been a no-trade or small loss. The second daily momentum bullish reversal was followed by a consistent rally of several points. The third and last daily momentum bullish reversal

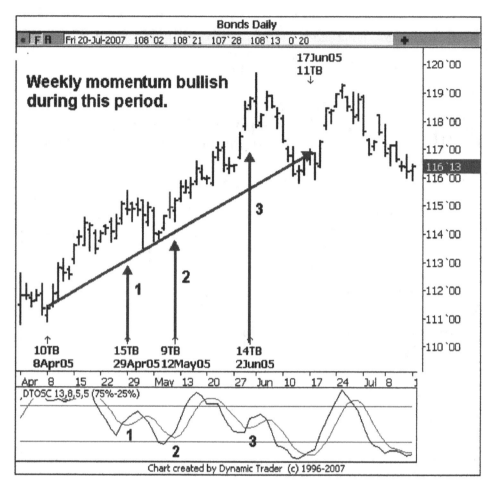

FIGURE 2.13   Smaller Time Frame Momentum Bullish Reversals, Period 5

for this weekly bullish momentum period was made just before bonds made a significant high—another no-trade or small loss.

I purposely chose this 18-month period for bonds and the weekly and daily data because it illustrates most conditions you will run into with Dual Time Frame Momentum Strategy setups. There were periods for strong winners; periods of price/momentum divergence that still would have resulted in some gains; periods of marginal gain because the smaller time frame reversals lagged the higher time frame momentum reversals; and at least one period that would have probably resulted in a small net loss.

I could have easily filled the chapter with unlimited examples of ideal setups that always resulted in massive profits, like so many other trading books and educational courses do. That is not the real world of trading. Yes, there can be some quick and significant gains. But there will always be periods when either the market does not set up for potential trades according to your trading plan or, regardless of your trade plan, the setups will not follow through with successful trades. That is the reality of trading. Believe it and you should be on the road to success.

The purpose of all trade strategies is to identify conditions with a high probability outcome and acceptable capital exposure. The Dual Time Frame Momentum Strategy is a completely objective approach to identify trade setups as just one part of a comprehensive trade plan.

This approach is applicable to any actively traded market and any time frame, from position-trading with monthly, weekly, and daily data to day-trading with intraday data. The principles and application are the same regardless of the market or time frame.

There are a couple of important questions about momentum studies and indicators that you should have come up with so far: Which indicator should you use, and what are the best settings or lookback periods to use? Let's address both of these now.

WHICH INDICATORS TO USE FOR MULTIPLE TIME FRAME MOMENTUM STRATEGIES

I've made the point several times in this chapter that most price indicators represent about the same thing, rate-of-change, and will give you about the same results for our purposes. In the examples so far, I've mostly used the DTosc, which is a proprietary indicator included with my Dynamic Trader software. Let's take a look at other indicators you can use and how to use them.

The stochastic (Stoch) indicator is very popular and included in all trading software. The Stoch has overbought (OB) and oversold (OS) zones plus a fast and slow line, both characteristics that are helpful for our purposes.

Overbought and *oversold* are not really good descriptive terms for an indicator that reaches extreme levels, but since these terms are commonly used, we will use them as well. Just because an indicator reached the OB zone at the upper extreme of the indicator range does not necessarily mean that the market itself is ready to turn down. It only means the indicator is near the extreme level. It will take some history and looking at many momentum cycles for the indicator to determine if price is usually at or near a position to make a reversal when the indicator reaches the OB or OS levels.

An indicator like the Stoch which has a fast and slow line is also helpful. The slow line of an indicator is usually just a moving average of the fast line. The slow line will react more slowly to momentum change. When the fast line crosses the slow line, we call it a *momentum reversal*. It warns that the rate of momentum is changing, which is often preceded or followed within a couple of bars by a directional price change.

If the fast line crosses above the slow line, it is called a momentum bullish reversal. If the fast line crosses below the slow line, it is called a momentum bearish reversal. We'll talk more about indicator settings and lookback periods later, but for now we just want to learn about how an indicator acts and reacts to price momentum changes and how we might use the OB/OS zones and momentum reversals as a trade setup.

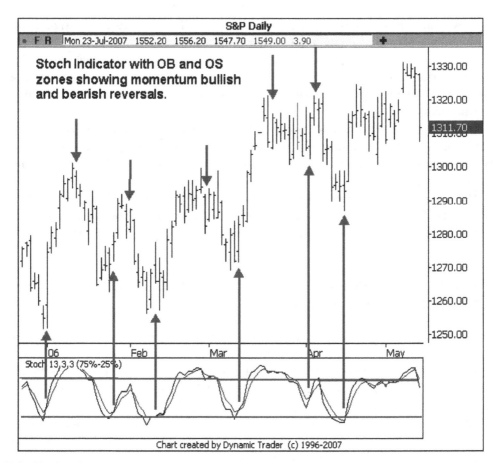

FIGURE 2.14 Stochastic Bullish and Bearish Momentum Reversals

Let's take a look at a couple of charts with a Stoch indicator. Figure 2.14 shows S&P daily data for about a four-month period. This period had a series of well-defined swings up and down with a bullish bias. I've drawn thick horizontal lines at the 75% OB and 25% OS zones, upward-pointing arrows for the momentum bullish reversals, and downward-pointing arrows for the momentum bearish reversals.

The Stoch did a very good job of making momentum reversals within a bar or two of each price reversal, which would make it a good momentum indicator for our purposes. The momentum reversals are not trade signals but conditions that must be met in order to consider a trade. Do you notice anything interesting about the position of the indicator reversals and the OB and OS zones?

For this series of S&P daily data, both lines of the Stoch reached well into the OB zone prior to a momentum bearish reversal. However, both lines did not typically reach the OS zone prior to the momentum bullish reversals. Why is that? The trend bias for this period was bullish. It is a characteristic of a Stoch indicator to hang in the OB zone if the trend is bullish and makes relatively shallow momentum corrections in the indicators, often not reaching the OS zone on price corrections. This is a characteristic that you should be aware of. The larger-degree trend bias will affect how the Stoch indicator cycles.

Let's take a look at more data. The next daily S&P chart (Figure 2.15) was for a four-month period with a strong bullish trend with only minor corrections. The chart has the same Stoch indicator with the same settings as the previous chart. Do you note any differences in how the Stoch cycled with the price cycles in this chart compared to the earlier one?

The Stoch hung in the OB zone for much of the trend, only making momentum declines below the OB line on the larger corrections that lasted several bars. Frequent momentum oscillations were made in the OB zone without a decline to below the OB line. This is a similar Stoch momentum pattern to what we saw on the previous chart, which had much larger corrections during the bullish trend. Even that chart showed a Stoch bias to hang in the OB zone and make relatively shallow momentum corrections.

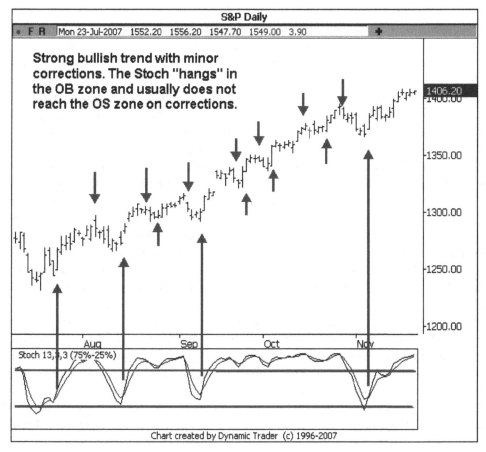

FIGURE 2.15 Stochastic Momentum Reversals

The momentum pattern on this chart is just more pronounced because of the stronger bullish trend.

So it looks like we need to make a set of momentum trading rules for the wide swinging periods with a modest bullish bias and a set of rules for a stronger bullish trend. That way, we can take full advantage of each market condition. At least, that is what some trading educators will teach you: different rules for different market conditions. But as we are well aware, *you never know what type of trend is developing on the right-hand side of the chart.* We can never have a different set of momentum rules for bull or bear or trading range, or for volatile or stable markets, or any other unique market condition, because *we never know what type of market lies ahead.* If we choose an indicator and a particular set of settings, we have to stick to them until we have a very compelling reason to change.

MACD Momentum Indicator

The moving average convergence divergence (MACD) momentum indicator is another very popular indicator found in all charting packages and familiar to most traders. The MACD measures the difference between two moving averages and is usually displayed in the indicator window as vertical bars in what is called a histogram. A shorter bar than a previous bar represents a narrowing range between the two moving averages and a loss of momentum. If a bar is made on the other side of the center line (signal line), it means the faster moving average has crossed above or below the slower moving average.

Many traders base their momentum decisions on the MACD, and lots of systems and trade strategies have been developed around MACD signals and patterns. Does the MACD hold the momentum secret for traders? Let's take a look at it.

Figure 2.16 shows the same S&P daily data we used to look at the Stoch indicator. The arrows show the momentum bullish and bearish reversals. A momentum bearish reversal occurs when a bar above the centerline (also called the signal line) is shorter than the previous bar. A momentum bullish reversal is made when a bar below the centerline is shorter than the previous bar. Each of these situations represents a narrowing spread between the shorter-term moving average and the longer-term moving average, or a decrease in the momentum. A change in momentum represents a change in the price rate-of-change. Usually it coincides with a change in the price trend, sometimes it does not.

Do these momentum reversals represented by the up and down arrows look familiar? They should. Every one of them is within one bar of the Stoch momentum reversals for the same data you saw in Figure 2.14. It looks like both the Stoch and MACD give about the same momentum information. This is no surprise since both are price indicators that represent about the same thing: a change in the rate-of-change of the price trend.

A difference between the MACD and the Stoch is that the MACD does not have OB and OS zones. This doesn't prevent you from using the MACD for Dual Time Frame Momentum Strategies. The change in bar heights works just fine.

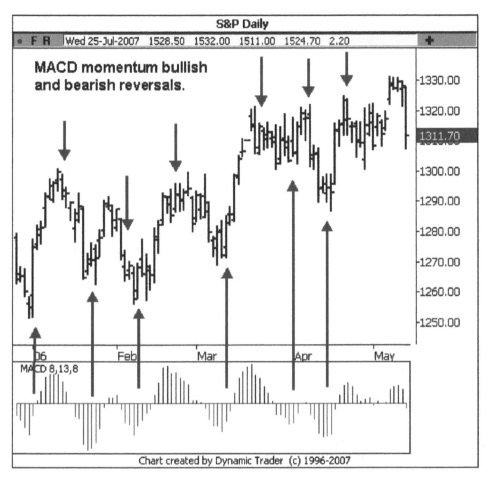

FIGURE 2.16 MACD Reversals

Figure 2.17 uses the same S&P daily data used in Figure 2.15. This S&P period was a strong bull trend with only minor corrections lasting a few days. The MACD made momentum bullish and bearish reversals within a bar or two of each minor price high and low. It would have been very effective to identify entry signals during the larger time frame bull trend.

So which indicator is best to use for the Dual Time Frame Momentum Strategy? You could just about throw a dart at a list of price indicators and use whichever is hit. I prefer to use an indicator like the DTosc, which is a combination of stochastic and RSI, or a stochastic itself or other indicator that has overbought and oversold zones. But the MACD or another indicator that you have used and are familiar with can be just as useful.

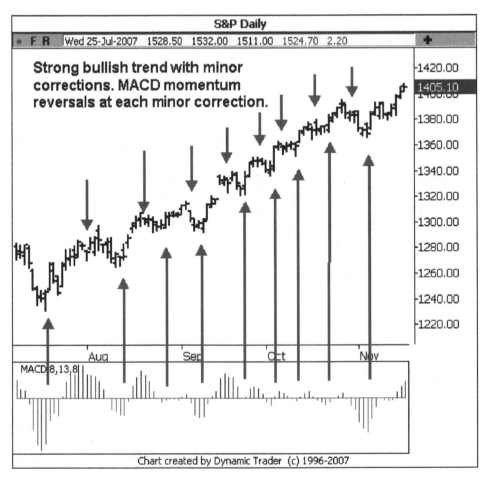

FIGURE 2.17 MACD Momentum Reversals during a Bull Trend

WHAT ARE THE BEST INDICATOR SETTINGS TO USE?

I wish I could give you the quick, easy, and definitive answer to this question. Unfortunately, there isn't one. Anyone who tells you there is such an answer is full of beans and, I suspect, has a very high-priced trading course or system to sell you.

For any given momentum indicator, there will usually be different settings for different markets and usually different settings for different time frames of the same market. Once you find the best settings for the recent data for a given market and given time frame, will those settings ever change? You bet they will. And anyone who tells you different is full of more beans.

The primary setting for any indicator is the lookback period. The lookback period is the number of bars back from the most recent bar that the indicator looks at to make the momentum calculations.

Why may the settings change? Momentum trends cycle from low volatility and relatively infrequent momentum reversals to high volatility and relatively frequent momentum reversals. Ideally, we would have a system or indicator that would warn us of the type of momentum cycles that will be made in the future. Unfortunately, no such system exists, any more than there is a system to project in advance when a market is going to be in a trading range or a consistent trend. So occasionally, we may adjust the settings for an indicator to reflect the most recent momentum volatility.

What is the primary variable for most indicators? It is the lookback period, or the number of bars, prior to and including the most recent bar the indicator will use to make its calculations. The current value of any indicator is the relationship of the last completed bar to the lookback period. Everyone is familiar with a simple moving average. It is the average price of the past x number of bars, usually the close. The lookback period is the number of bars used to calculate the moving average.

A longer lookback period will be less sensitive to price change than a shorter lookback period. It will take a longer period of recent momentum change to influence the longer lookback period momentum indicator. The upside to the longer lookback period is there should be fewer false reversals made by short-term momentum changes. The downside of the longer lookback period has the potential for a lag between price and momentum reversals; price may have made a reversal several bars before the momentum indicator makes the reversal.

Let's take a look at a few charts and indicators and lookback periods. We'll begin by looking at the same data with different indicator lookback periods to see which may be more useful. Figure 2.18 is daily S&P Index (SPX) data with the DTosc with a 21-day raw lookback period. The DTosc indicator is a combination of Stoch and RSI. Four numbers show in the indicator window. The first number is the raw lookback period while the other numbers are periods the raw data is smoothed. Don't get hung up on the details of the indicator; just grasp the concept of how the indicator acts and reacts to price trends based on the lookback period. How useful would this indicator have been to signal overbought and oversold positions and price reversals?

Two things are immediately obvious. While the indicator oscillated nicely with the price swings, most of the indicator momentum reversals did not reach the OB or OS zone. For a two-line indicator like the DTosc, stochastic, and others, both the fast and slow line must be in the OB or OS zone to consider the indicator OB or OS. If an indicator has an OB and OS zone, we want to use it to our advantage and ideally use an indicator lookback period so the indicator reaches the OB or OS zone most of the time before a momentum reversal is made.

The second important factor is that most of the momentum reversals which are made when the fast line crosses above or below the slow line were made several bars after the extreme swing high or low and after price had moved a significant distance from the high or low. If an indicator momentum reversal is part of our trade plan setup before an

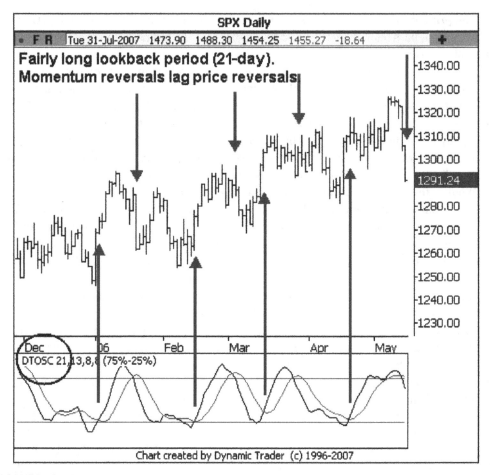

FIGURE 2.18 SPX Daily Data with a 21-Day Lookback Period

execution can be made, stops would typically have to be a long way from the entry price with a relatively long lookback period.

The 21-day lookback period is probably too long to use for this data because both lines of the indicator usually do not reach the OB and OS zones before a reversal is made, and the lag from price reversal to momentum reversal is usually several bars when price has moved a significant distance from the swing high or low.

Let's take a look at a shorter 8-day lookback period. Figure 2.19 shows the same period as the SPX 21-day lookback but with a little less data so you can see the momentum reversals more clearly. The up and down arrows show most of the momentum reversals. I've also circled a couple of periods in the indicator window when the momentum became choppy with reversals every few bars.

There are a couple of obvious factors from this data and indicator chart. First, at the price highs and lows the momentum reversals tended to be made in the OB and OS zones and right on or within just one or two bars of the price high or low. For any indicator

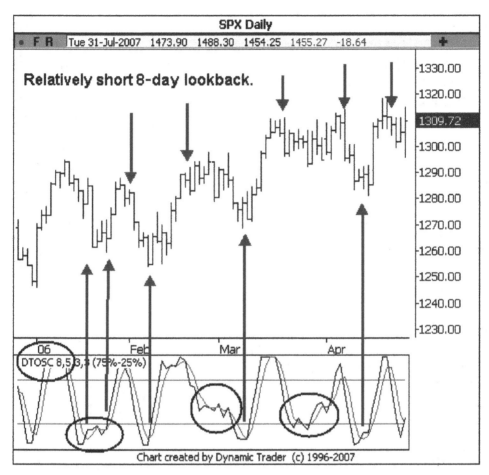

FIGURE 2.19 SPX Daily Data with an 8-Day Lookback Period

a relatively shorter lookback period will always result with the indicator making momentum reversals very close to the price-swing highs and lows. This would seem to make a short lookback period ideal. However, the more timely signals come with a cost.

A shorter lookback period will usually have lots of false momentum reversals, when very short-term momentum changes cause an indicator reversal that is quickly reversed again as the trend continues. I've circled three areas on the indicator window when the indicator became choppy and gave momentum reversal signals that were again reversed within a bar or two. Too short a lookback period will produce too many momentum whipsaws.

There must be a reasonably happy medium, and there usually is. Figure 2.20 shows the same SPX data with the same indicator but a 13-day lookback period.

What do you notice about this 13-day lookback setting compared to the prior two charts? The characteristics are (1) the indicator reaches the OB or OS zone at most

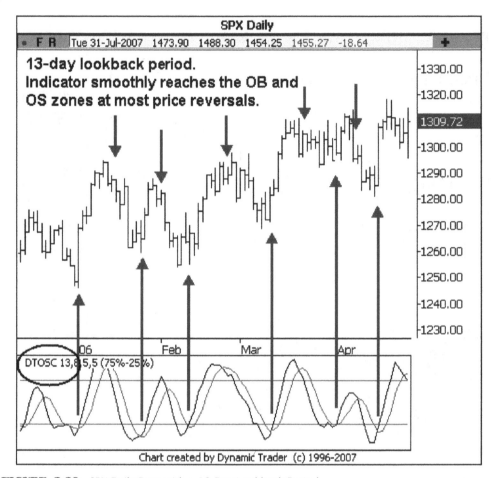

FIGURE 2.20   SPX Daily Data with a 13-Day Lookback Period

of the momentum reversals (2) the momentum reversals are within a couple of bars of the price highs and lows; and (3) there are no false momentum reversals between OB and OS zones. Of the three lookback periods we have looked at for this data, the 13-day is the best. Let's take a look at all three lookback periods on the same chart (Figure 2.21).

While the 8-day lookback period usually made momentum reversals from the OB and OS zones right on or within a bar or two of most price-swing highs and lows, it also made a lot of whipsaw reversals mid-range that quickly reversed again. While the 21-day lookback period was very smooth with no mid-range fake-out reversals, the momentum reversals usually lagged the price reversals several bars, and most did not reach the OB and OS zones. The 13-day lookback period made most of the reversals from the OB and OS zones and within a bar or two of the price-swing highs and lows.

This is how I decide which settings or lookback period to use—it's very simple: Test a few settings on recent data and see which best meets the criteria for a useful indicator.

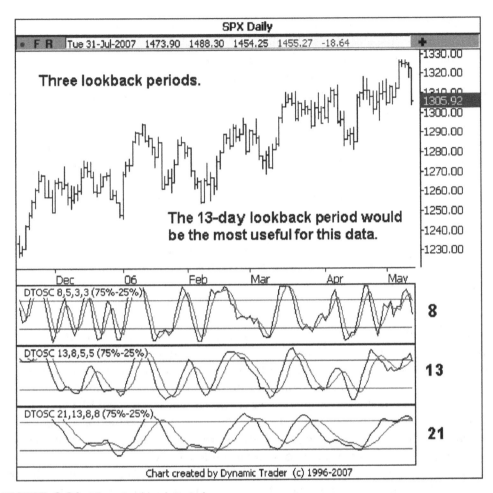

FIGURE 2.21 Three Lookback Periods

When I occasionally do a live workshop, I'll ask the students to write down any stock, ETF, futures, index, or Forex symbol of any time frame and I'll be able to choose the best settings for any indicator within one minute. I do the entire analysis and trade strategy for any market and any time frame within three minutes. You'll be able to do this yourself when you've finished this book. There are only so many variables and so much useful data needed to make a trading decision. Once you have developed a trade plan, you can very quickly understand the probable position of a market and what the market must do for you to consider a trade.

This has only been one example from a limited set of data. The concept and process is the most important thing for you to learn. Once you've learned it, the exact same concept and process is used for any market, any time frame, and any indicator.

You should have a big question about now: "You chose the best settings for this limited period of just a few months of SPX daily data. That's easy. It's called optimizing the historical data. Are these settings going to continue to be useful in the future?" The answer to that is "Usually." I wish I could say "Always." Some trading educators claim there is one best set of settings for an indicator that you use all of the time. These guys have probably never actually traded, because I can guarantee there will be periods when market volatility and momentum cycles change and the indicator settings you have been using will be much less useful.

So here's how it works. Look at a series of data for any market and any time frame. Test out a few lookback periods for your favorite indicator over two or three different periods of time for the data and choose the most useful settings. Assume that these settings will continue to be useful. *That's the best you can do, and don't let anyone tell you otherwise.* You're not Nostradamus. You can't see into the future. You can never know if the volatility and momentum cycles will change in the future. You have to assume they will continue.

If a market changes trend speed and volatility in the future and the best settings you have found in the past are no longer optimal after a few momentum cycles, you may need to shorten or increase the lookback period.

Figure 2.22 shows the data for several months following the examples I used previously.

The same settings that were found to be useful for the earlier few months continued to be useful for months after. Near the end of the data shown in Figure 2.22, it looks like the bull trend became stronger and the corrections smaller in time and price so the indicator did not reach the oversold zone on the corrections. That doesn't mean the indicator was not valuable, because if the larger time frame trend is bullish, any smaller time frame momentum bullish reversal below the OB zone is a setup for a long trade. If the indicator made a couple more oscillations without reaching the OS zone on the corrections, we would probably change to a shorter lookback period.

It is a quick and easy process to find the best indicator settings for any indicator and any market or time frame, as I have described. You are not looking for perfection. It doesn't exist. You are looking for the best fit, and that is as good as it is ever going to get. If you are ever taught by a book or course that there is one indicator and one setting that will consistently make reversals at price highs and lows, drop the book or walk away from the classroom. You are not being taught the truth by an experienced and successful trader.

Trading is like any other business. You have to use the information available, study, gain experience, and *make decisions*. I wish we had room in the book to put a hundred more examples of Dual Time Frame Momentum Strategy setups, indicators, and their settings. But this is just one chapter and just one part of the trading plan. It is much more important to understand the principles, concepts, and applications than to see lots of repetitive examples. If you understand the concepts and applications, you will be able to use this information with any indicator, any market, and any time frame.

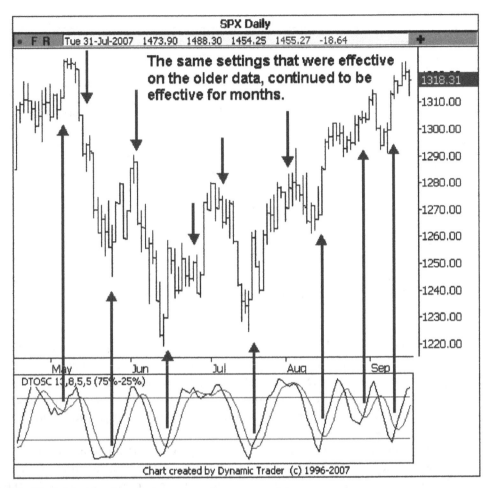

FIGURE 2.22 Indicator Settings Continue to Be Useful

DUAL TIME FRAME MOMENTUM STRATEGY RULES

The Dual Time Frame Momentum Strategy identifies when a market is in a position to consider a trade. It is the first filter for a potential trade. It is one part of the trading plan that will have completely objective rules, regardless of which indicator is used.

All you have to do is define what is a momentum reversal for the indicator you want to use, and you are set. If the indicator you use has overbought or oversold zones, you will incorporate them into the rules based on how the indicator typically acts and reacts to changes in momentum.

First let's take a look at the rules we would set up if using the DTosc, which tends to reach the overbought and oversold zones with most price swings. We can put the rules in

TABLE 2.1 Dual Time Frame Momentum Strategy Trade Setup Rules (DTosc)

Higher Time Frame Momentum	Smaller Time Frame Momentum
Bull, not OB	Long following a bullish reversal as long as bullish reversal is made below the OB zone.
Bull, OB	No new long position. Possible short position following a bearish reversal.
Bear, not OS	Short following a bearish reversal as long as the bearish reversal is made above the OS zone.
Bear, OS	No new short position. Possible long position following a bullish reversal.

a simple table (Table 2.1). The first column lists the four possible positions of the higher time frame momentum. The second column is the trade strategy given the position of the smaller time frame momentum.

The Dual Time Frame Momentum Strategy setups are not trade execution signals, but objective conditions that must be met to consider a trade:

Row 1: If the higher time frame is *bullish and not OB*, only long positions should be considered following a smaller time frame momentum bullish reversal. This is the ideal Dual Time Frame Momentum Strategy go-long setup. Two time frames of momentum are going in the same direction. The setup is made immediately following the smaller time frame momentum bullish reversal in the direction of the larger time frame bull momentum.

Row 2: If the higher time frame is *bullish but OB*, the upside should be limited and no new long positions should be taken. Short positions may be considered following a smaller time frame momentum bearish reversal. If the higher time frame is OB, the upside is usually limited before a momentum high is made, and there usually is not enough profit potential to execute a new long trade. A higher time frame overbought momentum is not a reason to exit an existing long position—it is merely a reason to avoid entering new long trades.

Row 3: If the higher time frame is *bearish but not OS*, a short position setup follows a smaller time frame bearish reversal. This is the ideal Dual Time Frame Momentum Strategy go-short setup. Two time frames of momentum are in the same direction, and the setup is made immediately following the smaller time frame momentum bearish reversal in the direction of the larger time frame bear momentum.

Row 4: If the higher time frame is *bearish but OS*, the downside should be limited and no new short positions should be taken. Long trades may be considered following a smaller time frame bullish reversal.

These conditions are simple, logical, and very powerful. There is no interpretation to the momentum position and how we use this information as part of a trading plan to make specific trade decisions. The Dual Time Frame Momentum Strategy is completely objective. Use it with any trading plan and I know you'll be very happy with your results.

These Dual Time Frame Momentum Strategy rules are good for any two time frames of data, from weekly/daily to 15m/5m.

Let's take a look at just one more example to illustrate the Dual Time Frame Momentum Strategy. Figure 2.23 shows 15m EUR/USD Forex data. The 60m data is the higher time frame and 15m data is the lower time frame. During most of the period of this 15m data, the higher time frame 60m momentum was bearish, as represented by the arrow line pointing to the right. The 60m momentum turned bearish just a few bars before the big pop up. The 15m momentum bearish reversals would be setups for short position trades as long as the lower time frame 15m bearish reversal was made above the OS zone.

There were eight 15m momentum bearish reversals made over about an 18-hour period following the 60m momentum bearish reversal. The second, third, and fourth 15m bearish reversals shown in Figure 2.23 were made with the market in a fairly narrow

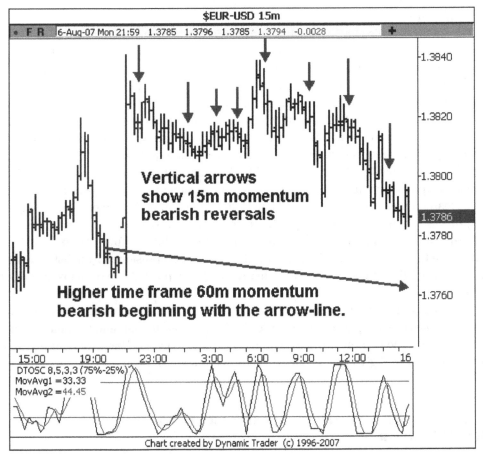

FIGURE 2.23 15m Bearish Reversals During 60m Bear Trend

TABLE 2.2 Dual Time Frame Momentum Strategy Trade Setup Rules (Stochastic)	
Higher Time Frame Momentum	**Smaller Time Frame Momentum**
Bull, not OB	Long following a bullish reversal as long as bullish reversal is made below the OB zone.
Bull, OB	No new long position. Possible short position following a bearish reversal.
Bear, not OS	Short following a bearish reversal as long as the bearish reversal is made above the OS zone.
Bear, OS	No new short position. Possible long position following a bullish reversal

trading range and turned out to have little if any profit potential, although we wouldn't have known that at the time they were made. The first and the last four 15m bearish reversals each were followed by strong moves down in the direction of the larger time frame 60m bearish momentum. Each would have resulted in great setups for short position day or swing trades.

I've set up the rules for the stochastic in Table 2.2 the same as I used for the DTosc, since the stochastic also has OB and OS zones. Figure 2.24 uses the same 15m EUR/USD data shown with the preceding DTosc example. The stochastic momentum turned bearish a few 15m bars before the DTosc did, but the first 15m stochastic momentum bearish reversal was also after the strong pop up.

While the stochastic didn't reach the OB zone on the momentum highs during this bear momentum trend, each 15m momentum bearish reversal was followed by a decline. All were good day-trade setups and most were good swing-trade setups.

What rules would you setup for an MACD, or any other indicator you are already familiar with and have used for other momentum strategies? That is your assignment. You've learned the principles of Dual Time Frame Momentum Strategies. The principles and process are the same for any indicator. Identify what the indicator activity is that represents a change in momentum, and devise the rules for the four conditions of the higher time frame momentum. Is a change of momentum represented by a fast and slow line crossover? By a higher or lower histogram bar? By a push above or below an OB or OS line?

Now that you know the principles for a Dual Time Frame Momentum Strategy, you can devise the rules for just about any price indicator. Identify minimum conditions that must be met on the two time frames to consider a trade, and you have the first part of a trading plan that will give you an edge in trade setup identification.

DUAL TIME FRAME MOMENTUM STRATEGY TRADE FILTER

The Dual Time Frame Momentum Strategy is a powerful filter to identify a trade setup. It may be used with any type of market and any two time frames. It is *not* a trade execution

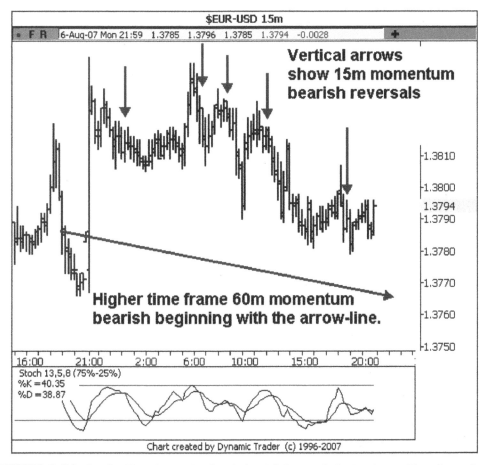

FIGURE 2.24 Smaller Time Frame Stochastic Bearish Reversals During Larger Time Frame Bear Trend

strategy. A later chapter will teach you specific trade execution strategies to use once you have identified the optimal trade condition.

The higher time frame identifies trade direction. The lower time frame momentum reversals in the direction of the higher time frame momentum are important filters to identify a high probability trade setup.

If you have the discipline to consider a trade only when a Dual Time Frame Momentum Strategy setup has been made, your trade results should improve dramatically.

CHAPTER 3

Practical Pattern Recognition for Trends and Corrections

Recognize Trend Position and Reversals for Trade Position

In this chapter, you will learn simple pattern recognition that will help you to identify whether a market is in a trend or correction, and what the position of the market is within the trend or correction. To be aware in advance if a market is at or near a reversal gives the trader a huge edge and will be an important part of any trading plan.

The prior chapter explained how to use dual time frame momentum position to identify the conditions for which side of the market to trade (larger time frame momentum) and the momentum reversal condition for a trade execution setup (smaller time frame momentum reversal). The dual time frame momentum position is 100% objective. There is no decision for the trader to make. Simply identify one of the four possible momentum positions (bull, bull OB, bear, bear OS) on two momentum time frames for the trade direction and trade execution setup.

As you also learned in Chapter 2, momentum trends do not always coincide with price trends. A momentum reversal may only represent the slowing down of the price trend, not necessarily a price trend reversal. Most important, a momentum reversal does not indicate where the market is within the price trend or if the trend itself is at or near a reversal.

The *pattern position* is the second of the four technical factors you will learn that provide the four key pieces of information you will use to make a trade decision.

Pattern Recognition Objectives
- Help identify whether a market is in a trend or correction.
- Ascertain whether the pattern conditions have been met that typically warn a trend or correction is at or near completion.
- Predict what is likely to follow the completion of the trend or correction.

This will be very valuable information for practical trade strategies for any market and any time frame as the trend position is another key to the trade direction and trade strategies.

In this chapter, you will learn the one important guideline that will indicate if a market is in a trend or correction and two simple patterns that will help to identify if the minimum conditions have been met that indicate completion of a trend or correction.

WHY IS IT IMPORTANT TO IDENTIFY A TREND OR CORRECTION?

It can be very useful, and by that I mean profitable, for a trader to be aware if a market is making a trend or correction and what the position of a market is within a trend or correction. Let's take a look at a few examples.

Figure 3.1 shows a strong bear trend making lower lows and lower highs. The last bar on the chart is a wide-range, outside-down day, often a trend continuation signal.

FIGURE 3.1 What Is the Position of the Bear Trend?

Would this be a great setup for a short trade and the continuation of the bear trend? It would be, *unless the bear trend is in the final stages and about to make a reversal.* Is there any way to know if the bear trend is in the final stages? If there is, we might not be so anxious to take a short trade following the outside down-day trend continuation bar.

If the pattern position suggests the bear trend is in a position to be complete followed by a substantial reversal up, we would probably avoid a short position on the daily outside down-day, bearish continuation signal or, at the least, only have minimum expectations for a continued decline and adjust the trade strategy accordingly.

Figure 3.2 adds several more bars to the prior chart. On the day following the last bar on the prior chart, which was a wide-range, outside-down day, this market reversed up for a substantial advance. A wide-range, outside-down day is typically seen as a trend continuation signal. But a short position following this wide-range down day would have been taken right at the low that preceded a significant advance and a losing trade.

The last bar on this chart is a wide-range up day, which took out a swing high and closed near the high of the day. Taking out a swing high is a traditional signal for a swing trader's go-long strategy. It looks like this market is very bullish and ripe for a long trade

FIGURE 3.2 Bull Trend or Correction to Bear Trend?

setup for a continuation of the bull trend. But what if the advance is just a correction to a bear trend? If so, the upside may be very limited before the market reverses to continue a bear trend to new lows. The pattern position may help to identify whether this is the case, which will have an important influence on the immediate trade strategy. We would be very cautious about taking a long trade if it is a corrective rally *with little upside potential* and would want to prepare for conditions for a reversal from a corrective high and a short trade to take advantage of a continued decline to a new low.

These are just a couple examples of how helpful it is to be aware of a few simple pattern position guidelines, to help identify if a market is in a trend or correction and whether the minimum conditions have been made to complete the trend or correction.

SIMPLE PATTERN RECOGNITION BASED ON ELLIOTT WAVE

The simple guidelines for pattern recognition and simple patterns in this chapter are based on Elliott wave (E-wave) analysis. You may have already had some exposure to Elliott wave analysis and become so confused by the overcomplicated approach to cycle degrees, subdivisions, and alternate wave counts taught by E-wave academics that your eyes are already starting to roll around. Stay with me, because in this chapter you are going to learn a very simplified, practical, and valuable approach to pattern recognition that you will clearly understand and immediately be able to put into practice.

E-wave analysis has been made way overcomplicated by E-wave academics. I know traders who have got bogged down in the paralysis of E-wave analysis for years and never figured out how to use it to make practical trade decisions. I'm going to teach you just one guideline and three patterns based on E-wave structure, which can be learned quickly and applied for practical trade strategies. You will learn how to look at any section of data of any market and any time frame and quickly determine if a market is likely in a trend or correction and if the pattern conditions have been made to complete the trend or correction. You will also learn how and why this information is valuable and how to make it a part of your trading plan. The pattern guidelines I teach for trends or corrections do not involve a complicated counting scheme or getting lost in the paralysis of analysis.

You will learn just one key guideline to identify if a market is in a trend or correction, and just three patterns to help identify trend and correction position. That is all we need to help make specific and practical trade decisions. Identifying patterns is only academic unless we can use the information to make specific and practical trade decisions, which, of course, is what this book is about.

TREND OR CORRECTION: THE OVERLAP GUIDELINE

There are two important pieces of information that we want the pattern position to tell us: Is a market in a trend or correction, and what is the position of the market within that trend or correction? Let's tackle whether a market is in a trend or correction first. This simple piece of information can be very helpful to a trade strategy.

The key is to identify if a market is making a correction. Why? If a market is making a correction, it should not take out the extreme that began the prior trend, but should eventually continue the trend direction prior to the correction and make a new extreme. Let's illustrate how this simple information can be very valuable.

Figure 3.3 shows a market that is making a decline following a strong advance. If the market is making a correction to the bull trend, it should not decline below the March 14 swing low shown on the chart and should eventually make a new high. It would be very valuable to have reliable information if the decline is a correction, because the downside potential would be very limited and the upside following the end of the correction would be very significant.

There is one simple pattern guideline that is very reliable to warn if a market is probably making a correction and not a new trend to a new extreme. If a market overlaps a section, more than likely it is making a correction. An *overlap* is when a market makes a new low or high, and then trades back into the range of the prior section.

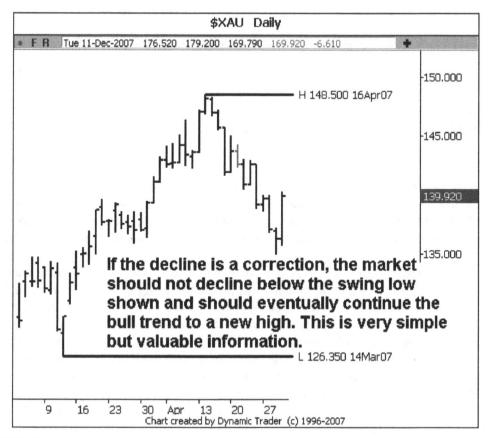

FIGURE 3.3 Trend or Correction

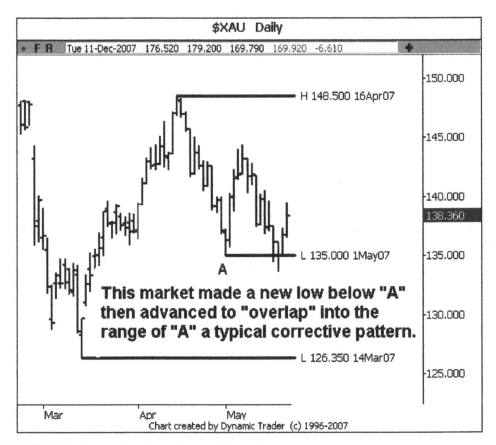

FIGURE 3.4 Section Overlap Indicates a Correction

In Figure 3.4 the Philadelphia Gold and Silver Index (XAU) made an initial swing low, labeled *A*, then a short rally followed by a new low below A, and then traded back up into the range of section A. The market overlapped, or traded back into, the range of section A, which warned the decline was probably a correction and not a bear trend to new lows.

The next chart, Figure 3.5, adds more data and shows how the market continued to make overlapping swings, confirming it was probably making a correction and would eventually make a new high without trading below the low on the chart. Bars later, the XAU did eventually make a new high as anticipated without trading below the low of the prior trend. Knowing early on that, following the first overlap, the XAU was probably making a correction and would eventually continue the bull trend to a new high gave the trader a huge edge. The downside should be limited with significant upside potential.

Figure 3.6 is another example of an overlap pattern that signals the decline is a correction and the mini Dow Jones Futures (YM) will eventually make a new high. This would be extremely valuable information particularly after the market had made such

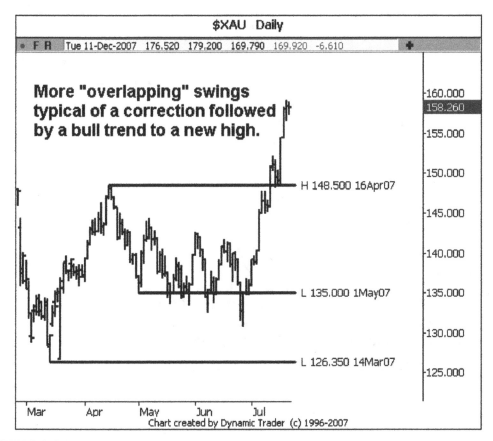

FIGURE 3.5 Overlapping Sections Are Typical of a Correction

a sharp decline, which would have made many traders bearish, just at a time when the market may be ready to take off to the upside following a corrective low.

Figure 3.7 adds more data to the previous chart and shows how the decline was a correction as anticipated by the overlap and the market did eventually make a new high, also as anticipated.

Wouldn't it be helpful to your trading to recognize, a few bars after the section C low, that the YM in the previous two charts was probably making a correction which would be followed by a new high without taking out the low shown on the chart? Let me answer that for you just in case you're not paying attention. *Very helpful.* You would then use the momentum, price, and time tools taught in this book to determine if the market was in a position to complete a correction for a long trade setup well before it continued to advance and take out a swing high. Pattern position signals can be a key component of any practical, real-world trading plan. The simple guidelines like the overlap guideline can give an early warning of the probable outcome of the current market position.

Have you ever read a book or taken a trading course where every example showed how every market responded to whatever signal was being taught? A better question may

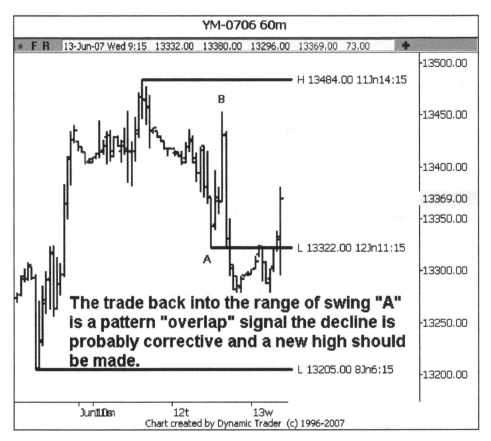

The trade back into the range of swing "A" is a pattern "overlap" signal the decline is probably corrective and a new high should be made.

FIGURE 3.6 Overlapped Sections Implies a Correction

be, have you ever read a book or taken a trading course that made a point that whatever was being taught did *not* work every time? This book is about the real world. No technical analysis technique, pattern signal, or trade strategy works every time.

A market may run against an ideal setup. An ideal pattern position that usually results in a corrective high or low may be followed by a strong trend continuation. I've said this before and you'll hear it again and again: The business of trading is to identify conditions with a high *probability* outcome and acceptable capital exposure. We will not be right all of the time. But we should be right most of the time, and when wrong, the cost is acceptable.

If you ever read a trading book or take a trading course where the author/instructor does not clearly state that whatever strategy he is teaching will not be profitable with every trade, and doesn't show examples that don't work out, get out as quickly as possible before it costs you a lot of hard-earned money. The author/instructor is not being honest and does not have your best interests at heart.

Not every correction will have an overlap of swings before the correction is complete. Not every overlap of swings will be part of a correction. Figure 3.8 is a 60-minute

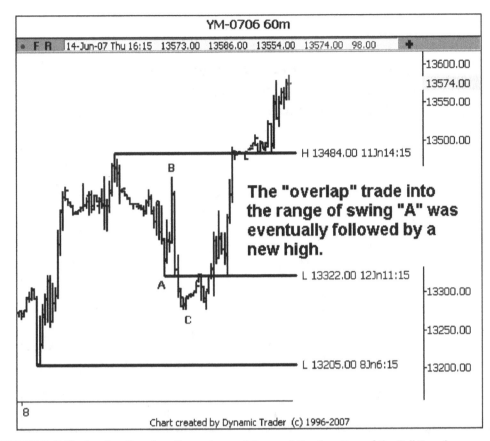

FIGURE 3.7 Overlap Signals a Correction and Eventual Continuation of the Bull Trend

chart of the S&P mini futures contract (ES) and shows a correction that was just one strong swing up followed by a continued bear trend to a new low. There was no overlapping swing in this correction.

Swings may overlap and not be a part of a correction. Figure 3.9 clearly shows the overlapping sections in the box which typically signal the market was making a corrective rally. However, the SPX eventually continued to advance to a new high for a failed overlap corrective pattern signal.

I actually had to do quite a bit of searching through several markets and time frames to locate these two failed pattern examples, because most corrections do have a swing overlap and most overlaps are a part of a correction. Of the two types of failed examples, the most infrequent is an overlap that is not part of a correction.

Always remember that there are no sure things with any type of trade strategy. However, we want to put the odds in our favor and give ourselves an edge by identifying conditions with a high probability outcome. If most swing overlaps are part of a correction, this guideline will be an important part of our trading plan that we can use to make specific low-risk, high probability trade decisions.

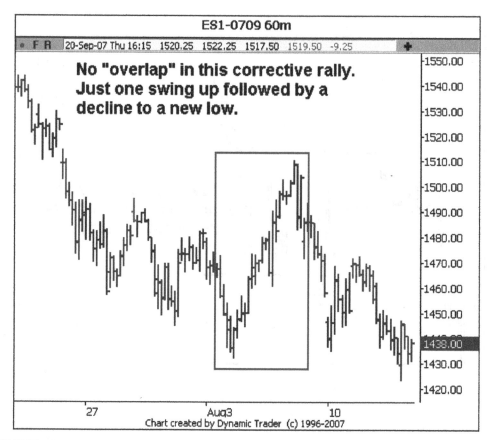

FIGURE 3.8   Not Every Correction Has Overlapped Sections

ABC AND AWAY WE GO

If overlapping swings are typical of a correction, it implies a correction will usually have at least three swings. A frequent type of correction for all markets and all time frames is three swings, called an *ABC correction*. However, corrections may take many forms and have more than three swings. Traders obsessed with Elliott wave have identified 13 complex corrective patterns, not including the so-called irregular ABCs. For our purposes, the most important piece of information is a correction should have at least three distinct swings.

We're going to keep it very simple, as usual, and always make the assumption that a correction will have at least three sections called a simple ABC—in E-wave terms, an ABC zigzag. A correction will often have more than three swings or a form other than a simple ABC, but we always first look for at least three sections. Let's take a look at a

FIGURE 3.9 Failed Overlap

simple ABC example and then learn the rules and guidelines and how this information can be used for practical trade decisions.

I'm going to use E-wave type nomenclature to identify the pivot highs and lows and usually call them *waves*. The terms *wave, swing,* and *section* are all used to identify the same thing. Waves that are a part of a correction are labeled with letters, such as Wave-A (W.A), Wave-B (W.B), etc.

Figure 3.10 is a daily chart of American Airlines (AA) showing an ABC correction followed by a bull trend to a new high. Following the Wave-C low, AA traded up into the range of Wave-A for an overlap and pattern signal that AA should be making a correction to a bull trend, not a bear trend to a new low. Once the overlap is made, we don't know if the correction has ended as a simple ABC or will develop into a complex correction. What we do know is that it probably is a correction and will eventually continue to advance to a new high. We also know that the minimum three sections for a correction are complete. A continued advance to above the Wave-B high is a pattern signal that the corrective low is probably complete and the advance will continue.

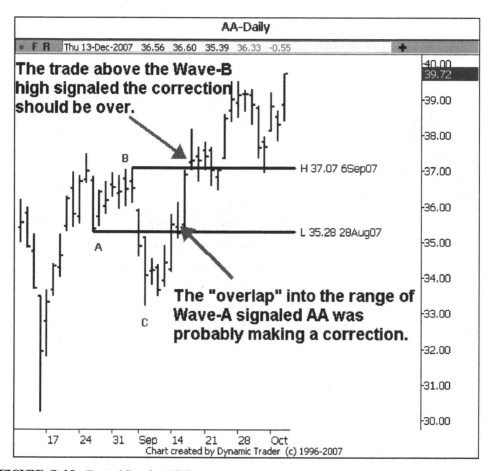

FIGURE 3.10 Typical Simple ABC Correction

This one example illustrates the three guidelines for ABC corrections, the minimum expected pattern for a correction:

ABC Guidelines

1. The Wave-C should exceed the extreme of Wave-A.
2. If the market trades back into the range of Wave-A, the minimum conditions for a correction are complete.
3. A trade beyond the Wave-B extreme is a pattern signal that the correction should be complete.

Figure 3.11 is the daily Russell 1000 ETF (IWD) and shows another ABC correction. IWD made three distinct sections up for a potential ABC and then traded into the range of Wave-A to signal it was probably making a correction and would eventually decline

FIGURE 3.11 ABC Correction Followed by New Lows

to a new low. IWD traded below the Wave-B low to signal the correction should be over and the bear trend should continue.

Let's review a few important things before we continue. We make a trade decision based on what we *know*. We use the information that we know to identify conditions with a high probability outcome. The assumption is that a correction will make at least three sections (also called swings or waves). If an overlap is made, it meets the three section criteria and is a pattern signal that a correction is probably being made. We know the market has made a section overlap and we know the minimum three sections are complete. At this point, we would only consider trades against the correction direction. If the Wave-B extreme is taken out, more than likely the corrective high or low has been made and is an all-out go long or short signal, depending if the Wave-B is a high or low, with a stop no further than the potential Wave-C extreme.

Notice that I continually use the words *potential, probable, more than likely,* and such. Why? Remember that the objective of all trade strategies is to identify conditions

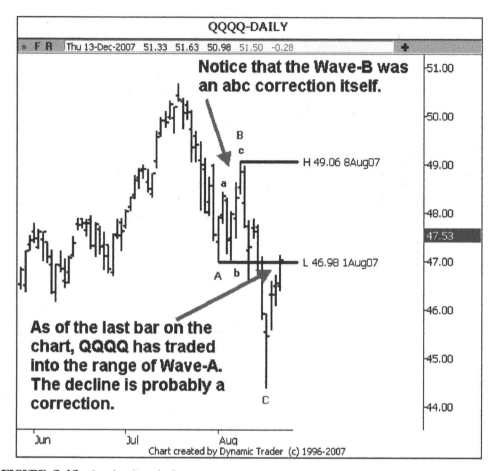

FIGURE 3.12 Overlap Signals Correction

with a high *probability* outcome and acceptable capital exposure. *Probability* is the key word, so I never imply that a particular strategy—whether pattern recognition, Dual Time Frame Momentum, price, or any other strategy—will always have the expected outcome. I am teaching you strategies and market conditions that will have a *probable* outcome.

As of the last bar on the daily QQQQ chart in Figure 3.12, QQQQ has traded into the range of Wave-A. The minimum conditions to complete an ABC correction have been made and QQQQ is likely to eventually continue to advance to above the high shown on the chart. It will still take a trade above the Wave-B high to confirm the corrective low should be complete. Notice that the Wave-B, which is a correction itself to the Wave-A down, made a small ABC. Since a Wave-B is itself a correction, its pattern should also meet the guidelines for a correction for what we call a smaller degree pattern. We are not going to complicate pattern analysis with subdivisions and degrees. While it can be helpful, it is an entire course of study in itself and is not necessary for the trading strategies taught in this book.

As of the last bar on the QQQQ daily chart in Figure 3.12, we don't know if an ABC correction is complete or if it will take a more complex pattern or even if the QQQQ won't decline to a new low. What we do *know* is the conditions for a correction have been made with the three sections and overlap trade into the Wave-A range. That information alone gives us an edge to immediately consider long trade strategies for a probable advance to a new high.

The weekly British pound chart in Figure 3.13 shows another ABC correction. The first weekly bar off the potential Wave-C low traded above the Wave-B high for a pattern confirmation signal that an ABC correction was probably complete and the bull trend would eventually continue to a new high without trading below the Wave-C low.

The corrective trade strategies are applicable to any actively traded market and any time frame, whether stocks, ETFs, futures, indexes, or Forex.

You've learned about simple ABC corrections and how to identify the initial signal that the market is in a correction and the initial conditions that signal an ABC

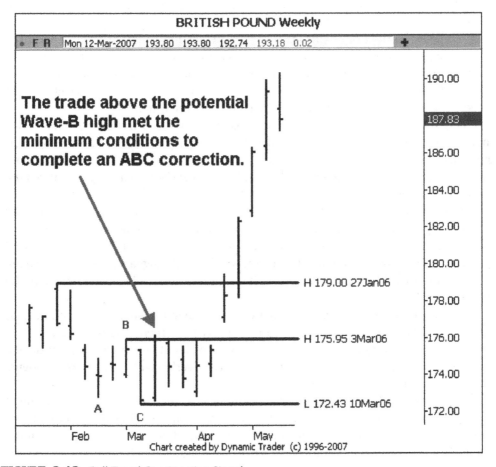

FIGURE 3.13 Bull Trend Continuation Signal

correction may be complete. In Chapter 4, you will learn how to identify *in advance* the high probability price target to complete an ABC and other corrections.

While the simple ABC correction is a frequent type of correction, a correction can take many forms. Let's take a look at complex corrections.

COMPLEX CORRECTIONS

A *complex* correction is any correction that makes more than three waves or sections. E-wave academics have identified 13 patterns of complex corrections. We are not going to examine the many patterns of complex corrections here. In fact, we're not going to examine any particular complex correction patterns because it serves little purpose for practical trade strategies. All that we want to do is recognize that a correction is probably being made. If we can do that, we know to orient our trade strategy to trade against the direction of the correction for a probable continuation of the trend to a new high or low once the correction is complete.

A complex correction typically has several sections that overlap. That's the key—overlapping sections. Once we identify that the market should be making a corrective pattern and eventually trend to a new high or low, we can use other strategies including Dual Time Frame Momentum, price, and time position to help identify if the correction is in a position to be complete and continue the trend.

Figure 3.14 is an example of a complex correction in the GBP/USD 60-minute data. While the last advance of the correction made a new high, the sections had already overlapped and even made a slight new low; the pattern signals a correction to the bear trend was probably being made, not a new bull trend. The GBP/USD eventually completed the correction and continued the bear trend to a new low.

Figure 3.15 shows another complex correction for the EUR/USD 15-minute data. I'll let you tear your hair out putting labels on each of the sections in the correction. The most important factor: Each of the small sections overlapped as the EUR/USD struggled higher. Eventually a swing low was taken out, which usually signals a correction is complete, and the EUR/USD continued to decline to a new low, below the low where the correction began.

It is always easy to show after-the-fact examples. Just remember what you need to learn here. If the sections overlap, more than likely a correction is being made. That information itself is very valuable and will help you to identify the probable position of a market and probable next major trend direction. The overlap will be an important signal to trade direction.

Figure 3.16 is a GM daily chart showing another complex correction. Near the end of the correction, GM traded to a new high for the correction but below the bull trend high shown on the chart, then traded back into the range of the first section up, signaling more than likely it was making a correction and would eventually continue lower. As soon as a market makes the overlap, it is a strong pattern signal a correction is being made. The

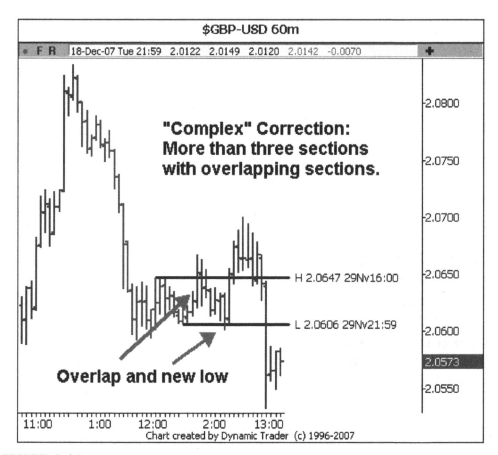

FIGURE 3.14 Complex Correction Sections Usually Overlap

market may continue in a complex correction, making several overlaps. Throughout, the strategy will be to identify the end of the correction in order to position for a trade in the direction of the trend. Later in this book, you will learn specific reversal and breakout trade strategies.

Wouldn't it be nice, and infinitely profitable, if every market and every time frame worked out as expected? Figure 3.17 shows 60-minute Dow Jones mini futures contract (YM) data. If we were to add bar-by-bar during the period shown in the box, the only conclusion from a pattern perspective would be that the YM was making a correction in a bull trend. We could call it a complex correction, a consolidation, a trading range or any other corrective name you want to give it. The main factor is the sections were overlapping, typical of a correction. How did it turn out? Eventually, the YM declined strongly to a new low, not a new high as would have been anticipated from the probable corrective pattern position.

As in any other business, the best data, strategies, and plans sometimes don't work out. Markets may do just the opposite of what is anticipated from the information

FIGURE 3.15 Overlapping Sections Typical for a Correction

available. And, just like with any other business, that is why strategies are so important to limit losses when things don't work out as planned. Trade strategies and trade management are just as important as the technical analysis that identifies the high probability setups. Later in this book, you will learn specific trade strategies and trade management from entry to exit that will help minimize losses when a setup does not work out, and maximize gains when it does.

OVERLAP IS THE KEY TO IDENTIFY A CORRECTION

We don't need to look at dozens of examples of ABC and complex corrections, since there is just one guiding principle to identify if a market is in a correction. Once the sections overlap, it is an early alert signal the market should be making a correction. While a market may continue to trade higher or lower depending on the direction of the

FIGURE 3.16 Complex Correction with Overlap

correction, the overlapping sections continue to signal that the market is in a correction, that it should not make a new extreme, and that it will eventually continue to trend in the direction of the trend prior to the beginning of the correction.

TRENDS AND FIVE-WAVE PATTERNS

You learned that corrections are usually at least three sections and the overlap of a section is the pattern guideline that signals the market should be in a correction and not a trend. A correction may make more than three sections for a complex correction, but once an overlap is made, more than likely the market is making a correction and will eventually continue in the original trend direction before the correction began, and reach a new high or low.

Trends usually make five sections, and the sections do not overlap. In E-wave terms, a trend is called an *impulse* wave. We are going to stick with the term *trend* because

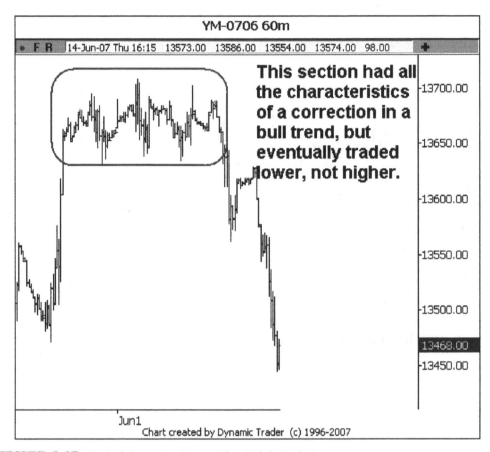

FIGURE 3.17 Typical Corrective Pattern That Didn't Work Out

all that we are concerned with is using pattern guidelines to identify two basic market conditions: trends and corrections.

We have used letters to label the sections of a correction (Wave-A, Wave-B, etc.). Numbers are used to identify the sections of a trend, such as Wave-1 (W.1), Wave-2 (W.2), and so on.

A trend usually makes five sections, or *waves*, in E-wave terms. There are three rules accepted by E-wave traders for five-wave trends. They are good rules with one modification, so let's learn them first and then take a look at a chart. Since I've modified one of the accepted E-wave trend rules, I'm going to call them guidelines instead of rules.

Trend Pattern Guidelines

1. Wave-2 cannot trade beyond the beginning of Wave-1.

2. Wave-3 cannot be the shortest in price of waves 1, 3, and 5.

3. Wave-4 cannot make a daily close into the closing range of Wave-1.

The one modification I've made to the accepted E-wave rules is the Wave-4 rule with daily data. The typical E-wave rule is Wave-4 cannot *trade* into the range of Wave-1. My modification to the rule is Wave-4 cannot make a daily close into the daily closing range of Wave-1. Over the past 20-plus years, I've seen a market trade a few ticks into the Wave-1 range and then continue the trend to complete an otherwise perfect five-wave trend so many times that I modified the rule, and it has served me and others very well over the years.

The SPX daily chart in Figure 3.18 illustrates the three trend rules.

Guideline 1, that a Wave-2 may not exceed the beginning of a Wave-1, is logical. If a market took out the beginning of Wave-1, it would have made a new high or low and voided any logical beginning of a new trend.

In Chapter 4, you will learn how we can use guideline 2, where the Wave-3 cannot be the shortest in price of waves 1, 3, and 5, to project the maximum trend price target in certain circumstances.

FIGURE 3.18 The Three Trend Pattern Rules

Guideline 3, where a Wave-4 may not close into the daily closing range of Wave-1, is related to the correction overlap rule. An overlap of the daily closing range of Wave-1 signals the market is probably not making a trend but a correction.

Before you learn more about the most typical trend pattern, I want to make something very clear. Not every trend makes a five-wave pattern that conforms to the trend guidelines. But many trends do, and knowing that a trend is usually at least five waves or sections provides us with valuable information to recognize when a trend May be in the final stages before a major trend reversal. Let's take a look at some trends and see how the probable trend pattern can help us to make practical trade decisions.

Figure 3.19 is the continuous British pound weekly closing data. As of the last data point on the chart, the BP has made an ideal five-wave decline to a new low, although the potential Wave-5 may not be complete. How does the pattern of the BP data through the last data point help us?

If most trends are complete with five sections that conform to the three trend guidelines, what we *know* is the BP has met the guidelines to complete Waves 1 through 4 and

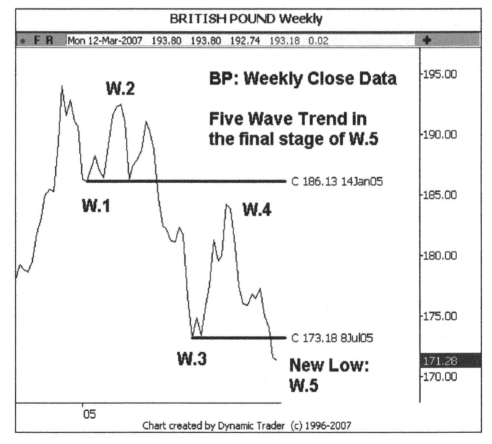

FIGURE 3.19   Potential Five-Wave Trend, British Pound

may be in the final section of the bear trend. The downside could be relatively limited. This itself can be valuable information. While the BP had been in a bear trend for months and just broke out to a new low, typically a very bearish signal for swing traders, we would be aware that the bear trend could be very near the end just at a time when many traders would be extremely bearish.

We are always making decisions based on the data through the last data point, but we trade the right side of the chart—the side to the right of the last data point. We're making the best guess possible based on the known data and probable market position. The information from the pattern position of the data on the weekly BP chart is that the downside may be limited and the next weekly swing low is likely to be followed by a rally greater in time and price than any since the beginning of the bear trend. That is valuable information. The momentum, price, and time position will help us to identify the next swing low and potential W.5 low.

Figure 3.20 is daily SPX data. What do we know as of the last bar on the chart? With the decline below the swing low labeled 3, there are four completed sections that meet

FIGURE 3.20 Potential Five-Wave Trend, SPX

the trend guidelines. The Wave-4 did not close into the closing range of Wave-1, and the SPX has made a new low for a potential Wave-5 to complete the bear trend. The downside should be limited before a Wave-5 low is made and a rally greater in time and price than any rally in the bear trend (the W.2 or W.4 corrections) begins. This is a description of what we know and the likely outcome.

How did it turn out? Go back to Figure 3.18, which illustrated the three E-wave guidelines for five-wave trends. It includes the same data on this chart plus a couple of additional weeks of data. The SPX made a sharp rally. The bear trend made five sections.

Don't make wave counting difficult. Think in logical terms. If a correction is greater in time and price than any previous correction of the trend section, we can count it as a completed wave or section. Let's illustrate this. In Figure 3.21 I've labeled a five-wave bull trend on the QQQQ daily chart. The Wave-2 decline lasted just four days but was greater in time and price than any correction during what is labeled the Wave-1 advance. Since that decline was greater in time and/or price, more than likely it is a completed correction to the trend section, or a Wave-2.

FIGURE 3.21   Five-Wave Trend, QQQQ

The QQQQ than made a significant rally to a new high above what is labeled a Wave-1 and, beginning with what is labeled the Wave-3 high, made a correction much greater in time and price than any correction since the Wave-2 low. It should be a Wave-4 low.

The QQQQ then made a new high to complete four sections. Since most trends are complete with five waves, the upside would probably be limited before the Wave-5 is complete and either a corrective decline greater than any correction within the five-wave trend or a new bear trend began. The key is, once the new high above the probable Wave-3 high was made, more than likely the QQQQ was in the final stages of the bull trend from the August low and a significant decline would soon begin. The decline below the Wave-4 low signaled the end of the five-wave trend.

Keep this whole business of counting or labeling waves or sections simple and logical. Don't fall into the E-wave paralysis of analysis trap. We are only interested in the two types of patterns that are useful to help us understand the position of the market and to make practical trade decisions.

Let's take another look at the QQQQ daily data. As of the last bar on Figure 3.22, the QQQQ has traded above the probable Wave-B swing high, confirming a three-wave

FIGURE 3.22 Correction Should Be Followed by at Least a Five-Wave Trend

decline. Trends should be at least five waves, so the market has clearly indicated by the pattern that a correction to the bull trend was being made. The correction may continue in a complex correction but—and here's the key information—the QQQQ should eventually make at least a five-wave trend to a new high. That is powerful information as of the last bar on the chart. The downside should be relatively limited and the upside has significant potential.

Let's add some more data to the chart. As of the last bar on the chart in Figure 3.23, the QQQQ has made a new high as anticipated. The new high signals a trend should be under way. Trends should be at least five waves. Only waves 1 and 2 could be complete as of the last bar. That means there should be waves 3 through 5 still to come, taking the QQQQ higher, possibly much higher. Again, this is powerful information based on simple correction and trend pattern recognition guidelines and the logical position of the market based just on the pattern as of the last bar.

More data is added in Figure 3.24. The last bar on the chart has made a new high following a probable Wave-4 low. Since most trends end with five sections, the upside should be relatively limited before the entire trend up from the W.C low is complete. You

FIGURE 3.23   Trends Are Usually at Least Five Waves

FIGURE 3.24   The Fifth Section or Wave Usually Ends the Trend

know what happened. I started this series of examples with the end result. A few bars later, a high was made, followed by a sharp decline.

I don't want you to become a so-called Elliott wave expert. I just want you to use simple logic on what trends and corrections usually look like, what guidelines to use to recognize the probable position of the market within a trend or correction as well as the probable outcome, and to think in a logical step-by-step manner as new data is added. No complex counting systems, no detailed subdivisions of subdivisions and waves of different degrees. Just know a couple simple patterns that are reliable and how to recognize them as the market unfolds.

GREATER IN TIME AND PRICE

Earlier, I identified corrections as "greater in time and price" than any prior correction in the section to help identify a new section in the trend. W. D. Gann called this an overbalance of time and/or price. It is a simple but reliable way to help determine whether a section is complete.

Figure 3.25 is daily QQQQ day and shows a four bar decline which is labeled a Wave-2. Up to this point in time, the largest decline was just two bars, which was much shorter in price than the four bar decline. Once the QQQQ made a new high, the larger four bar correction is probably a Wave-2 correction to the bull trend up to that point.

No matter what approach to technical analysis you use, you always have to make assumptions based on the information at hand. The outcome is *never* certain, but using the "greater in time and/or price" correction assumption is a good one, at least until more data is available that may prove it wrong.

The other "greater in time and/or price" assumption is that once a trend is complete, the minimum expectation is that a correction greater in time and price should follow than any correction within the trend. In other words, the minimum expectation is a correction greater than either the Wave-2 or Wave-4 corrections (if a five-wave trend) should be

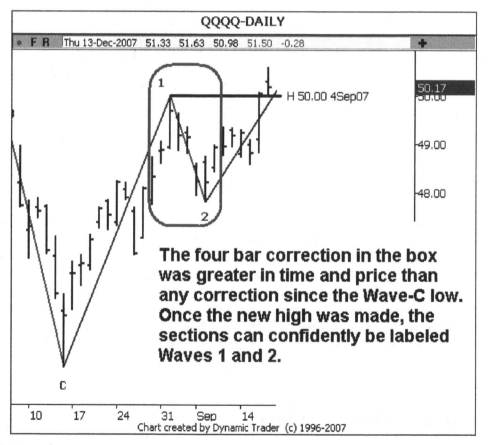

FIGURE 3.25   Wave-2 Greater in Time and Price

made. This is very valuable information that you will use over and over again. Note that I said the "minimum expectation." Once a trend is complete, either a correction to that trend will be made or a new trend in the opposite direction may begin. It depends on the position of the just completed trend within the larger time frame trend. If we were going to get into different degrees or time frames of trend, we would just complicate matters and have to learn about subdivisions of trends and more. Frankly, that is an entire course in and of itself, and we just don't need it to make practical, high probability trade decisions day by day.

FIFTH WAVES ARE THE KEY

The most valuable piece of information regarding trends is that once waves 1 through 4 are confirmed, the trend should be in the final stages. In our *DT Reports* we often say, "The trade to a new high (if a bull trend) confirms a Wave-4 should be complete and the upside should be limited before a Wave-5 high is complete, which should complete the bull trend." If a market is making new highs, the natural inclination for most traders is to be very bullish. This is a good inclination in the early stages of a trend. It can be a very costly inclination in the later stages of a trend. If we are aware that all of the guidelines to complete Waves 1 through 4 have been met, the swing to a new high could be a Wave-5 and the probable last swing up in a larger time frame. This information will be a huge advantage and help us to be prepared for a top and major reversal just when most traders are very bullish.

If we just focus on this one pattern tendency of trends to usually make at least five sections with no overlaps, that information alone will be of enormous benefit if four sections are complete. If a market is in a probable Wave-5, the next momentum reversal could be the early signal the Wave-5 is complete and we can adjust our trade management strategies accordingly. I will teach you more on how to use momentum to confirm pattern position in the chapters to come.

Figure 3.26 is General Motors (GM) daily close data. Based solely on the probable pattern position, what would you anticipate for GM in the days or weeks ahead?

GM has made a new low, so the decline should be a trend, not a correction. If so, three waves could be complete. If this is the case, following the completion of a Wave-4 corrective high, GM should make a new low. Not good news for the stockholders, given that GM has already declined over 30% in a month. And, based on the pattern position, more than likely GM will continue lower before the decline is complete. Ouch—unless you're short.

Figure 3.27 is 15-minute data for the GBP/USD. What should you anticipate as of the last bar on the chart?

The GBP/USD has made a five-wave decline, confirmed by the trade above the probable Wave-4 high. What do we anticipate following a completed five-wave trend just based

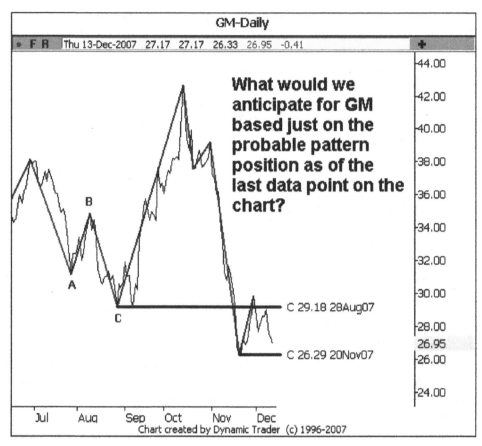

FIGURE 3.26 GM Pattern Position

on pattern? At least a corrective rally greater in time and price than any correction within the bear trend should follow. More than likely, the GBP/USD should be sideways to up for a while longer before the bear trend has the potential to continue.

Corrections usually have overlapping sections. Trends usually do not. But markets don't always follow the rules! Figure 3.28 is daily SPX data for more than a two-year period. The SPX was in a relentless bull trend, making higher highs and higher lows, but each bull section overlapped with the prior section. A trend structure is not supposed to do that. But sometimes they do. Within the larger time frame overlapping sections, the S&P made lots of tradable minor trends and corrections.

That is why pattern position is not the only factor on which to base a trade decision. It is one of the four key factors, which also include the momentum, price, and time position, plus low-risk, high probability trade strategies that make up a complete trading plan. Let the Elliott wave obsessives go crazy with a labeling scheme for this bull trend. All we want to do is make money and use practical pattern guidelines to help us make high probability trade decisions.

FIGURE 3.27 GBP/USD Pattern Position

Before we go on to the next chapter and learn how to make high probability price targets in advance for support, resistance, and trend reversal, let's take a quick look at how we will use what we have learned so far about momentum and pattern position to help make trade decisions.

MOMENTUM AND PATTERN POSITION

In Chapter 2, you learned how to use dual time frame momentum position as the filter to identify probable trade setups. How do we use what we have learned so far about momentum and pattern together to up the odds for a successful trade and lower the initial capital exposure?

Let's revisit the QQQQ daily chart with Figure 3.29, and include a momentum indicator. The pattern signal that a five-wave trend is complete occurs if the market takes out the Wave-4 extreme, in this case a low. The Wave-4 extreme may be far from what

FIGURE 3.28 Overlapping Trend Waves

may end up to be the Wave-5 high. Ideally, we have a much earlier signal than a decline below the Wave-4 low. As of the last bar on the chart, the momentum made a bearish reversal. The QQQQ price was well above the probable Wave-4 low. The pattern position of a probable Wave-5 high with a momentum bearish reversal is a setup to signal the Wave-5 is probably complete. It is a setup for a short trade with very minimal capital exposure. As you will learn as we put all of the factors together to develop a simple but comprehensive trade plan, it is when several completely independent factors all indicate the same position that the best setups with the highest probability outcome and smallest capital exposure are made.

Figure 3.30 is the AA daily data we used for an example in the correction section. The initial pattern signal that an ABC correction may be complete occurs if the market trades into the range of the potential Wave-A low, making an overlap. As of the last bar on this chart, AA has clearly made a three section decline for a potential ABC correction and has made a bullish momentum reversal. Pattern position and momentum reversal

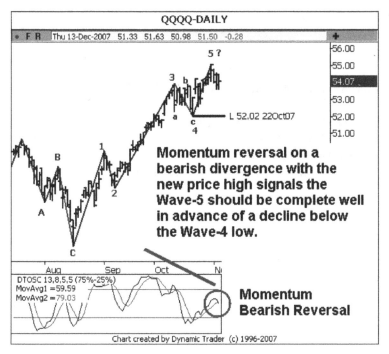

FIGURE 3.29 Pattern and Momentum Setup

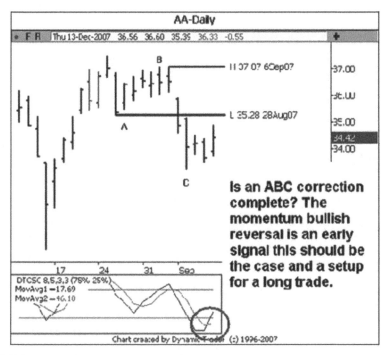

FIGURE 3.30 ABC and Momentum Reversal

together are giving an early warning of an ABC low setup for a long trade before an overlap is made.

MOMENTUM AND PATTERN NOT ENOUGH

Potential pattern position and momentum reversals are a powerful combination to identify trade setups, which you will learn much more about in the chapters ahead. But the combination of just these two factors is not as powerful as when we add the price and time position, which you will learn in the next two chapters.

CHAPTER 4

Beyond Fib Retracements

High Probability Price Targets for Support/Resistance and Trend Reversal

In this chapter, you will learn new and unique ways to project in advance very narrow-range price targets for any market condition. The Dynamic Price Strategies you learn will put you miles ahead of traders who only use typical Fibonacci retracements.

Are you ready to learn how to identify *in advance* narrow-range price zones for trend and countertrend reversal? I'm not talking about just identifying support and resistance. I'm going to take you beyond simple support and resistance and teach you how to project high probability trend reversal price targets for any market and any time frame. That's information every trader can use every day and make an important part of a trading plan.

Many trading books talk about Fibonacci (Fib) retracements and imbue them with magical properties that will result in endlessly profitable trade strategies. Fib retracements by themselves can be useful, but they are only entry-level price strategies compared to the more comprehensive Dynamic Price Strategies you will learn in this chapter. Fib retracements are only one type of price technique and fail to include key ratios for a complete price strategy approach.

Most trading software includes a Fib retracement routine. While many corrective highs and lows are made at Fib retracements, most traders have not been taught how to identify *in advance* which retracement is likely to be support, resistance, or trend reversal. Plus, the Fib ratios are a limited set of ratios that do not include other important geometric ratios that are equally important for a complete price strategy. It is not enough to know that a reversal should be made near one of the retracement levels. With three, four, or five retracement levels on a chart, it is imperative that the trader have some method to identify which retracement level is likely to be the support/resistance or trend reversal.

In this chapter, I teach you not only how to identify in advance which retracement level is likely to be the target for a trend reversal high or low, but some new and very important ratios to project the end of trends and corrections that are not typically used by most traders. In addition, you will learn unique and very effective ways to identify high probability price target zones to use for practical trade strategies.

In this chapter, you will learn the difference between internal and external retracements and alternate price projections, and how together they identify not just support and resistance, but narrow-range price zones where corrections and trends usually end. Even if you are familiar with Fib retracements, don't skip through this chapter as there should be a lot of new information for you. Prepare to take your price analysis to a whole new level with real-world, practical price trade strategies.

I have taught this approach for almost two decades to all types of traders, from day traders to position traders and for all types of markets, including Forex, futures, stocks, exchange-traded funds (ETFs), and even mutual funds. I call this approach to price *Dynamic Price Strategy*. Why not just call it Fibonacci price strategies? For two reasons. One, we use some ratios that are not a direct part of the Fibonacci series but are just as important as the typical Fib ratios. And two, we use the ratios in ways other than the typical retracement approach usually taught.

I have refined and simplified the Dynamic Price Strategy approach over the years to get to the core of practical, real-world price strategies that you can use for any market and any time frame. Let's begin by learning *internal retracements*.

INTERNAL RETRACEMENTS AND CORRECTIONS

There are two types of retracements: *internal* and *external*. The price retracements with which most traders are familiar are what I call *internal retracements*. If it is necessary to distinguish between internal and external retracements in this chapter, I will use the label *In-Ret* for internal retracements.

Internal retracements are less than 100% and are primarily used to identify the price target to complete a correction. Even if you are familiar with so-called Fib retracements, don't skip this section. I want to be sure we are on the same page with the language, terms, and specific ratios used with the Dynamic Price Strategy.

The ratios used for internal retracements are .382, .50, .618, and .786. They are often expressed as a percentage. The first three ratios, .382, .50, and .618, are commonly called Fib retracements, although .50 is not actually a Fib ratio. The fourth ratio, .786, may be new to you unless you've taken some of my courses over the years. It is not a Fib ratio but is closely related and an important retracement ratio that should always be included; it is the square root of .618.

I won't go through the history of the Italian Fibonacci and the ratios named after him. The history and significance of the ratios is thoroughly covered in other trading and non-trading books. There is a huge body of trading and mathematical literature about Fibonacci numbers and ratios for those interested. The history is simply not relevant. I think I have almost every book relating to Fibonacci, sacred and philosophical geometry, sacred architecture, and related subjects available in the past 30 years. including many that are out of print. It is a very, very interesting subject. But all those books and three dollars will get you a cup of cappuccino at the local overpriced coffee shop. We'll just stick to the practical application. All you need to know are the numbers for trading. Feel free to spend your spare time learning about the fascinating history and historical application of these geometric and harmonic numbers and ratios. It is time well spent but not relevant to the course of study at hand.

I'm also not going to discuss why markets seem to respond to these price (and time) harmonics. That is another fascinating subject, not yet fully understood, but there is a lot of evidence that our brains are hardwired to respond to these proportions. Since market trends and corrections are simply the consequence of crowd psychology, a natural consequence is for trends and countertrends to be in the proportion of these harmonics. Robert Prechter has done a good job of addressing the whys and hows of these harmonics in price data in his books *Socionomics: The Science of History and Social Prediction* and *Pioneering Studies in Socionomics* (New Classics Library, 2003). If you want more background, knock yourself out with this fascinating study.

But I digress. Back to internal retracements: What are they and how do we make and display them on a chart?

Figure 4.1 shows the four key internal retracements for a bull section of the 60-minute data for an S&P mini futures (ES) contract.

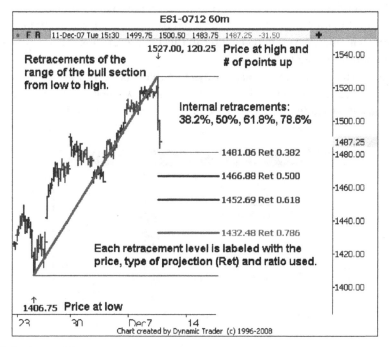

FIGURE 4.1   Internal Retracements

Trading decisions are based on key information and on having the key information quickly and clearly available. On the charts in this book, swing highs and lows are often labeled with an arrow pointing to the high or low, as shown on the chart in Figure 4.1. These are called *date labels* in the Dynamic Trader software. The user has a choice of what information to include with the labels, such as the date, time (if intraday data), price change, percentage change, number of trading bars or calendar days, and the rate-of-change (ROC). The Dynamic Trader software automatically calculates the price change, percentage change, number of trading bars or calendar days, and the ROC from the last date label, so the user may have a lot of information included with the label. It is helpful if your trading software is able to at least label the date/time and price of swing highs and lows on any chart.

In Figure 4.1, the ES made an advance of 120.25 points from 1406.75 to 1527.00. The low and high are labeled on the chart and the range of the advance is shown in the top label. The range of 120.25 is proportioned by the four key ratios with the results subtracted from the high price to arrive at the four retracement levels.

Most trading software will have a retracement function. If yours doesn't, your trading software is probably not fully functioning or it is not designed for professional traders, and you need new trading software. Your trading software should allow you to enter any ratio you choose and should allow you to choose to make the retracements by either the range of price (highs and lows of the bars), as shown on the chart, or by closing prices.

Figure 4.2 is the Price Retracement Ratios menu from my Dynamic Trader program. The menu includes all of the possible options to choose ratios and how they are displayed and labeled, including the thickness and color of each line. Your trading software should at least give you the ability to choose any ratios to include for retracements, including ratios greater than one. As you will see later in this chapter, ratios greater than one are a key component of the Dynamic Price Strategy.

Because internal retracements are always less than 100%, they are used to help identify price targets for corrections. Why is it helpful to know the key retracement price levels for any market we trade? *Most corrections in every actively traded market and time*

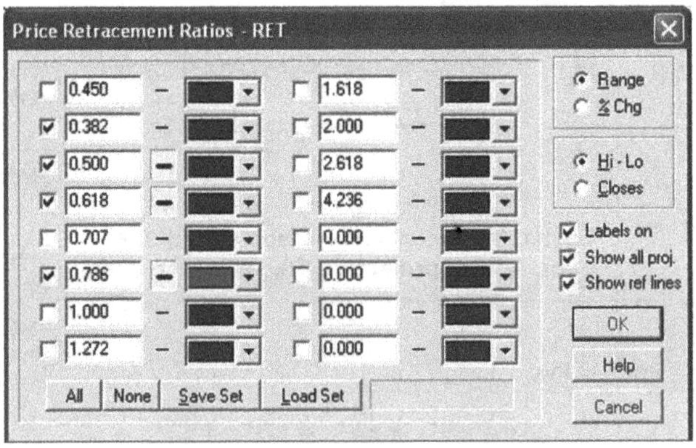

FIGURE 4.2 Price Retracement Menu

frame end at or very near one of the four key retracements. That is why retracements are a key to help identify where a correction will end and why Dynamic Price Strategies are a very important part of a trading plan. Figure 4.3 includes about two years of weekly SPX data and shows that the four primary corrections during this period were each made at or very near one of the key internal retracements.

Each corrective low for the SPX for this period was not made exactly at one of the key retracement levels, but all were made within just a few points of either the 50% or 61.8% retracements during this period. I could put up dozens of charts of many markets and time frames and show how almost every corrective high and low is made at or very near one of the four key retracement levels. But that wouldn't be instructive at this point, so let's just assume it to be the case for now. Even given that assumption, which I have found to be fact over the past 20-plus years, you have to be asking yourself (or really asking me) the big question: If there are four key retracement levels, how do I know

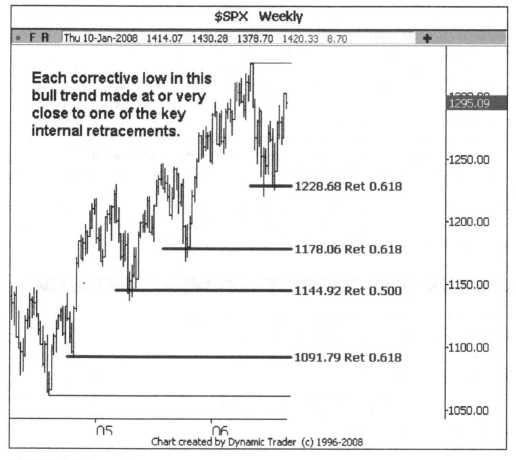

FIGURE 4.3 Internal Retracements

which retracement level is likely to end the correction? Am I supposed to make a reversal trade every time a market reaches one of the four retracement levels?

Showing simple Fib retracements is usually as far as most trading educators go. But this chapter is called "Beyond Fib Retracements." I promised to take you to another level with price strategies, and that is exactly what I am going to do. Retracement levels by themselves are not of much use for practical trade strategies. You could go broke making trend reversal trades every time a market reached a retracement level. There has to be more to the price strategy that will help identify which retracement level is most likely to be the end of a correction. We are not just looking for support or resistance; we want to identify the price level that will complete a correction so we can either cover a countertrend trade or enter a trade in the direction of the larger time frame trend at the end of a correction. Plus, we must be able to discern if there is a relatively narrow-range of price around the retracement level that is a trend reversal price zone, so we don't get hung up expecting the reversal to be made right at the retracement price.

I'm not going to show you dozens of examples of highs, lows, and corrective trend reversals made at the retracements. It is not instructive at this point. For now, all you have to know is that most corrective highs and lows are made at or very near one of the four internal retracements and how the retracements are made.

How do we identify *in advance* which retracement level is most likely to be the price near where a correction is complete? We do this by also making *alternate price projections* and *external retracements* which will help to identify the internal retracement level that is likely to end a correction and not just be temporary support or resistance. Even though external retracements are more closely related to internal retracements, we are going to first learn how to make and use alternate price projections to help qualify which internal retracement is most likely to be the price target for a corrective trend reversal.

I also want to emphasize at this point that the objective is not just to identify temporary support or resistance. That is not particularly helpful. The objective is to identify the probable price target that should end the entire corrective or trend structure.

INTERNAL RETRACEMENTS

The four internal retracement levels are 38.2%, 50%, 61.8%, and 78.6%

- Most corrections end at or very near the 50% or 61.8% retracement.
- The 38.2% retracement level usually does not end a correction, but is only temporary support or resistance.
- The 78.6% retracement is typically the maximum retracement for a correction. If a market closes above the 78.6% retracement, typically it is not making a correction but will continue to trend to a new high or low.

ALTERNATE PRICE PROJECTIONS QUALIFY INTERNAL RETRACEMENTS

Alternate price projection (APP) is the second method for Dynamic Price Strategies. An alternate price projection compares swings that are in the same direction (alternate swings), while a retracement compares sections that are in opposite directions.

The ratios used for alternate price projections for a corrective structure are .618, 1.00, and 1.62. The ratios used for a trend structure are .382, .618 and 1.00. Let's first look at alternate price projections and a corrective structure.

Figure 4.4 shows the APPs on a USD/JY daily chart. The objective is to identify a probable target for the next swing up that may complete an ABC correction. Swing O–A is measured; it is proportioned by .618, 1.00, and 1.618; and these proportions of swing O–A are projected from the B low.

Each APP is labeled on the chart with the price of the APP, the type of projection (APP), and the ratio used. We are only interested in potential targets above the A high. The .618 APP is below the A high so is not relevant.

Most corrective highs are made at or very near an APP. If most corrective highs are also made at or very near an internal retracement, *a corrective high is likely near the In-Ret that is near an APP.* In other words, if an In-Ret and an APP are near each other, they form a relatively narrow-range zone from where a corrective trend reversal is probable. The APP points to which In-Ret is likely to be the corrective high or low *in advance.*

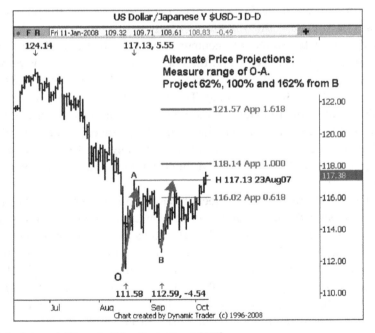

FIGURE 4.4 Internal Alternate Price Projections (APP)

FIGURE 4.5 Alternate Price Projections

Figure 4.5 is the same data as the previous figure but includes the In-Rets along with the APPs. The 100% APP is just a few ticks above the 50% retracement, labeled Zone 1. The 162% APP is so close to the 78.6% retracement for Zone 2 that the numbers can't be read. There are no APPs near the 61.8% retracement.

With no APP near the 61.8% retracement, more than likely the 61.8% retracement will not be significant resistance or end the corrective rally. If the JY is making a corrective rally, it is likely to end near either the 50% retracement or the 78.6% retracement and not near the 61.8% retracement. The 100% APP is the most frequent APP target where highs and lows are made, so the odds are a corrective high would be made near 117.66 to 118.14 (Zone 1), which includes the 50% retracement and the 100% APP. If the JY continued higher beyond this zone, it would likely continue all the way to near the 78.6% retracement before a corrective high would be made, bypassing the 61.8% retracement.

Figure 4.6 is the Alternate Price Projection menu from the Dynamic Trader software. Like the Retracement setup menu, any ratio may be used and projections may be made from swing ranges (Hi-Lo) or closes and by price range or percentage change of price.

Your trading software should have similar choices. In some software, this routine is called *extensions* instead of Alternate Price Projections. *Extensions* is not a properly descriptive term, but as long as you are able to make a projection from three points (two points to measure the range, and make the projections from a third point), you will be able to accomplish the same thing. Alternate price projections are an equally important price strategy as retracements. Be sure you are using trading software that allows you to make these key price projections.

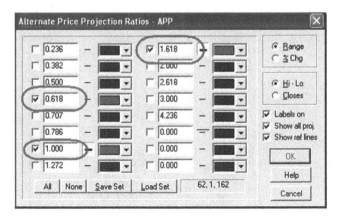

FIGURE 4.6 DT Alternate Price Projection Menu

Let's make a short review of the key price factors you've learned to be sure you have the concepts down cold before we continue.

- Most corrective highs and lows are made at or very near one of the four key internal retracements.
- The most likely retracement for a corrective high or low is a retracement that has one of the three key alternate price projections near it. In other words, the APP helps to identify in advance which retracement is likely to be the price target to complete the correction.
- The focus is always on the 100% alternate price projection.
- The retracement and alternate price projection often result in a relatively narrow-range zone for trend reversal.
- If an APP does not fall relatively near a retracement, it is not significant for other than minor support or resistance, and the focus for a corrective high or low is on the retracements.

Figure 4.7 shows another ABC correction which made a bottom right at the narrow-range zone that included the 61.8% retracement and 100% APP. The 162% APP was far from the 78.6% retracement, which suggested, *in advance*, that the most probable target for a corrective low was near the 61.8% retracement.

Once again, I could take up a lot of space and amaze you with dozens of examples of corrective highs and lows made right at the narrow-range zones created by a retracement and alternate price projection. My objective is not to impress you with a myriad of perfectly executed after-the-fact examples, but to teach you how to do it. The objective has been to show you how the alternate price projections are made and how they often identify in advance which retracement level is likely to complete a correction. There will be many more examples of how to use the internal retracements and alternate price projections later in this chapter and especially in Chapter 6.

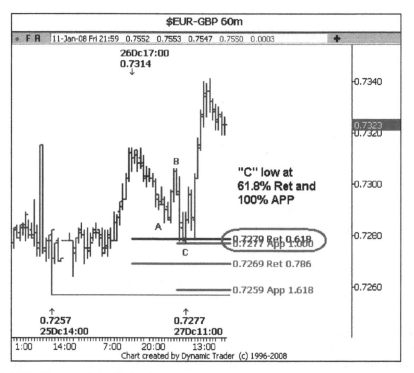

FIGURE 4.7 Alternate Price Projections

Needless to say, often the alternate price projections do not fall near a retracement to create a narrow-range target zone. But when they do, the odds increase significantly that a narrow-range zone made at the confluence of these two important price projection techniques will complete a correction and offer a great low-risk trade setup. Always remember, the objective is to identify conditions with a high probability outcome and acceptable capital exposure, not to trade any particular market all of the time. Focus on being a successful trader and not on trading activity. Focus on having the patience to only consider a trade when the conditions are optimal.

MORE ALTERNATE PRICE PROJECTIONS

Figure 4.8 is the S&P mini futures contract of 60-minute data. The period shown is a bear trend and I've labeled the pivots from 0 through 4. Alternate price projections can help to identify the probable high or low price target for a trend just as they were used in previous examples to help identify the high or low price target for a correction. The chart shows the 100% APP of the two completed bear sections (0–1 and 2–3) projected from the 4 high.

Frequently, a high or low is made at or very near the 100% APP of a past section within the trend structure. Sometimes all of the sections are approximately the same length in price. We always want to be aware of the 100% APPs of each prior trend section.

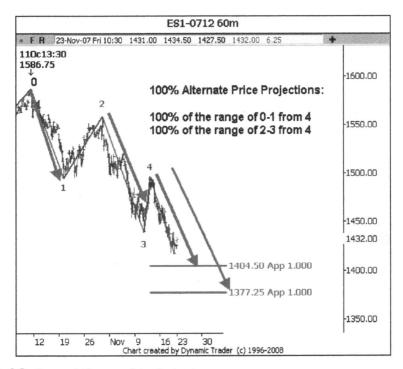

FIGURE 4.8 External Alternate Price Projections

The 100% APPs by themselves are not enough for high-confidence price targets. Other price projections should fall near them to create a relatively narrow-range zone with two or more of the key projections near each other.

Figure 4.9 is the same ES 60-minute data with different alternate price projections. On this chart, I've measured the range from the 0 pivot high to the 3 low, proportioned it by 38.2% and 61.8% and projected from the 4 high. The two projections shown on the chart are the result. These two APPs can also be described as the 38.2% and 61.8% APPs of the range of waves 1 through 3, projected from the Wave-4 extreme. A trend Wave-5 is often made at or very near one of these two APPs.

Figure 4.10 includes both sets of projections shown on the previous two charts. The 100% APP of 0–1 from 4 and the 61.8% APP of 0–3 from 4 are only one point apart, which is why the labels overlap each other and are difficult to read. The narrow-range price zone where these two projections coincide, at 1404.50–1405.50, is a high probability price zone for the next pivot low and potentially to complete the bear trend.

Figure 4.11 is the EUR/USD 15-minute data and shows another use for alternate price projections. Corrections within a trend are often very similar in price range. The chart shows the 100% APPs of the A–B and C–D corrections projected from the E pivot high. The prior two corrections were similar in price so the two 100% APPs made a relatively narrow-range target for another minor correction. The next minor corrective low was made right in the target range and the EUR/USD then continued to a new high.

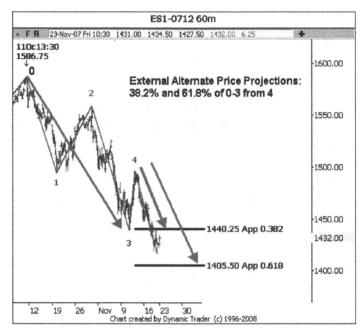

FIGURE 4.9 More External Alternate Price Projections

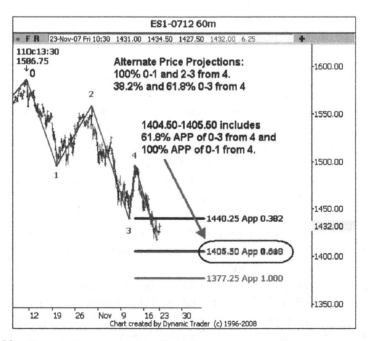

FIGURE 4.10 Alternate Price Projections Target Low

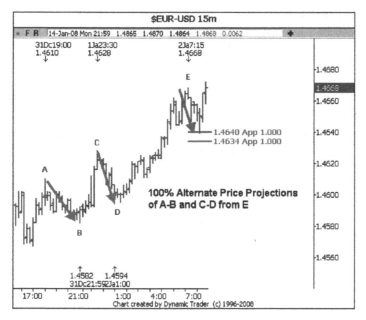

FIGURE 4.11 Alternate Price Projections for Support

Most market reversals are made at one or more proportions of prior sections of the trend or correction. Don't ask me why markets have this symmetry over and over again in all actively traded markets and all time frames. The why isn't relevant. The fact that it happens over and over again provides the basis of the Dynamic Price Strategy where we proportion the various sections of the trend or correction, make the projections, and identify if there is a narrow-range price zone that includes at least two or three projections. The beauty of this approach is we are working with a relatively limited number of key projections and ratios which allow us to identify *in advance* probable support, resistance, and, best of all, trend reversal.

ALTERNATE PRICE PROJECTIONS

Corrective sections: 61.8%, 100%, and 162%
Trend sections: 38.2%, 61.8%, and 100%

- The most frequent APP of a corrective structure is the 100% APP. Be very alert if a correction reaches a narrow-range zone that includes one of the key internal retracements and the 100% APP.
- Corrective sections rarely exceed the 162% APP.
- The 38.2% and 61.8% APPs for trend targets are used to project the range of multiple sections, such as waves 1 through 3, from a Wave-4 high or low of a potential five-wave trend.

EXTERNAL RETRACEMENTS HELP IDENTIFY THE FINAL SECTION OF A TREND OR CORRECTION

There is a second type of retracement that many traders do not use but should. An *external retracement (Ex-Ret)* is greater than 100%. The ratios usually used are 1.27, 1.62, and 2.62 and are often shown as percentages rather than ratios. Ex-Rets are made just like the more familiar In-Rets. The external retracements are most useful to identify the final section of a trend or countertrend such as a Wave-5 of a five-wave trend, the Wave-C of an ABC correction, or the final section of complex correction. Of course, we never know for sure if a market is making the final section of a trend or countertrend, but if the pattern conditions have been met such that it could be the final section, the external retracements are an important factor to help identify the probable price target for trend reversal.

Figure 4.12 is the same USD/JY daily chart used in an earlier APP example but only shows the three external retracements.

The 127%, 162%, and 262% external retracements are shown for the A-B range. The two most typical Ex-Rets where a trend reversal is often made are the 127% and 162%, which we always focus on. In this example, the 262% Ex-Ret is above the high of the bear trend section, so it is not relevant to identify the end of a correction for this data. Let's add the In-Rets and APPs to the chart to see if there are one or two relatively narrow-range zones that ideally include one each of the three sets of projections.

Figure 4.13 is the same USD/JY daily data. I've zoomed in a bit so it will be easier to see the labels for the projections. The chart includes all three types of price projections

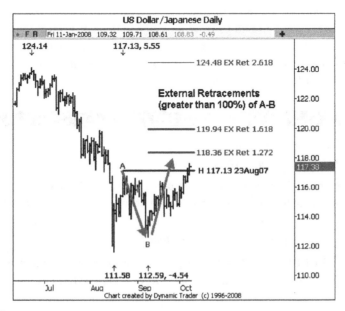

FIGURE 4.12 External Retracements Greater Than 100 %

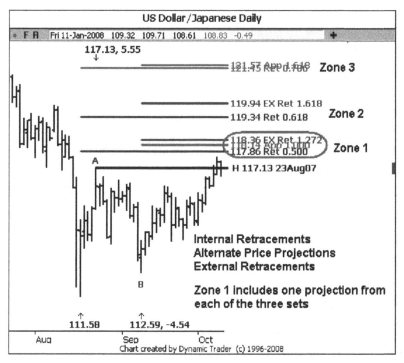

FIGURE 4.13 External Retracements Project Target for Correction

you have learned so far: internal retracements, alternate price projections, and external retracements.

I have labeled three relatively narrow-range price zones that include at least two projections. Zone 1 includes the 50% internal retracement, 100% alternate price projection, and 127% external retracement. Zone 1 is the only zone to include one projection from each of the three sets. Therefore Zone 1 is the most probable target for an ABC corrective high. Figure 4.14 shows that the corrective high was made in Zone 1. followed by a decline to a new low.

External retracements are used primarily to help identify the end of the last section of a correction or trend. The preceding examples have shown how they are used to help identify the end of the last section of a possible correction. The next example, Figure 4.15, shows Dow Jones Industrial Average (DJIA) daily data and how the last section of a five-wave trend was made right at the 162% Ex-Ret of the Wave-4 correction.

Figure 4.16 is another example of a low in the 60-minute EUR/USD made at the 162% Ex-Ret.

Not every trend ends with just five sections, as you learned in Chapter 3, but many do. If a market has met the guidelines to have completed four sections, always include the 127% and 162% external retracements of the potential Wave-4 as probable price targets to complete a Wave-5.

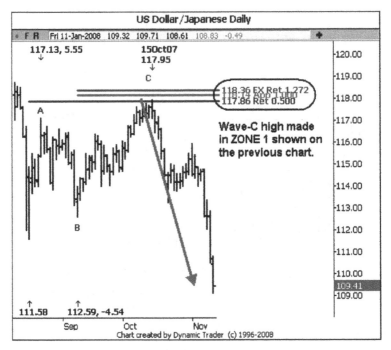

FIGURE 4.14   Wave-C High Made in Zone 1 Price Target

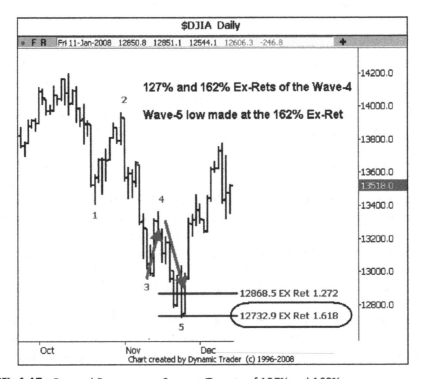

FIGURE 4.15   External Retracement Support Targets of 127% and 162%

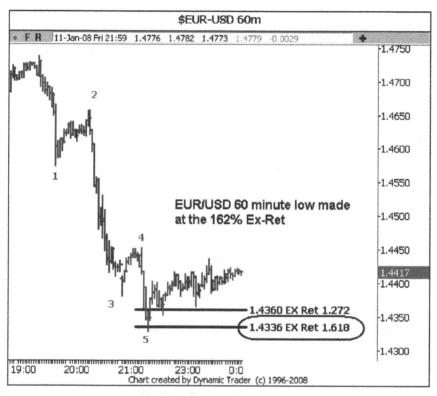

FIGURE 4.16 Wave-5 Low at External Retracements

EXTERNAL RETRACEMENTS

The ratios usually used for external retracements are 127%, 162%, and 262%

- External retracements are important to help identify the final section of a trend or countertrend.
- External retracements are not used on their own for price targets, but to confirm an alternate price projection and/or internal retracement.

PATTERN PRICE TARGETS

In the past 20 years, I've identified the most consistent price targets typically reached for each of the most frequent E-wave patterns. I call this approach end-of-wave (EOW) targets. In Chapter 3, I focused on just the two most frequent patterns for all markets and all time frames, the ABC correction and five-wave trend patterns. Of all the potential patterns, they are the simplest, most useful, and most reliable patterns to project the specific price target where they will complete. Many traders who have learned from my practical trading educational material over the years focus on just these two patterns for all of their trades. You might also consider specializing in just one or two types of very high probability setups for your trading as well. You may have fewer trade setups but, like specialists in other businesses, there is a good chance your success will be greater.

While many corrections make a pattern other than an ABC, if the minimum conditions for an ABC have been made, it is essential to consider the potential for an ABC and project the price target for a Wave-C. While many trends do not complete with five sections or waves that meet the guidelines for an E-wave five-wave trend, if four sections are complete that meet the guidelines for a five-wave trend, it is essential to make the price projections for a possible Wave-5 which may complete the entire trend. This does not mean that the Dynamic Price Strategies are not useful for any other pattern structure. Later in this book, I include lots of examples of how all the trade strategies are useful for non-three-wave ABC corrections and non-five-wave trends. Since the three-wave, ABC corrections and five-wave trends are so prevalent in all markets and all time frames, we will focus on making the high probability end-of-wave (EOW) price targets for each of these patterns.

ABC Price Targets

A simple ABC correction is a frequent type of correction. An ABC correction is also called a Gartley pattern. It has well-defined minimum guidelines to recognize if two sections are complete. Once two sections are complete (waves A and B) there are very specific price strategies to help identify the EOW-C price target.

The probable End-of-Wave-C price target is identified *in advance* by making three sets of projections you have already learned. In fact, a couple of the earlier examples used projections for an ABC price target. We can never know for sure if a market is making a correction. What you are going to learn to project is the probable price target if the market is making an ABC correction.

END-OF-WAVE-C PRICE TARGET PROJECTIONS

In-Rets of prior trend: 38.2%, 50%, 61.8% and 78.6%
APPs of Wave-A: 61.8%, 100% and 162%
Ex-Rets of Wave-B: 127%, 162% and 262%

- The ideal target zone for a Wave-C includes one projection from each of the three sets.
- In-Rets are first in the order of importance of the three sets of projections, since most corrections end near one of the four In-Rets.
- The second most important are the APPs.
- The third most important are the Ex-Rets.
- A high probability Wave-C target zone should include an In-Ret and an APP.

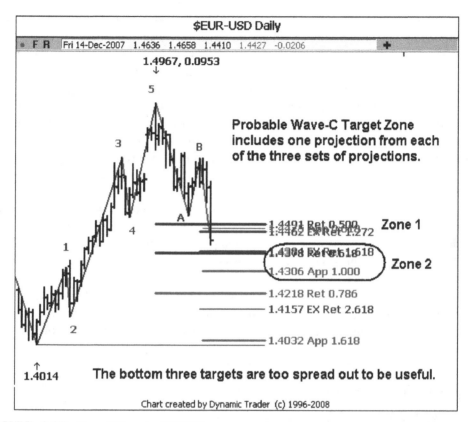

FIGURE 4.17 Wave-C Targets, EUR/USD

When the three sets of projections are made, the ideal target zone(s) will be a relatively narrow-range zone that will include one projection from each of the three sets. The order of importance of the three sets of projections is In-Rets, APPs, and Ex-Rets. A target zone should include at least one In-Ret and one APP.

Figure 4.17 is the EUR/USD daily data and shows all three sets of projections. At first glance, it would seem there are so many price lines on the chart that a low will inevitably be made at or very near one of them. You are correct in thinking this. The big question is, can we identify *in advance* the probable target to complete a corrective ABC low out of the many targets shown? The answer, of course, is yes.

Two zones in Figure 4.17 contain a relatively tight grouping that includes one projection for each of the three sets. Zone 1 includes the 50% In-Ret, 62% APP, and 127% Ex-Ret. The last daily bar on the chart is a wide-range bar that took out the Wave-A low and closed below Zone 1, all in one day. Zone 1 would not be relevant.

Zone 2 includes the 62% In-Ret, 100% APP, and 162% Ex-Ret. If the EUR/USD is making an ABC correction, the probable target for a Wave-C low is the Zone 2 range. The bottom three projections do not provide a relatively tight grouping for a potential support zone. Of 10 separate price projections, we are able to identify *in advance* which relatively narrow-range zone is likely to complete a corrective ABC low.

We *never know* in advance if a market is making a correction, but we often make assumptions as to whether it is, based on the larger time frame momentum, price, pattern, and time position. We *never know* if a correction will be a simple ABC or something more complex, but we always assume a correction will be at least three sections.

We can make completely objective price projections and identify relatively narrow-range price zones based on the three sets of price projections, with the focus on the internal retracements, and be prepared *in advance* for the high probability price target to complete an ABC correction. If a market reaches that zone, it has met the price conditions for a probable reversal. Trading, like every other business, requires that you identify what you know, what you don't know, and what is probable. This is the information from which decisions are made.

Figure 4.18 is the Gold/Silver Mining Stocks Index (XAU) daily close data. All three sets of projections have been made for the probable Wave-C price target. The one relatively narrow-range zone that includes one projection from each of the three sets is circled. If the XAU is making an ABC correction, this is the zone where a Wave-C low is likely to be made, based on daily closing data.

For these last two ABC price target examples, I have purposely not shown the outcome. The objective right now is for you to learn how to make the projections and identify *in advance* the high probability target zone(s) near one or more of the key

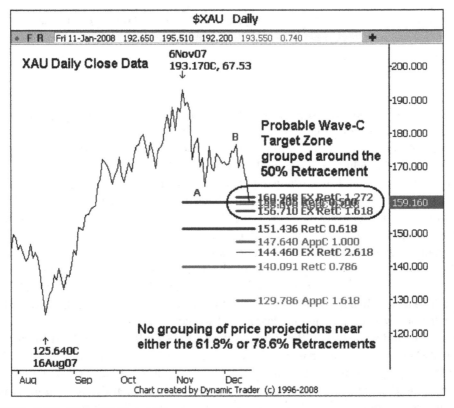

FIGURE 4.18 Wave-C Target, XAU

retracements. Once you are able to do this, you are set to be prepared for a corrective trend reversal for any market and any time frame. I have been making these trend reversal target zones for almost 20 years. We do it virtually every day in our daily DT futures, stock/ETF, and Forex reports on most of the major markets, from intraday to monthly data. Once you incorporate these Dynamic Price Strategies in your trading plan, you will be amazed at how often reversals are made at the trend and correction price targets that you have projected and for which you are prepared in advance.

I've often had students over the years initially complain that it is too much work to make all the projections to identify the probable support/resistance and trend reversal zones. My answer has always been, "If you're not willing to do the work necessary for the information you need to make a trade decision, you have no business with a trading account." In recent years, wannabe traders have a distorted view of what it takes to be successful in the business of trading because of all of the trading software available and scam system sellers. No specific software or system will make you a successful trader. Powerful computers, comprehensive trading software, and inexpensive data have not made anyone a trading success. All that each of these can do is provide you with the information you need to make trading decisions more quickly and accurately. They will never be the cause of success. Only your own work, knowledge, and experience can result in trading success, the same as with any other business.

End-of-Wave-5 Target Zones

As you learned in Chapter 3, a five-section trend is the most frequent trend pattern. Not all trends complete in five sections that meet the E-wave guidelines you learned in Chapter 3, but whenever four sections are complete, you should always anticipate the trend is likely to be complete once the fifth section is complete.

Over the years, I have identified the key price targets where a Wave-5 is usually complete. It happens over and over again, as we demonstrate daily in our DT Reports, so be sure and make these projections and identify the narrow-range EOW-5 target zone whenever four sections are complete.

END-OF-WAVE-5 PRICE TARGET PROJECTIONS

APP of waves 1 to 3 from Wave-4: 38.2%, 61.8%, and 100%
APP of Wave-1 from Wave-4: 100%
Ex-Ret of Wave-4: 127%, 162%, and 262%

- The ideal target zone for a Wave-5 includes one projection from each of the three sets.
- The order of importance of the three sets of projections is the 38.2% or 61.8% APP of waves 1 to 3, the 100% APP of Wave-1, and the 127% or 162% Ex-Ret of Wave 4.
- The 100% APP of waves 1 to 3 and the 262% Ex-Ret of Wave-4 are rarely met except for commodity market fifth-wave extensions.

Figure 4.19 is the ES 60-minute data used for an earlier alternate price projection example. I have made the three sets of projections for the EOW-5 price target on the chart. The three sets of projections are (1) the 100% APP of the range of Wave-1 (points 0 to 1) from the Wave-4 extreme; (2) the 38.2% and 61.8% APPs of the range of waves 1 to 3 (points 0 to 3) from the Wave-4 extreme; and (3) the 127% and 162% Ex-Ret of the range of Wave-4 (points 3 to 4). There is one very narrow-range zone that includes one target from each of the three projections: 1404.50 to 1405.50. This zone includes the 100% APP of Wave-1 from the Wave-4 high, the 61.8% APP of waves 1 to 3 from Wave-4, and the 162% Ex-Ret of Wave-4.

If the ES continued to decline and reached 1405.50, we would be very alert to any momentum or pattern reversal signal for a potential Wave-5 low. How did it turn out? That is not important at this point. What is important is that you learn how to make the EOW-5 price targets whenever four sections are complete. It would be easy to show you dozens of after-the-fact examples that worked out perfectly, but we need to take this one step at a time. As you progress through the book, you will learn how to integrate

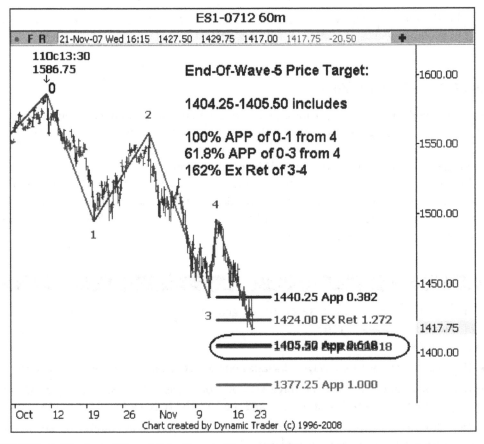

FIGURE 4.19   End-of-Wave-5 Price Target, ES

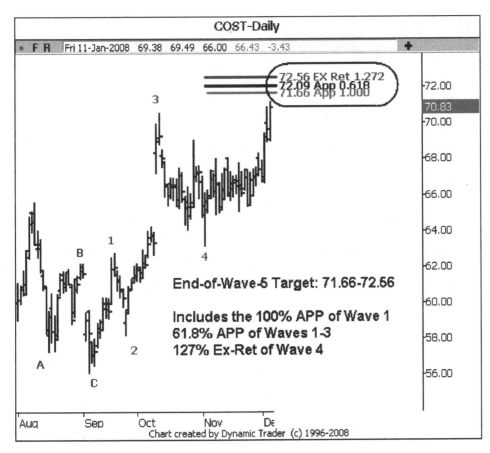

FIGURE 4.20 EOW-5 Price Target Zone, Costco

the momentum, pattern, and time position with practical, low-risk trade strategies from entry to exit to take advantage of this critical information.

Figure 4.20 is Costco daily data and another example of a high probability, EOW-5 target zone. The three sets of EOW-5 projections were made. The 71.66–72.56 zone includes one projection from each of the three sets. As of the last bar on the chart, Costco is only a couple points from that zone. While Costco had a strong bull run for three months and made a new high as of the last bar on the chart, a trader should be very alert that the upside may be very limited and a significant decline may be forthcoming.

In this section, you have learned to identify *in advance* the probable price target(s) for the two most frequent patterns, the ABC correction and five-wave trend. Don't fail to be prepared for a possible Wave-C high or low if two sections of a probable correction are complete, and for a possible Wave-5 high or low if a trend has completed four sections. You will find that these end-of-wave and Dynamic Price Strategies will be a very important factor of your trading plan and will give you a huge edge for your trade strategies and trade management.

PRICE, PATTERN, AND MOMENTUM

If price strategies were able to pinpoint the exact support, resistance or trend reversal at every market reversal, that is all we would need to make a trading decision. While the Dynamic Price Strategies you learned in this chapter are the most quick, easy, and reliable of any price strategy I have devised or seen from other traders or educators for the past 20-plus years, not every high and low is made right on a key price target identified in advance. If we don't make trade decisions based solely on the price position, how do we use these support, resistance, and trend reversal strategies as part of a complete trading plan?

In the previous two chapters you learned about the momentum and pattern factors. I want you to see how we are building up a complete trading plan, step-by-step in each chapter. So let's take a look at just a couple of examples of how the momentum, pattern, and price factors all work together to set up conditions for a high probability trade.

Figure 4.21 is the XAU daily close data that was used earlier to illustrate the price projections for an end-of-Wave-C target. I only show two of the projections that are part

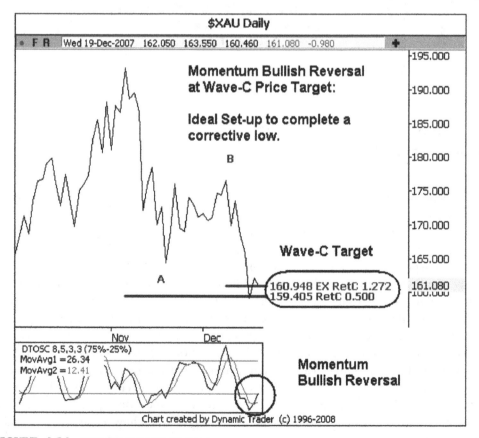

FIGURE 4.21 Price/Momentum Reversal

of the target zone so you can clearly see the price labels on the chart. Note the *C* that is just after the description (Ex Ret and Ret) on the price lines. When a price projection is made from closing data in Dynamic Trader, the *C* for *close* is included in the price line labels.

The decline was recognized as a *potential* ABC correction. XAU reached the Wave-C price target, which was *identified in advance*. Two days after the XAU tagged the EOW-C price target zone, the daily momentum made a *bullish reversal* from the oversold zone. Pattern, price, *and* momentum conditions had all been made to complete a Wave-C corrective low, which should be followed by an advance to a new high.

As of the last daily close on the XAU chart, we *don't know* if the XAU has made an ABC corrective low. For all we know, the XAU may immediately continue to decline to a new low or work out a complex correction. What we do *know* is the XAU has met the minimum pattern conditions typical for a correction (three sections), it has reached the ideal Wave-C price target zone, and the daily momentum has made a bullish reversal. Remember, we trade what we know. We *know* the conditions are in place for a high probability outcome with acceptable capital exposure.

You don't need any fancy and expensive trade management software or spreadsheets to know that the initial capital exposure for a long trade would be just 2 to 3 points (the difference between the last bar's close and the lowest daily close so far), and the potential gain 35 points or more (to above the high on the chart where the potential correction began). If these conditions were in place, would it seem like a worthwhile trade to you? If it doesn't, close the book now, go out and play golf or whatever you do for fun, and come back later when you've gained some sense and understanding about what the business of trading is all about!

Figure 4.22 is the ES (S&P mini) 60-minute futures data that was used to illustrate the end-of-Wave-5 price targets earlier. You might remember that the three key targets all fell within less than two points of each other for a high probability target zone. Only the 100% APP is shown on this chart so it can be easily read.

As of the last bar on the chart, the S&P has reached the high probability price target for a Wave-5 low and made a momentum bullish reversal on a bullish momentum/price divergence. This is an ideal setup for a long trade with minimal capital exposure and a lot of upside potential.

Once again, what do we *know*? We know the pattern, price, and momentum are all in a position typical to complete a five-wave trend low. We know the downside is relatively limited to find out if a low is complete, and the upside is substantial. We *don't* know if the S&P has made a trend reversal low that will be followed by a substantial advance; the S&P may continue lower. However, we have identified "conditions with a high probability outcome and acceptable capital exposure," the objective of all trade plans. That is what trade setups are all about.

These have been just a couple of examples to give you a preview of how the momentum, pattern, and price factors are each used as part of a trading plan. You will see lots more in Chapters 6 and 7, plus specific entry-to-exit plans. We'll get there before long, but first you will learn about the time factor in the next chapter.

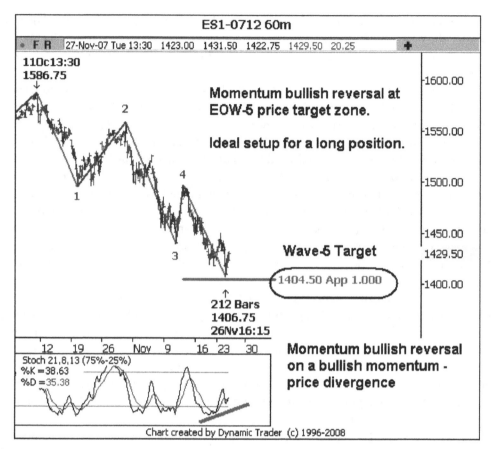

FIGURE 4.22   Price/Momentum Bullish Reversal

NO EXCUSE

Twenty years ago, I used to do all of the price strategies you learned in this chapter with hand-drawn charts and a calculator. Then I graduated to spreadsheets. In the late 1980s to mid-1990s there were only one or two trading programs that could do the retracements and alternate price projections and allow the user to include any ratio they chose. I used the best one until its development and distribution was discontinued.

I decided to design my own charting and trading software so all of the routines would be complete and easy to use, and would properly display the output on a chart. In the late 1990s, I released Dynamic Trader Version 1 with many routines not found in any other trading software. Today many charting programs have caught up, with more complete price functions that will allow you to do the retracements and alternate price projections with any ratio you choose. If yours doesn't, find one that does. The cost of the proper trading tools is minimal to the business of trading so you have no excuse not to have the right tools to provide you with the best information to make trade decisions. If you are interested in only a few markets, knock yourself out with hand-drawn charts and a calculator. I did for years.

However, there is one type of software to avoid like the plague. A few programs are available that claim to make support, resistance, and trend reversal price targets automatically. Like software that makes Elliott wave counts and system software, they cater to the inexperienced, unknowledgeable, and lazy wannabe traders who believe a software program can automatically give them the buy-sell signals. These auto price target systems must make assumptions based on the data that can lead you into big trouble because not all the variables can be programmed. Since a software program is nothing but instructions to a glorified calculator, the computer, the quality of the output is limited to the quality of the input algorithms.

As the late Bruce Babcock, editor of the *Commodity Traders Consumer Report*, said, "You can't buy success." If you want to be successful in the business of trading, you have to take the time to gain the education and experience and make your own decisions. Sounds like every other business doesn't it? That's because it is. If you are willing to learn to make logical decisions based on relevant information, you have a good chance to become a successful trader. If you believe you can buy success through a trading system or any sort of automatic price or time system, find a deserving charity for your trading funds instead of donating them to the educated, serious, and successful traders. Because if you think you can buy success, you are in for a very expensive lesson.

Up to now, we have been primarily concerned with identifying conditions for a trade entry. In later chapters you will learn about specific, objective entry strategies, stop-loss adjustment, exit targets, and more, as part of a complete trading plan. We are taking it one step at a time.

It is time to learn about the fourth and final technical factor of the trade plan: market timing.

CHAPTER 5

Beyond Traditional Cycles

In this chapter, you will learn how to project in advance very narrow range time targets for support, resistance and trend reversal for any market condition. The Dynamic Time Strategies you learn will put you miles ahead of traditional cycle analysis with timing tools for practical trade strategies.

When most traders think of market timing, they think of traditional cycle strategies. Traditional cycle strategies project a low or a high based on an average length of low-low or high-high cycles of past data. This type of cycle analysis makes assumptions that usually prove to not hold up in reality.

Traditional cycles are based on an average cycle length. An average cycle length is usually pretty useless because it does not consider how tight or widespread are the range of numbers used that make the average. If most of the cycle repetitions that were used to come up with the average cycle were tightly grouped, the average would be useful. Unfortunately, an average can be made of any series of numbers which may be widely dispersed. The average may be meaningless to predict the next repetition.

Traditional market cycle analysis also assumes a cycle length is static and the static cycle will continue indefinitely into the future. It just doesn't work that way. Price and volatility cycles change over time. What might have been a fairly regular cycle in the past may no longer be evident in recent market activity. Cycles are not static, but dynamic. The typical L-L or H-H cycle length are generally different for bull and bear markets and will fluctuate over time as volatility and price cycles fluctuate. Plus, markets generally make their highs and lows at dynamic proportions of past trends and countertrends.

Just as you discovered in Chapter 4 that most trend and corrective highs and lows are made at or very near proportions of recent sections of the trend or correction, a similar approach to dynamic time proportion will help identify time targets for reversal. In this chapter you will learn a logical and practical approach to time target analysis that I have developed over the past 20 years. I have taken the Dynamic Time Strategies from a very complex to a simplified approach that every trader should make a part of his trading plan. In many cases, you will be able to identify *in advance* high-probability, narrow range time targets of just three to four bars for trend reversal for any market and any time frame. Let's begin by learning about *time retracements*.

TIME RETRACEMENTS AND CORRECTIONS

Time retracements are made in the same way as price retracements except time units are used instead of price units. If most corrections are made at or near one of the key price retracements, why shouldn't they also be made at or near a time retracement? That is a question I asked myself many years ago when studying Gann price and time strategies. Gann price and time analysis often seems very complicated but for the most part, it boils down to a simple concept: *Most highs and lows are made in proportion to one or more previous sections of the trend or countertrend.* In Chapter 4 you learned how to make price retracements and alternate price projections to help identify in advance the probable price target for support, resistance, and, most important, reversal of trends and corrections. If most reversals are made at or very near the key proportional price target zones, shouldn't they also be made near key proportional *time* target zones?

Over the past 20 years, I have found this to be the case. Time retracements are made just like price retracements but on the time axis, and they use some of the same ratios used for price retracements. The ratios for time retracements are .382, .50, .618, 1.00, and 1.618. In most cases, we just use the .382, .618, and 1.00 proportions to help identify time targets for corrections. The ratios are often expressed as percentages, just like with price retracements.

Figure 5.1 is daily XAU data. From mid-August to early November, the XAU made a strong bull trend for 58 trading days. The date-time range label above the high on the chart shows the top was made November 7, 2007, 58 bars (trading days) from the August 16 low. As of the last bar on the chart, the XAU has made a sharp decline. Along the bottom of the chart, the .382, .618, and 1.00 time retracement dates are shown. The 58-bar bull trend was proportioned into the .382, .618, and 1.00 ratio segments and the results projected forward in time from the November 7 high.

The time retracements were made in the exact same way as price retracements. The number of time units of the bull or bear trend is measured, then proportioned by the time retracement ratios, and the results are projected forward in time from the last bar of the bull or bear trend. A correction to a bull or bear trend is usually complete in the 38% to 62% time retracement (TR) zone. With internal price retracements, we look at a specific price for each retracement. With time retracements and corrections, we first look at the relatively broad 38% to 62% TR zone as the high probability target where a three-section correction is usually complete. This simple piece of information itself—the 38% to 62% time retracement zone for a simple correction—is very useful. If a market is making a

FIGURE 5.1 Time Retracements (TR)

correction, it will probably not be complete prior to the 38% time retracement. And it will probably be complete by the 62% time retracement unless the correction develops into a complex structure.

If a market is correcting into a price target and momentum reversal but has not reached at least the 38% time retracement, more than likely the best to expect is temporary support or resistance. It is not likely to complete a correction. If the correction reaches price or momentum support and is in the typical time retracement zone for a correction, the setup is complete to make a corrective high or low.

Figure 5.2 is the menu for the "Time Projection Ratios Using 2 Dates" function in the Dynamic Trader software. It looks similar to the Price Retracement Ratios function. This function is used whenever time projections are made using any two points. The time range between the two points is measured, proportioned by the ratios the user chooses, and projected forward from the second point. The time projections are shown along a horizontal line on the chart with the ratios and target dates, as shown in Figure 5.1.

If your software does not have the ability to make these types of time projections, they can easily be done with a spreadsheet for daily data. That's how I made them for

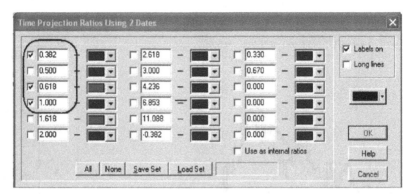

FIGURE 5.2   Menu for Time Projection Ratios Using Two Dates

years. It is not so easy to make intraday time projections using a spreadsheet, so if you want to do this type of time analysis, you should use a trading software that allows you to make the projections on a chart, or stick with daily data for the longer time frame trends.

The 38 to 62% time retracement zone may be a fairly broad time range. Are there other time factors that may narrow a relatively broad time zone to pinpoint the probable time target for a corrective high or low? Alternate time projections (ATPs) are the second time factor. Sound familiar? They are made in the same manner as the alternate price projections, but on the time axis instead of the price axis.

Time Retracements

    38.2%, 50%, 61.8%, 100%, 162%

- Most simple three-section, ABC corrections are complete in the 38.2% to 61.8% time retracement zone.

- If a correction makes a complex structure, the maximum time retracement typical to complete the correction is the 100% time retracement.

ALTERNATE TIME PROJECTIONS NARROW THE TIME RETRACEMENT RANGE

Alternate time projection (ATP) is the second time factor for Dynamic Time Strategies. An ATP compares the time range of swings that are in the same direction, in the same manner that alternate price projections compared alternate price swings.

The ratios used for alternate time projections for a corrective structure are .618, 1.00, and 1.618—the same ratios used for alternate price projections. Let's see how an ATP is made.

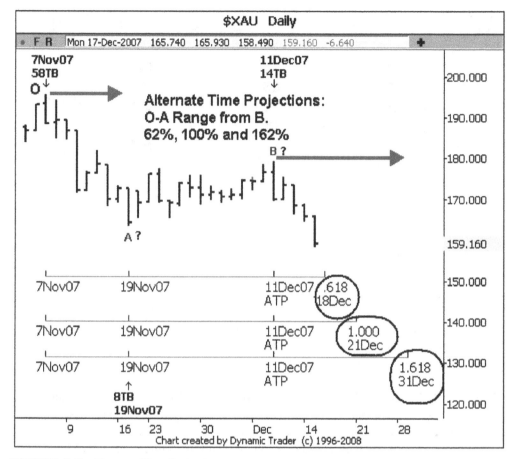

FIGURE 5.3 Alternate Time Projections

Figure 5.3 is the same daily XAU data used for the time retracement example except I'm only showing the data from the November high. The time range from O to A is measured (eight trading days), proportioned by the three key ATP ratios, and the results projected from the potential December 11, Wave-B high.

The three alternate time projections are shown on the chart. Typically, all three time projections are shown on one horizontal line. Since in this case the three projections are fairly close to each other and the labels would overlap each other if shown on the same line, I've made each projection separately and stacked them so the results can be easily displayed and read on the chart.

The 62% ATP should be the minimum time target for the third swing in a three-section, ABC correction. In this case, it falls on December 18. The 100 % ATP is the most frequent ATP target where a Wave-C is made. In this case, it falls on December 21. The third section of a correction will usually not exceed the 162% ATP, which in this case is December 31.

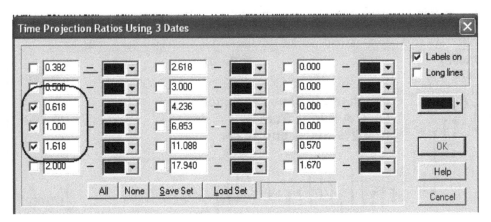

FIGURE 5.4 Menu for Alternate Time Projections with Three Dates

We've accomplished two important things by making the three alternate time projections: We've established the probable minimum and maximum time target for the third section of an ABC correction, and we are able to eliminate any of the three ATPs that fall outside the 38.2% to 61.8% time retracement zone. Time retracements and alternate time projections work together in a logical manner to help identify specific time targets to complete a correction.

Figure 5.4 shows the Time Projection Ratios Using 3 Dates menu. The user may choose any set of ratios. The time range of the first two data points is measured and the proportions are made from a third data point.

The three ATPs give us a minimum, probable, and maximum ATP to complete the third section of a correction. By themselves, they provide useful timing information. When used with the time retracements, they provide even more important information.

Figure 5.5 is the same XAU daily data with both the time retracements and alternate time projections shown on the chart. The first important thing to note is that all three of the alternate time projections fall within the December 11 to January 2, 38% to 62% time retracement zone. The minimum 62% ATP is December 18 and the maximum 162% is December 31, so right away, the target zone for a corrective low is narrowed by several days from the time retracement zone. Because the 62% ATP is December 18, more than likely a corrective low will not be complete prior to December 18 and typically would be complete around December 21, the 100% ATP. The maximum time target to expect a Wave-C low is December 31, the 162% ATP.

So far, you can see how time retracements and alternate time projections work together to help identify a time target in the same manner as price retracements and alternate price projections. They are both made in the same way using price units or time units. Alternate price projections qualify which price retracement is likely to be where support/resistance or trend reversal is likely to be made. Alternate time projections help to narrow a relatively wide time retracement zone to a narrower time target for reversal.

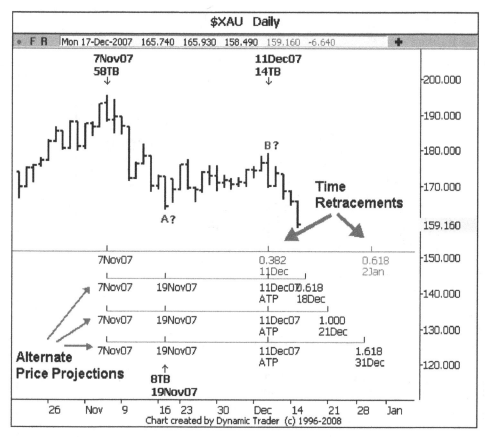

FIGURE 5.5 Time Retracements and Alternate Time Projections

Let's add one more time factor and see if it will help us to narrow the time range for a corrective low even more.

MORE TIME FACTORS

There are several other possible time factors or proportions of prior sections that can be made. The most important is the recent high-high or low-low cycles. If projecting for a possible low, the time range of recent lows will help to identify when the next low is probable. If projecting for a possible high, the time range of recent highs will help to identify when the next high is probable. This approach is similar to traditional cycle analysis but focuses on the most recent few cycles, particularly the last completed cycle.

Figure 5.6 is again the same XAU daily data. The chart shows the most recent 100% low-low projection on December 19. Since the last several low-to-low cycles have been in the 16-20 day range, a low around December 19 is probable.

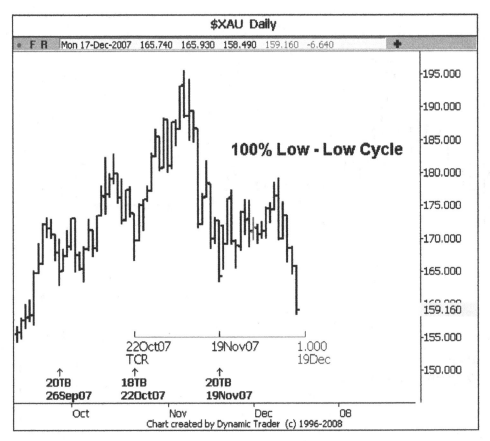

FIGURE 5.6 Low-to-Low Cycle

If the recent cycles have been in a relatively tight range, project the range forward from the last completed high or low for a time range when the next low is probable if the recent time rhythm continues. Figure 5.7 shows the recent low-low time range projected forward from the last completed low. If the recent low-low time rhythm continues, the next low is probable in the December 13–19 period.

THE TIME TARGET ZONE

It may seem like there are projected dates all over the place but there is method to the madness. All of these time projections are not just a bunch of random dates without specific meaning. Each set of projections provides a unique piece of information. There is a logical progression arriving at a probable time target based on all of the projections.

We initially assume a correction will be at least three sections, or a simple ABC. It may not turn out that way. A correction may eventually continue to a complex

FIGURE 5.7 Low-Low Time Range

corrective pattern but we never know that ahead of time. We make an assumption based on the minimum expectations. Most three-section corrections are complete in the 38.2 to 61.8% time retracement zone. That is our first focus of attention. This time zone can be relatively broad, depending on the time range of the prior trend. The objective is to use the alternate time projections and low-low or high-high time projections to help narrow the relatively broad zone.

Once two sections of a potential correction are complete, the 62%, and 162% alternate time projections may be made. The next swing low and potential end of the correction is likely to fall on or very near one of the three key ATPs. Any of the three ATPs that fall outside the time retracement zone are eliminated.

Next, make the 100% low-low (or high-high) projection. If the recent low-low (L-L) cycles have been in a relatively narrow range, the next low is likely to fall near the 100% L-L projection. Or you can also make projections for the minimum to maximum range of the recent low-low cycles if they have been in a relatively tight range. The most recent cycle is the focus.

Each set of time projections has a specific reason and purpose. Each is a logical proportion of prior sections. We begin with the broad time retracement range and narrow the time range with the position of the ATP and cycle projections. If a relatively narrow time range is made from the three sets of projections, it is a high probability time target to complete a corrective low. Does this approach sound familiar? It is the same basic approach used with the Dynamic Price Strategy to identify *in advance* the probable price zone or zones for a corrective high or low.

Figure 5.8 includes all three sets of time projections. I realize the chart is a bit crowded, showing all six projections together, but let's see how we can make a logical choice for a probable time target for a Wave-C if the XAU is making an ABC correction.

The last bar on the chart has made a new low on December 17 from the November 7 high. The XAU has already reached the December 11 to January 2, 38% to 62% time retracement zone. So far, so good. The three alternate time projections range from the 62% on December 18 to the 162% on December 31, with the 100% ATP on December 21. Because the 62% minimum ATP and 100% typical ATP are only three days apart, we should focus on the December 17–22 period, one bar plus or minus these two ATPs.

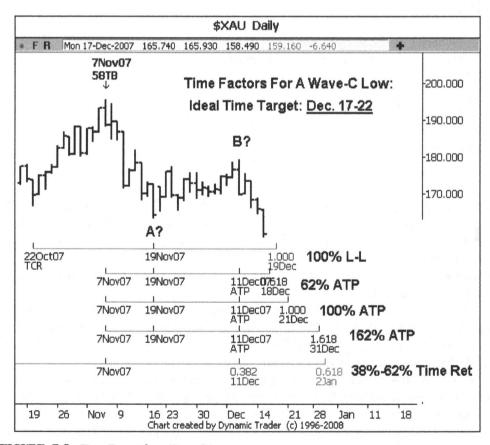

FIGURE 5.8 Time Target for a Wave-C Low

They are too close together to focus on each individually. The 100% low-low projection is December 19, right in the middle of the ATP projections. The ATPs and the low-low cycle projection have narrowed the relatively broad time retracement zone to December 17–22, a four trading day range (a weekend is in this period) when a Wave-C low and possible end of a corrective decline is probable.

This is powerful information based on the actual time range of sections of the recent trend and possible correction, not based on so-called historic cycles which are likely to be no longer relevant to recent market trends and volatility.

Figure 5.9 shows how it turned out. A Wave-C low was made on December 18, right in the December 17–22 time target for a low which was projected *in advance*. The XAU reached a price target for the low where the 50% price retracement and 62% alternate price projection coincided, also projected *in advance*, and where the daily momentum was oversold and made a bullish reversal two days after the extreme low in price and time. Time, price, pattern, and momentum were all pointing to the same thing: a probable Wave-C low and ideal setup for a continuation of the bull trend to a new high.

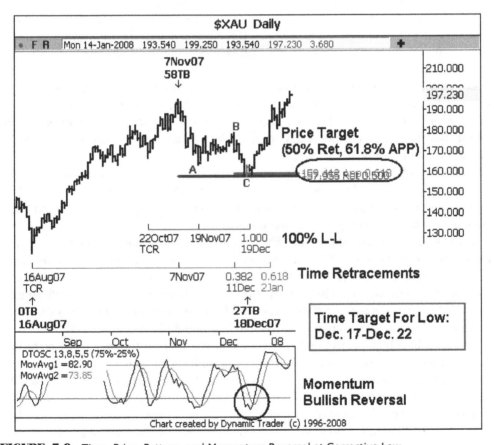

FIGURE 5.9 Time, Price, Pattern, and Momentum Reversal at Corrective Low

Is every corrective low made in the 38 to 62% time retracement zone? No, but most simple corrections are. At the least, this range gives us the typical minimum time target for a corrective low, a very valuable and practical piece of information itself, to warn us that a new low made prior to the 38% time retracement is not likely to complete a correction. Is every simple corrective low made at one of the three alternate time projections? No, but most are, so they are very valuable to help identify when a corrective low is probable. Is every corrective low made at the recent 100% low-low (or high-to-high) projection? No, but many are, particularly if several of the recent low-low cycles are in a relatively narrow range.

The Dynamic Time Strategy is used in a logical sequence of time projections to narrow a relatively wide time target zone to a narrower zone, sometimes as little as just two or three bars. This same strategy is used on all actively traded markets and all time frames.

So far, we've used one example of a simple ABC correction to illustrate the whole process. The Dynamic Time Strategy is used for all market conditions, not just simple ABC corrections. We never know in advance what form a correction may take. For that matter, we don't even know for sure if a correction is being made or a new trend. But if the larger time frame trend analysis suggests a correction is being made, the first assumption is it will be at least three sections. If it continues beyond three sections, don't despair—the Dynamic Time Strategy will still help provide the time target to complete the correction.

Let's take a look at a couple of more examples. Figure 5.10 is 15-minute EUR/GBP data covering less than two days of data. I don't want to encourage day trading. In the final chapter you'll read my thoughts about day trading and why most traders should avoid it. But even if you're not a day trader, you can use intraday setups to position yourself for a swing or position trade.

The EUR/GBP made a five-wave decline to the low on the chart, followed by a choppy advance. The advance had overlapping sections, which warns it is probably some sort of complex corrective advance and not a new bull trend. The objective is to identify the probable time target to complete a corrective high.

The top horizontal line shows the 62% and 100% time retracements. The advance has already gone beyond the 38 to 62% time retracement zone, which is the typical time target for a three-section, ABC correction. Most complex corrections will be complete by the 100% time retracement. This is logical. The time range of a corrective section will usually not exceed the time range of a trend section. The 100% time retracement is just a few bars past the last bar on the chart. A corrective high should be complete soon.

The 100% high-high projection is just a couple of bars past the high made as of the last bar on the chart, another sign a high is due soon if not already complete. The alternate time projections are not shown with the horizontal lines like in previous examples because it would crowd the chart. However, the last two low-high time counts were five and seven bars. The last high shown on the chart was eight bars, which is just one bar beyond the most recent alternate time projection of seven bars. This is another time factor that suggests at least a minor high is at or near completion.

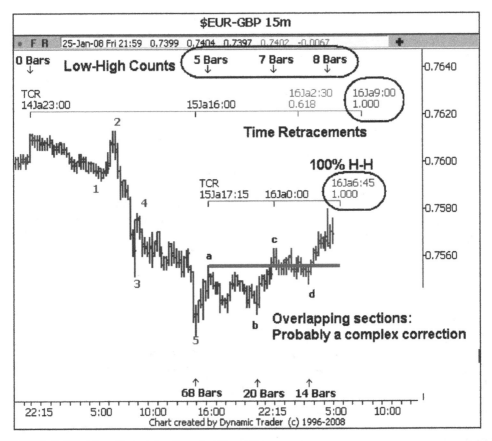

FIGURE 5.10 Time Target for Complex Correction

If the EUR/GBP is making a corrective rally as the overlapping pattern suggests, the corrective high should be complete within the next few bars, if it is not already complete as of the last high on the chart. Consider the logic of the time factors. The 100% time retracement of the five-wave bear trend is just a few bars away. The 100% time retracement is typically the maximum time retracement for a complex correction. The 100% high-high cycle is just a couple of bars away. The last high on the chart is within one bar of the recent low-high counts (alternate time projection). All three time factors suggest the corrective rally is at or near completion. If this is the case, the EUR/GBP should soon begin a decline *to a new low*, not just a minor decline. The pattern and time factors don't suggest merely a short-term high, but the final minor high of a complex correction that will be followed by a continuation of the bear trend to a new low. Is this valuable information you could use to make a specific trade strategy? You bet it is.

Figure 5.11 shows what followed. The EUR/GBP tagged the 62% price retracement, made a momentum bearish reversal, and soon declined to a new low. The time factors didn't point to the precise 15m bar of the high. They did clearly warn the trader that the

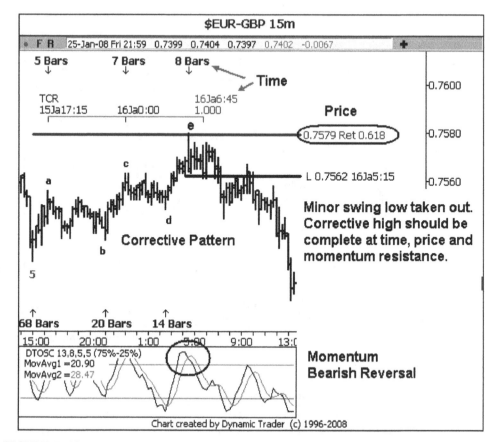

FIGURE 5.11   Time, Price, Momentum and Pattern to Complete a Corrective High

EUR/GBP was within a few bars of the maximum time probable to complete a complex corrective high, and to prepare to establish short positions for a probable decline to a new low. Not just a short-term day trade, but a short position based on 15m data that would probably last at least several days and make a new low.

While time factors often project a very narrow range time target to complete a trend or corrective high or low, their value is often to warn what is probable and not probable. In this case, they warned the trader the EUR/GBP was very near the probable maximum time for a corrective high and to be prepared with trade strategies to take advantage of a probable decline to a new low.

When the time position is considered with the pattern, price, and momentum position, the trader has a *very powerful* set of strategies for high probability trades with minimal capital exposure.

Figure 5.12 is 15-minute ES (S&P mini) futures data. If the advance off the low on the chart is a correction in a bear trend, what is the probable time target for a corrective high? With 15m data, we can often identify the time target for a corrective high within just an hour or two range. How helpful do you think this would be for your trading?

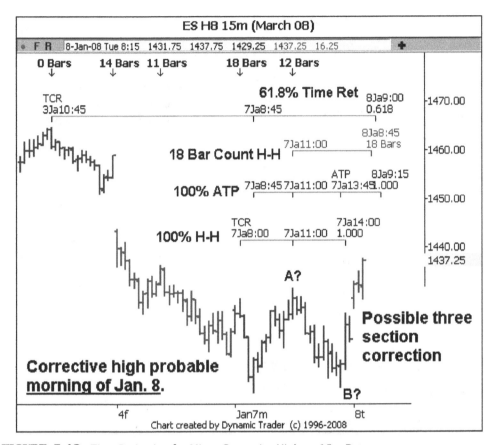

FIGURE 5.12 Time Projection for Minor Corrective High on 15m Data

Do you also see how it could be helpful to identify when to enter a position on a minor correction, in order to hold a position in the direction of the larger time frame trend?

The chart shows the 61.8% time retracement (9 A.M. January 8), typically the extreme of a three-section, ABC correction; plus the 100% ATP (9:15 A.M. January 8) and the 100% H-H projection (2 P.M. January 7). I've also added the 18 bar H-H count from the last high. Since the beginning of the bear trend shown on this data, the longest high-high count has been 18 bars, so we would anticipate the next high should be complete by the 18-bar count (8:45 A.M. January 8).

As of the last bar on the chart, the ES has already made a new high beyond the 100% high-high projection. All three of the other time factors fall within a 45-minute range, from the 15m bar ending 8:30 through 9:15. If the ES is making a three-section corrective rally, the probable time target to complete a corrective high is from 8:30 to 9:15 the morning of January 8.

Before we look at the results, once again consider the logic of how we used the three key time factors to identify a probable corrective high. We never know what form

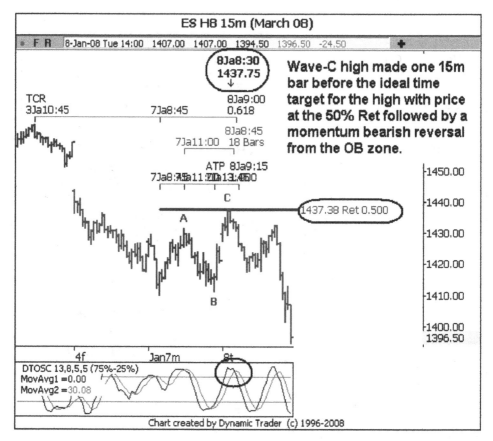

FIGURE 5.13   Reversal at Time Target

a correction may take, but the ES is in a position to complete an ABC, three-section correction. Typically, an ABC correction is complete by the 62% time retracement and near the 100% alternate time projection. The maximum recent high-to-high count has been 18 15-minute bars. All three of these time factors are within three 15m bars the morning of January 8. If the ES continues to advance into this narrow-range time zone, we would be very alert to the price and momentum position for a probable corrective high and go-short strategy for a probable decline to a new low.

Figure 5.13 shows the outcome. The ES made a Wave-C high on the 8:30, 15m bar, just one bar prior to the three-bar range projected for a Wave-C high. The ES was at the 50% retracement with the momentum OB. An ideal time, price, momentum, and pattern setup to complete a corrective high followed by a decline to a new low.

Not every corrective high or low is made when all four factors of time, price, pattern, and momentum are in place for a reversal, but many are. Your job is to identify *in advance* the conditions with a high probability outcome and be prepared to take advantage of those conditions. That's the objective of all technical analysis and trade strategies.

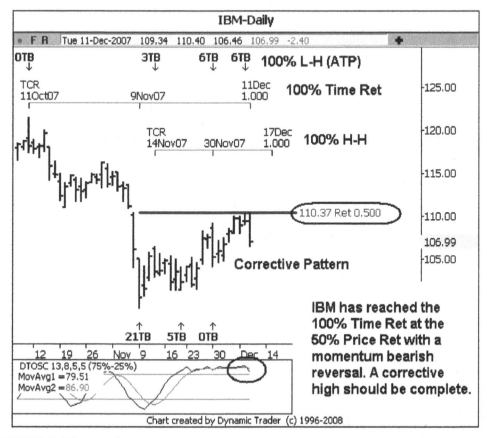

FIGURE 5.14 Time for a Top?

Figure 5.14 is IBM daily data. The advance up from the low has all the characteristics of a corrective pattern. There is not a tight group of time factors but as of the last bar on the chart, IBM has reached the 100% time retracement on December 11. This is typically the maximum time retracement for a complex correction. The last minor swing up was six trading days, the 100% low-high ATP. The recent 100% high-high (H-H) factor is almost a week away. Based on the time factors, IBM has reached the maximum probable time extreme to complete a corrective high. It has also tagged the 50% price retracement and made a momentum bearish reversal. Looks like another ideal setup to complete a correction followed by a decline to a new low.

Figure 5.15 shows how it turned out. IBM declined for several days and then advanced to a new high. The final corrective high was made on December 26, nowhere near any of the time factors. Once IBM made a new high beyond the 100% time retracement, the Dynamic Time Strategy you have learned so far is not of much use. I wish I could tell you every high and low will be made at the projected time target, but they are not. What we have is a time strategy approach that identifies relatively narrow range time

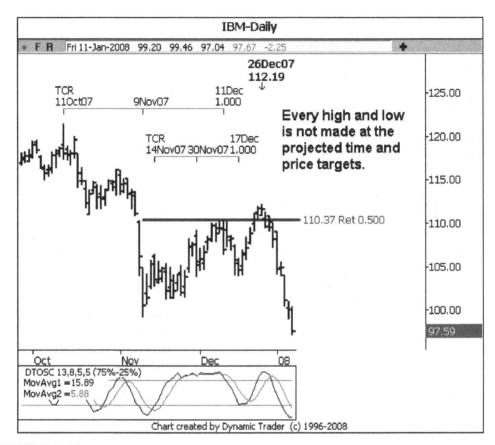

FIGURE 5.15 Corrective High Not Made at a Time Target

targets and maximum time targets when a reversal is *probable*, but not certain. That is the best we can ask for and expect. If the trade strategies you learn in a chapter later in the book execute a trade, the loss will be acceptable and part of the business of trading. Remember, the objective is not to be right every time. That's not going to happen. The objective is to identify conditions with a high probability outcome and acceptable capital exposure.

TIME BANDS

Time Bands are similar to the traditional style of cycle analysis but with a more relevant and useful approach. Walter Bressert, who is considered the father of financial cycle analysis, developed this approach in the early 1980s. This approach to identifying time targets for a low or high in any market and any time frame is quick and simple to do. As usual, let's jump right into a real-world example to learn how to make Time Bands.

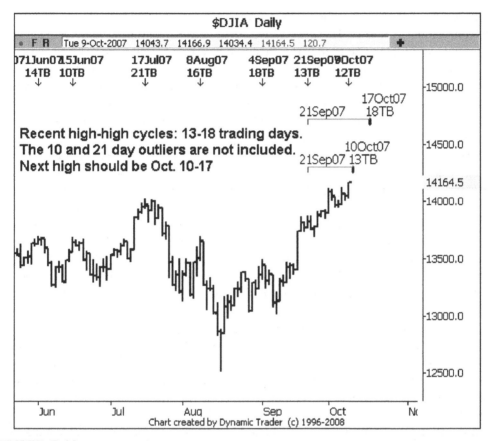

FIGURE 5.16 High-to-High Counts

Figure 5.16 is several months of DJIA daily data. The date and time range markers along the top of the chart point to some of the highs made during the period. The date markers show the date of the high and the number of bars between the dates. Of the highs shown, plus several to the left of the chart not shown, the high-high periods range from 10 to 21 trading days. If this H-H time rhythm continues, the next high would be made 10 to 21 trading days from the last completed high made on September 21. This is too broad a range to be of much use.

There are two H-H outliers: the 21-day and 10-day H-H counts in June and July. If most of the periods are grouped in a relatively small range, I eliminate the extreme short and long outliers when making the counts. In this case, the range of all the high-high periods, not including the extreme short and long outliers, was 13 to 18 trading days. Interestingly, in this case, the back-to-back 21- and 10-day periods total 31 days, which is about twice the average of the rest of the high-to-high periods.

The last complete high was made September 21. If we count forward 13 and 18 trading days from the September 21 high, the result is October 10 and October 17. If the recent high-to-high time rhythm continues, the next comparable high should be made between October 10 and 17. This is a relatively narrow range of time to anticipate a high, but we should be able to do even better than that and narrow the range to fewer days.

Before you learn how to complete the Time Band for a more narrow range time target, a few comments are necessary. First, you have to use some judgment in choosing the high or low pivots. In most cases the relevant pivots are the obvious swing highs and lows, but also look for periods of market consolidation that fit in with the typical high-high counts that have been made.

Over the past 20 years, I've tested many approaches to automatically identify the cycle highs and lows, including percentage change of price movement, factors of average true range, Gann swing charts, momentum cycles, and more. None has proved satisfactory, and each of these approaches has inherent weaknesses that either miss relevant pivots or include irrelevant pivots. I have built into the Dynamic Trader software an auto swing mode which will pick highs and lows either by percentage change in price or by factors of the average true range. While it saves a lot of time on the first run through to pick the highs and lows, in almost every case when the auto swing mode is used, I find I need to edit the swing file because not all the relevant pivots were picked by the auto mode.

Beware of any so-called cycle software that allegedly identifies pivots without any user input. As I've said many times before, all aspects of trading are like any other business. You can't buy success. You have to gain knowledge and experience and make decisions. While identifying the relevant pivots for Time Band targets is 80% or so objective, with any set of pivots you will have to use some common sense and make some decisions which pivots to include.

Another decision you will have to make is whether to eliminate outlier counts. In most cases, it is obvious. If most of the periods are within a relatively narrow range like the DJIA in Figure 5.16, and there is one outlier on each end of the range, they can be eliminated. If the periods are fairly evenly spread through a wide range with no obvious outliers, the entire range of periods is used but will probably result in too wide a range for the Time Band projection to be useful. You have to use whatever information the market provides and then make decisions to arrive at the best results.

The final decision is how many repetitions are enough for a reliable Time Band projection. Probably not as many as you think—as few as five or six are enough. I rarely go back more than 10 or 12 pivot highs or lows. If cycle periods have stayed within a relatively narrow range of time, the assumption is the recent time rhythm will continue. We are interested in the *recent* time rhythm of the market, not the time rhythm of the distant past. We are trading today's market and are interested in the current trends, volatility, and time rhythms, not what happened months or years ago.

Let's complete the Time Band with the second set of counts and see if we can narrow the relatively wide high-high band to a more narrow range.

The second set of counts when making a Time Band for a high is the low-to-high (L-H) counts using the same high pivots used to identify the high-high cycles. On the chart in Figure 5.17, I've marked the lows between the high pivots. The new time

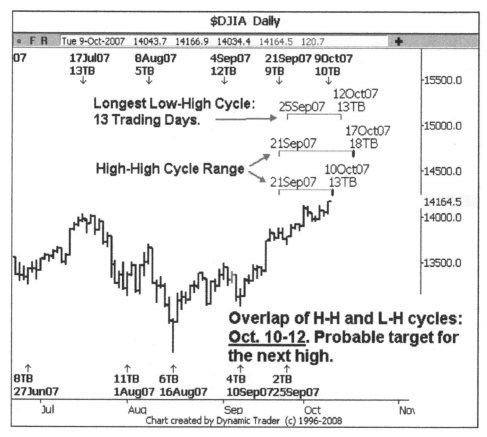

FIGURE 5.17 Overlap of L-H and H-H Cycles

counts that are part of the high markers now represent the low-to-high counts of each advance.

I've reduced the number of bars so the pivot markers can be read. The range of low-to-high counts is from 5 to 13 trading days. There were several counts on the data to the left of the chart not shown that were in the low end of the 5 to 13 trading day range. There were no obvious outliers, so the entire 5 to 13 trading day range is used. This is a very broad range, and not of much use by itself. I have only shown the maximum 13-day low-high count on the chart since the DJIA is already well past the minimum part of the low-high range. The 13 trading day count from the last low on September 25 is October 12. If the recent low-high time rhythm that has been made for the past several months continues, a comparable high should be made by October 12.

The Time Band combines the high-high count range and the low-high count range. *The overlap of the two ranges is the Time Band* and a high probability time target for the next comparable high. Just with the information in Figure 5.17, we can see the overlap period would be October 10 (minimum H-H count) to October 12 (maximum L-H count).

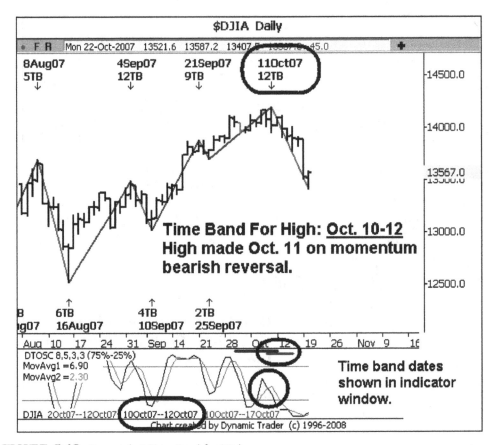

FIGURE 5.18   Reversal at Time Band for High

Figure 5.18 shows the result. A high was made on October 11, right in the October 10–12 Time Band for a high. The Dynamic Trader software includes a Time Band function and displays the Time Bands in the indicator window. The center range of dates along the bottom of the indicator is the Time Band of the H-H and L-H overlap period (October 10–12). The Time Band range is also displayed in the overbought zone above the indicator, so we have an easy visual of the Time Band and momentum position.

On October 11, right in the Time Band for a high, the DJIA made an outside reversal day with a momentum bearish reversal. Nice setup for a short trade. Earlier you may have noted that I said a "comparable" high should be expected. A high made in the Time Band should be comparable to the highs made for the period of the raw data for the Time Band. In this case, since the DJIA was in a bull trend during the period, the declines off the recent highs have been from a few days up to two weeks.

The Time Band itself does not provide any information as to whether the high will be more significant than recent highs, only that a high comparable to the recent highs should be made. That itself is good and useable information for a trade strategy. If the pattern and/or price and/or larger time frame momentum position suggested the market is in

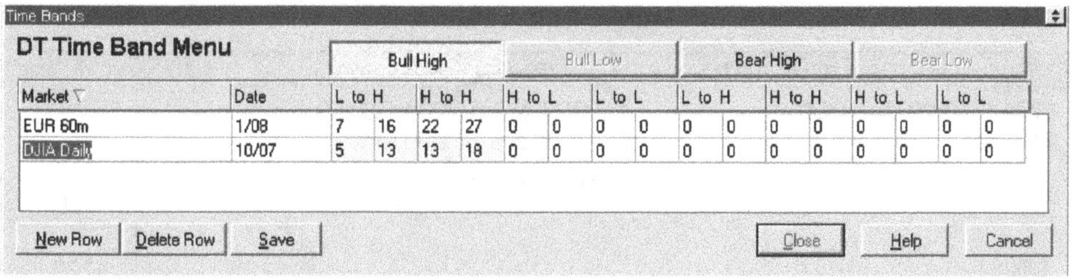

| Time Bands | | | | | | | | | | | | | | | ⬍ |

DT Time Band Menu		Bull High		Bull Low		Bear High		Bear Low	
Market ▽	Date	L to H	H to H	H to L	L to L	L to H	H to H	H to L	L to L
EUR 60m	1/08	7	16	22	27	0	0	0	0	0	0	0	0
DJIA Daily	10/07	5	13	13	18	0	0	0	0	0	0	0	0

New Row | Delete Row | Save   Close | Help | Cancel

FIGURE 5.19   DT Time Band Setup

a position to make a larger time frame reversal, the Time Band would be very helpful to identify the narrow-range time target when the larger-degree high or low should be complete. With each part of the trade strategy, the lower time frame can help to identify a narrower range of time, price, momentum, or pattern when a higher time frame reversal may be made.

Figure 5.19 is the Time Band menu in the Dynamic Trader software. The first column identifies the market or symbol and the time frame of the Time Band, such as daily or 60 minutes. In the case of the daily DJIA example we just looked at, the 5 to 13 low-to-high and 13 to 18 high-to-high ranges are entered and the Time Band result is displayed in the indicator window, as shown in the prior figure.

The DT Time Band menu contains columns labeled Bull High and Bull Low as well as Bear High and Bear Low. The time rhythms in bull and bear markets are often different, so we include a section for each.

Time Bands can be made on any market and any time frame of data. The next example is for the EUR/USD on 60-minute data. The highs are marked on Figure 5.20. Only a limited amount of data is shown so the markers will not overlap and be unreadable. The highs going back several more repetitions to the left of the chart were in the 22 to 27 bar range. One high-to-high count shown on the chart was 57 bars, which is about twice the range of the other counts. We'll eliminate the 57-bar outlier and use the 22 to 27 bar range of all the other counts, which include several repetitions to the left of the chart.

Figure 5.21 shows the same EUR/USD data with both the lows and highs marked. The bar count with each high label is the low-high count. The low-to-high range of counts is from 7 to 16, which includes several L-H counts to the left of the data on the chart. The overlap of the H-H and L-H ranges of counts is a Time Band for a high from the 8 P.M.. (20:00) bar on January 24 to midnight (0:00) January 25. If the recent time rhythm from the last few weeks continues, a high lasting at least from 10 to 18 bars should be made in this Time Band.

The last 60m bar on the chart is the 8 P.M. (20:00) bar on January 24, which is the first bar of the Time Band range for a high. Momentum is overbought in a position where highs lasting at least several hours have been made. The EUR/USD is in a position to make a high lasting at least 10 to 18 hours, a comparable high to recent highs, not including the outlier that made a 43-bar decline.

How did it turn out? Figure 5.22 shows the results.

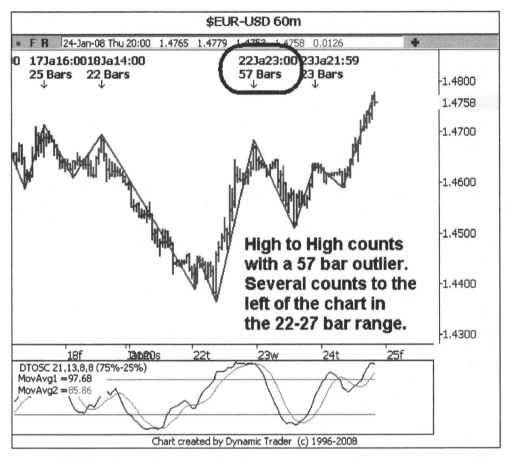

FIGURE 5.20   High-to-High Counts with Outlier Count

Note that I frequently stated, "If the recent time rhythm continues . . . " No matter how narrow the range of the recent cycles, we never *know* if the next high or low will continue the recent time rhythm, so I'm always careful what I say—which reflects what I believe. As stated over and over again through this book, every trade strategy or technical analysis approach only has a probability of divining what the future holds. In this case, a market could make a high earlier or later than the Time Band, but since the Time Band was made based on the recent time rhythm, we have to consider that it will probably continue and the next high or low has a *high probability* of being made in the Time Band. A *high probability* outcome is the absolute best we can expect. It is enough to use for low-risk, high probability trade strategies.

Time Bands are a very logical and effective approach to identify in advance high probability time targets for any market and any time frame to make highs and lows. If you include Time Bands as part of your trading plan, I know you will find them extremely

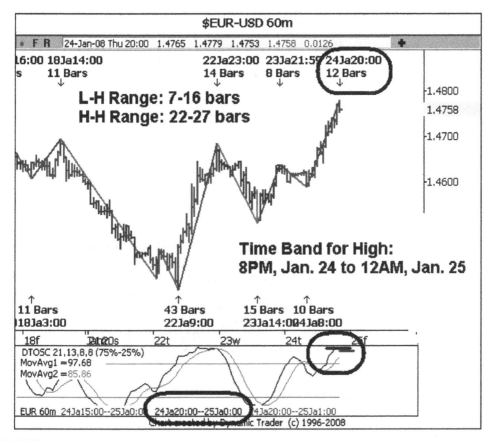

FIGURE 5.21 Time Band for EUR/USD 60m High

useful and they will become a regular part of your strategy to identify conditions with a high probability outcome and acceptable capital exposure.

MORE TIME FACTORS

In the preceding sections on the Dynamic Time Strategies, I have taught you how to identify time targets to complete a correction. If you can identify the conditions with a high probability to complete a correction, you are in a position to enter a trade in the direction of the major trend, which is why we put a lot of focus on corrections.

The same approach is used to identify in advance the time targets to complete five-wave and other trend structures. I have not included Dynamic Time Strategies for trend targets because they involve more sets of projections and more ratios from a wider variety of sections. They are also more difficult to do unless you have the Dynamic Trader software to make the projections. So we'll have to leave Dynamic Time Strategies for

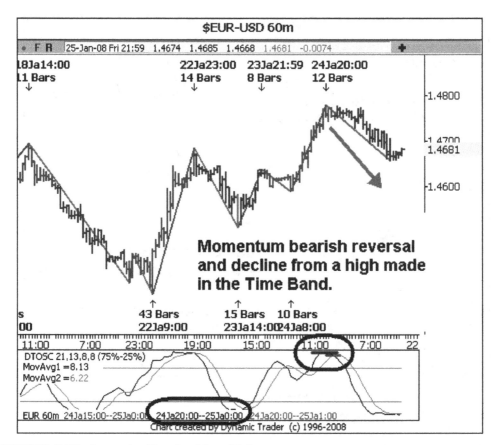

FIGURE 5.22   Reversal at Time Band for a High

trend targets to another time, but don't despair—they aren't necessary for the complete trade plan from entry to exit that you will learn in the chapters to come.

As you have seen from the time strategies outlined here, a chart can become crowded if all of the time projections are made and saved to a chart. The Dynamic Trader program has several unique time projection routines, including the Dynamic Time Projection (DTP) report. The DTP routine makes all of the sets of time projections you learned here, plus a few additional ones that are unique to different pattern structures, and displays the results as bars in the indicator window. The bars represent those times in the future with the greatest number of hits. The bars are a visual representation of the clustering of the time retracement, alternate time projection, and high-high and low-low projections that you learned earlier, plus a few others.

Figure 5.23 shows the Wave-C Dynamic Time Projection for the XAU example used earlier. The highest scoring date was December 18, the same time target we arrived at by looking at all the individual time factors. The DTP report uses the same information you've learned in this chapter, but crunches the numbers instantly to arrive at the time targets.

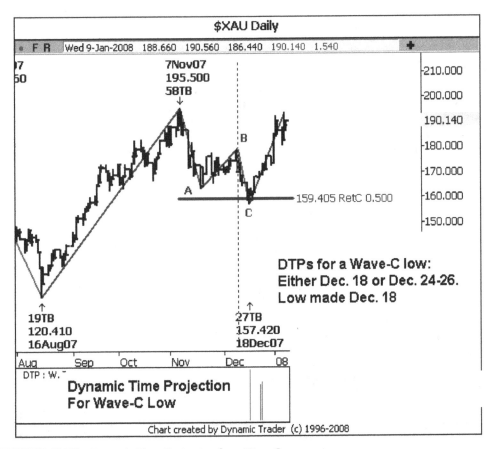

FIGURE 5.23 Dynamic Time Projection for a Wave-C

A Dynamic Time Projection target can be made for any pattern structure. Figure 5.24 shows the DTP for a Wave-5 low for 60m ES data. This is the same data used in Chapter 4, where you learned to identify the probable price target for the five-wave trend low. The highest DTP score was for a Wave-5 late afternoon of November 26, right when the low was made.

If you want to make the Dynamic Time Strategies a regular part of your trading plan for all market conditions, you might check out the Dynamic Trader program on our web site. You don't need it to do what I've taught you so far, but it can save you a lot of time.

CONCLUSION

In this chapter you've learned some practical time strategies including Time Bands and Dynamic Time Strategies. Use them every day for every market and time frame and you should make a great advance in your trading results.

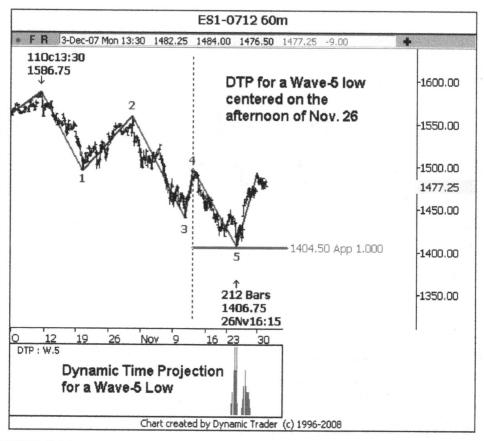

FIGURE 5.24   Dynamic Time Projection for a Wave-5 Low

In the chapters so far, we've focused on identifying conditions with a high probability outcome to consider a trade. Now it's time to learn trade execution, including the
specific entry and initial protective stop price in the next chapter. Then you will learn
exit strategies and trade management to round out a complete trading plan from entry
to exit.

CHAPTER 6

Entry Strategies and Position Size

In this chapter you will learn two completely objective entry strategies, including the specific entry price and initial protective stop for all market conditions, plus the maximum position size for any trade. Objective entry strategies are a key to a successful trade plan. They will eliminate the emotion and indecisiveness once the trade decision is made. Knowing the maximum position size for any trade will be a key factor in your trading success.

So far you have learned the four factors of multiple time frame momentum, pattern, price, and time used to identify market conditions with a high probability outcome to consider a trade. This doesn't mean a trade should be entered every time these conditions are made. It just means there is a potential trade.

Now we set the specific conditions to execute the trade including the entry price and initial protective stop-loss. Most of the time a trade will be executed. However, sometimes the market will not react as anticipated and will not meet the trade execution conditions.

While there is some judgment involved to identify the best trade conditions based on what you have learned so far, the trade entry strategy is completely objective. Once the conditions are in place for a probable correction reversal or trend reversal, there is no more thinking, and no more judgments to be made. The entry strategy is objective.

In this chapter, you will learn just two specific entry strategies. Both are similar in that they require the market to move in the anticipated direction before the trade is entered. This is crucial. I don't recommend buying or selling at a price target. There is too great a risk of the market continuing through the price target. Why not wait for the market action itself to give some evidence that it is going to do what you anticipate it should do, before entering the trade?

An entry strategy must have a specific buy/sell price and a specific initial protective stop price. You may have been taught vague strategies in the past such as "you could buy around here and place your stop around here." That's not a strategy—that's a suggestion. You can't place an "around this price" order with the broker. Brokers don't take vague or approximate orders. They take specific price orders, so that is what you are going to learn: practical, simple, and, most important, logical entry strategies based on the market position.

Stops are always placed at the exact price that will void the setup. That's the key to stops. What can the market do that will void the very condition that prompted the trade? That is where the stop-loss is placed. If a market voids the condition that caused the trade to be taken, there is no reason to remain in the position. You want to be out quickly with an acceptable loss rather than potentially ending up with an unacceptable and possibly ruinous loss.

This chapter is just about entry strategies, which include the specific entry price and initial protective stop-loss. It is not about how to adjust the stop-loss if the market moves in the anticipated direction, and it is not about exit strategies. Those are the subjects of Chapter 7. For most of the examples in this chapter, I focus on the specific entry strategy and don't go into much detail about the momentum, pattern, price, and time position that made the probable trade setup. Some of these other factors are shown, but the focus is on the specific entry strategy. We'll put all of the factors together in a more comprehensive way when you learn to plan a trade from entry to exit in later chapters.

In this chapter you will also learn about other completely objective decisions, including the maximum capital exposure (risk) and maximum position size for any trade, under any conditions, and for any market.

ENTRY STRATEGY 1: TRAILING ONE-BAR ENTRY AND STOP

The *trailing one-bar-high* (or low) entry (Tr-1BH/L) is very simple and logical and will usually put you into the trade with a very close stop. Once the conditions are in place for a reversal and following the lower time frame momentum reversal, trail the buy-stop or sell-stop to enter the trade one tick above the high or below the low of the last completed bar. Place the initial protective stop one tick beyond the swing high or low made prior to entry.

Let's take a look at an example. Figure 6.1 is the XAU daily data. As of the last bar on the chart, the XAU has reached the 50% retracement, is near the 100% low-low cycle, and has made a daily momentum bullish reversal. There are several other time and price factors for support that you've learned in previous chapters, but the ones shown here are just a couple that demonstrate the XAU is in a position for a possible Wave-C low. We'll assume for now the higher time frame weekly momentum was either oversold or bullish, which are the higher time frame momentum conditions to consider a long trade following the lower time frame daily momentum bullish reversal. In Chapter 2 we saw that if a market has reached a higher time frame oversold position, the immediate

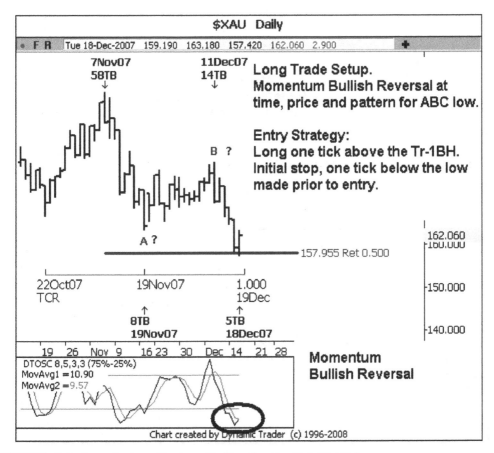

FIGURE 6.1 Setup for Long Trade on Trailing One-Bar-High (Tr-1BH)

downside should be limited, and the next momentum bullish reversal on the lower time frame is likely to be quickly followed by a bullish reversal on the higher time frame. A higher time frame oversold momentum is in a position to prepare for a long trade.

Since the XAU is at time and price support for a potential Wave-C low and the smaller time frame daily momentum has made a bullish reversal, the entry strategy is to go long one tick above the daily trailing one-bar-high (Tr-1BH) and place the initial protective sell-stop one tick below the swing low made prior to entry.

Figure 6.2 shows the results. The next day, the XAU took out the high of the prior day and continued to advance in the days ahead without hitting the stop. At this point it is not relevant how far the XAU advanced or how the stop was adjusted or trade exited. We are only concerned with how the trade was executed once the conditions were in place for a reversal.

The Tr-1BH(L) entry/stop strategy is very simple and logical. The market must make some positive action in the anticipated direction by taking out a bar high before the trade is entered. The entry will not always be executed on the next bar. It may take several bars

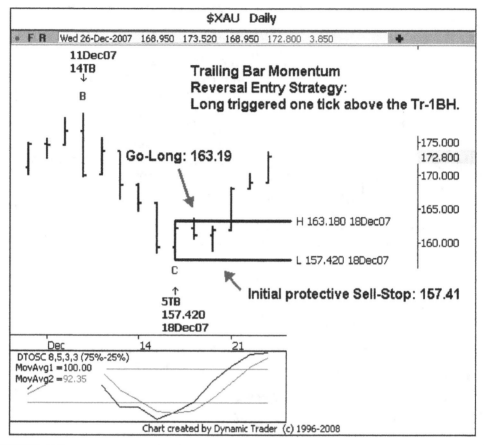

FIGURE 6.2 Long Trade Executed on Tr-1BH

before the trailing one-bar-high or low is taken out and the trade executed. Figure 6.3 is a close-up of a momentum bearish reversal and how the TR-1BL entry was adjusted at each bar until executed.

The bar labeled 1 was the bar when the momentum bearish reversal was made. Beginning with the next bar, a sell-stop one tick below the low of the last completed bar is placed to enter a short trade. Neither the bar 2 or bar 3 low took out the prior bar's low, so no short trade was executed. Bar 4 took out the trailing 1BL and executed the short trade. The initial protective buy-stop was placed one tick above the bar number 3 high, the highest bar made since the momentum bearish reversal and recent swing high.

Following the lower time frame momentum bearish reversal, the Tr-1BL entry strategy continues as long as the momentum remains bearish and does not reach the oversold zone. If the momentum makes a bullish reversal or reaches the oversold zone before a 1BL is taken out and the trade executed, the entry is canceled. The lower time frame momentum conditions are no longer valid for a short entry. It may take several bars before the trade is executed, if executed at all. The beauty of the Tr-1BL(H) strategy is that if

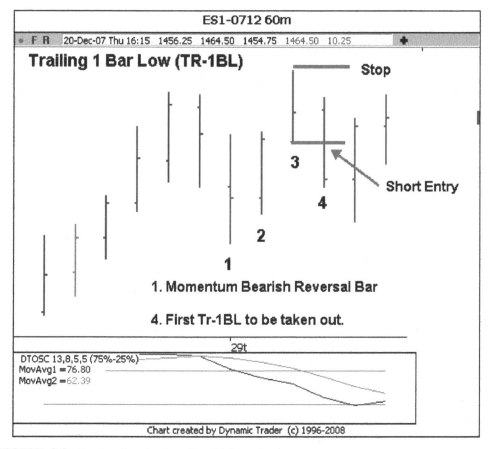

FIGURE 6.3 Trailing One-Bar-Low (Tr-1BL) Entry Strategy

the market does not immediately begin to trend in the anticipated direction, the entry is often at a better price and/or less capital exposure than if the entry was immediately taken following the reversal.

Figure 6.4 shows a situation where the entry strategy would have been voided before a trade was executed. The bar labeled 1 is the first bar following a momentum bearish reversal. Using the Tr-1BL entry strategy, for the next three bars the low of a prior bar was not taken out, so no short trade would have been elected. Four bars later at the bar labeled 2, the momentum made a bullish reversal, voiding any further short setup. The Tr-1BL entry strategy is canceled. Another short setup would not be made until the momentum made the next bearish reversal, as long as the higher time frame momentum was still bearish and not oversold.

As of the last bar in Figure 6.5, the 60m momentum made a bullish reversal at potential Wave-5 support. Let's assume the higher time frame daily momentum was either bullish or bear OS, creating the momentum conditions to consider a long trade following a smaller time frame, 60m momentum bullish reversal. We begin to trail a buy-stop to go

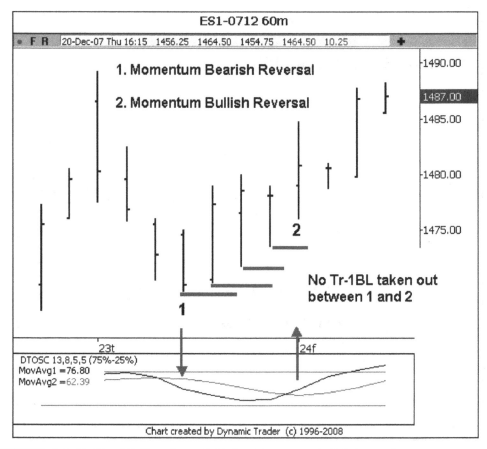

FIGURE 6.4 Trailing 1BL Short Setup Voided on Momentum Bullish Reversal

long, one tick above the last completed bar's high, which so far is 1431.25. If the trade is executed, the initial protective sell-stop is one tick below the swing low made prior to trade entry, in this case 1406.50. If the swing low is taken out, it is not a valid reversal, which was the basis for entering the trade. The trade conditions would be voided and there would be no reason to remain in the trade.

If this long trade were executed at 1431.25 (one tick above the 1BH), the stop must be placed at 1406.50 (one tick below the swing low) for a capital exposure of 24.75 per contract. The stop cannot be placed closer to the entry as only a trade below the swing low would void the setup, not some arbitrary price somewhere between the entry and swing low. A 24.75 point capital exposure per contract is a larger capital exposure than a highly leveraged futures trader would probably accept (including me). We don't determine the entry price, stop price, or initial capital exposure. The market does so by the range of bars it is making. We don't control the potential risk of the setup. We do control whether to accept the risk or not, and we do control the position size. Later in this

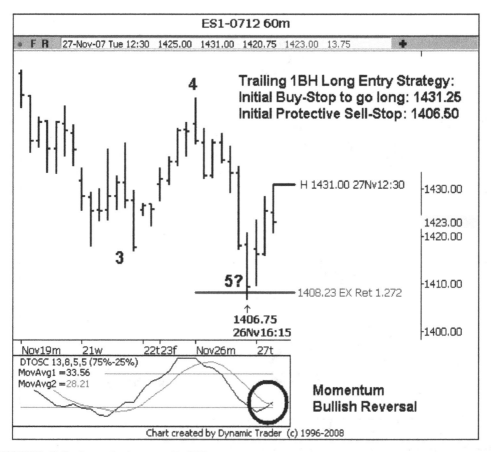

FIGURE 6.5 Setup for Long on Tr-1BH

chapter you will learn how to objectively determine the maximum capital exposure and position size for any trade.

There are two solutions to an unacceptable capital exposure such as with this setup. First, once the setup is made on the 60m data, you could move down to the next smaller time frame like the 15m data, and wait for the setup to be made there after the 60m setup is made. There is no guarantee a trade setup will be made on the 15m data, but if it is, the initial capital exposure is likely to be much smaller. Or you can take the trade with less or even no leverage with an exchange-traded fund (ETF) such as the SPY that represents the S&P. Take advantage of all the work you've done to identify the high probability setup and take the trade with less capital exposure on an unleveraged or low leveraged market. There will be much more on the choices of markets in later chapters. For now, let's continue to focus on entry strategies.

Figure 6.6 is IBM daily data. Assume the higher time frame weekly momentum was either bearish or bull OB for a short setup on the smaller time frame daily data. In mid-December, the Stoch daily momentum made a bearish reversal with price at the 50%

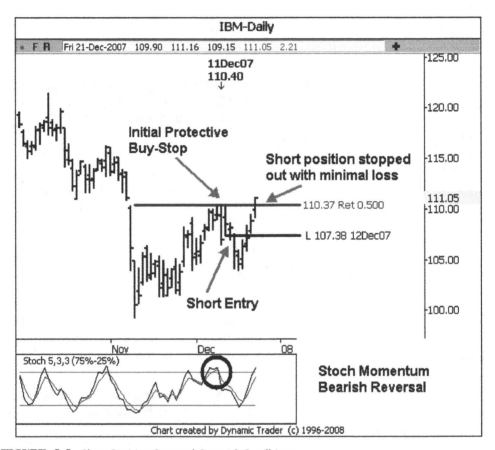

FIGURE 6.6   Short Position Stopped Out with Small Loss

retracement. Two days later, IBM took out the Tr-1BL to execute a short trade with an initial protective buy-stop one tick above the swing high made prior to trade entry. Several days later, the short trade was stopped out with a small loss.

The entry price and the initial protective stop are completely objective with the Tr-1BH(L) entry strategy. The beauty is that the entry is usually very close to a reversal and the capital exposure is usually very small in the event of a loss.

If stopped out of a trade, continue with the same strategy *as long as the trade conditions are in place.* In the case of IBM, as long as the higher time frame weekly momentum is still bear or bull OB, the next daily momentum bearish reversal is another setup for a short position. The rally in IBM still appeared corrective, so any daily momentum high could result in the final minor swing high of the correction.

Figure 6.7 is the daily EUR/GBP which has reached a Wave-5 price target zone. As of the last bar on the chart for January 15, the daily momentum made a bearish reversal. The strategy for entry is to go down a time frame to the 60m data for a trade execution setup.

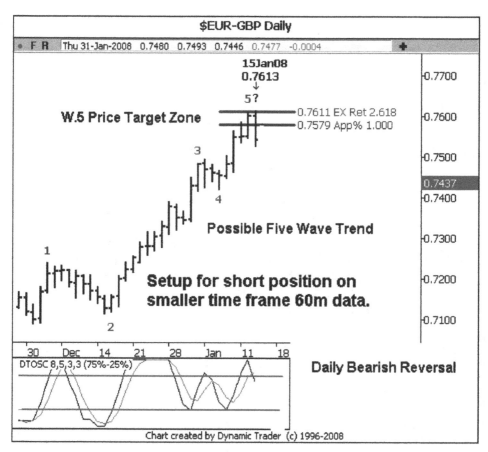

FIGURE 6.7 Short Setup on Higher Time Frame Daily Data

Figure 6.8 is the 60m data for January 15-16, just following the higher time frame daily momentum bearish reversal. The morning of January 16, the EUR/GBP tagged the 61.8% price retracement just a couple of bars short of the 100% time retracement. The pattern up has all the characteristics of a correction. The 60m momentum made a bearish reversal to complete the setup to initiate the Tr-1BL entry strategy on the 60m data. Two bars after the 60m momentum bearish reversal, the Tr-1BL is taken out to execute a short trade with the initial protective buy-stop one pip above the corrective high.

If you want to make real money trading, trade the major trends. There is probably no better trending market than currencies (Forex). Trade the weekly/daily setups for the major trends. Trade for points, not for ticks, or, in the case of Forex, pips. Figure 6.9 is weekly EUR/USD data. As of the last weekly bar on the chart, the weekly MACD made a shorter bar from below the signal line, a bullish reversal for the MACD. Since the MACD doesn't have OB and OS zones, we have to wait for a momentum reversal (shorter bar from below the signal line) before we can consider it has made a higher time frame setup.

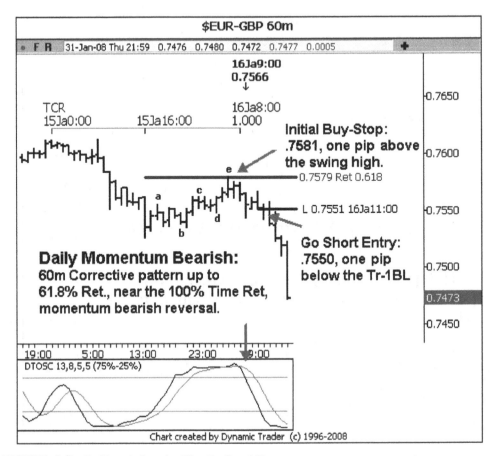

FIGURE 6.8 Go-Short below the 60m Trailing 1BL

Price had tested the 38.2% price retracement three times in a probable corrective pattern. Traditional chartists and swing traders would wait for the breakout above the trading range high to go long. This would require a very wide stop. With the dual time frame momentum setup and Tr-1BH entry strategy, a long trade can be made with a relatively small capital exposure. If the EUR/USD doesn't end up making a bull trend, the loss will be very small.

Figure 6.10 is the smaller time frame daily EUR/USD. The weekly momentum bullish reversal was made the week ending October 20. I've marked the daily October 20 bar at the top of the chart. The objective entry strategy is to execute the daily Tr-1BH following a momentum bullish reversal on the daily data as long as the weekly momentum remains bullish. Three daily bars after October 20, the daily MACD made a momentum bullish reversal (longer bar from above the signal line). The following day, a long trade was executed one tick above the prior day's high with a stop one tick below the swing low made prior to the bullish reversal. Currencies frequently have consistent trends that last for weeks and months. Using the weekly and daily data are the ideal time frames to enter

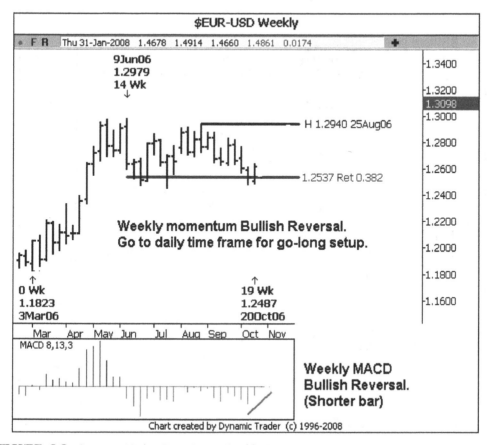

FIGURE 6.9 Setup on Higher Time Frame Weekly Data

position trades with minimal capital exposure and significant profit potential. Currency ETFs can be used for minimal to no leverage for potential long-term positions.

The trailing one-bar-high (low) entry strategy is completely objective and usually sets up with minimal capital exposure. It has some superb benefits. The trade will not be executed unless the market moves in the anticipated direction by taking out the trailing one-bar-high or low. The initial capital exposure is always known before the trade is executed because the setup defines the exact entry and stop prices. If the capital exposure is too large to be accepted, either pass up the trade or trade a minimal leveraged or un-leveraged market such as an ETF or mutual fund instead of a futures contract or highly leveraged Forex position.

If the market doesn't immediately move in the anticipated direction and take out the immediate 1BH(L), the trade may be entered within the next few bars, possibly at an even better price or with less capital exposure. If the setup conditions are voided by a smaller time frame momentum reversal against the higher time frame momentum direction, the trade is voided until the next setup is made.

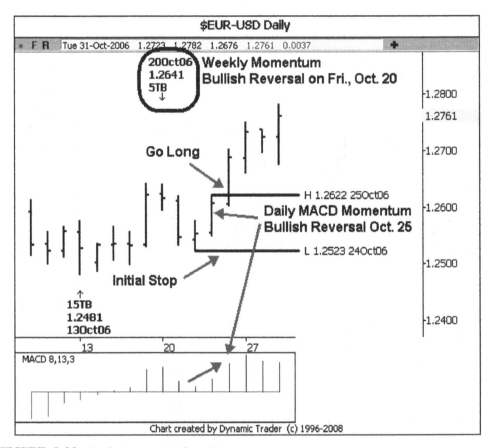

FIGURE 6.10   Trade Entry on Trailing 1BH

Most of the preceding examples showed successful trades where the trade was executed and the market moved in the anticipated direction. The objective was for you to learn the entry strategy and exactly where the entry and stop prices were in each situation. You'll have plenty of losses where the entry is executed and the market immediately turns around to stop out the trade. But the losses will be relatively small and the potential gains relatively large. Plus, there will be many setups that are just not executed as shown in an example near the beginning of this chapter. In the next chapter, you will learn the stop-loss adjustment and exit strategies to manage the trade from entry to exit and hopefully take advantage of the majority of any trend that develops.

Now let's look at the second entry strategy, the swing entry.

ENTRY STRATEGY 2: SWING ENTRY AND STOP

Concepts are important. The concept has to make sense before an action is taken. In the case of entry strategies, the concept is that the market must move in the anticipated direction and take out a swing high or low before a trade entry is made. It is the same concept for the trailing bar entry strategy. The initial conditions are the same as with the trailing bar entry strategy. The dual time frame momentum, price, pattern, and time conditions for a corrective or trend reversal must first be in place. The higher time frame momentum is either bull or bear OS for a long trade, or bear or bull OB for a short trade. The smaller time frame momentum makes a reversal in the direction of the higher time frame. Once these conditions with a high probability outcome are in place, the swing entry strategy requires the market to take out a swing high or low in the direction of the anticipated trend.

With the swing entry (SE) strategy, the capital exposure is usually greater than with the TR-1-BH(L) strategy because the entry price is usually further away from the initial protective stop price. On the plus side, the SE strategy should have a higher rate of success. Every entry strategy has a trade-off. An entry strategy made very soon after a smaller time frame momentum reversal may have a lower rate of success but a smaller capital exposure, while an entry strategy with a higher rate of success will often have a larger capital exposure.

Don't confuse the swing entry strategy with swing trading. *Swing trading* has become a buzzword the past few years and doesn't represent any one particular strategy. Pure swing trading is buying each new swing high or selling each new swing low to enter in the direction of the trend. It's a great strategy in a strongly trending market, but you get killed if the swing is the final section of a trend or a market is entering a choppy, trading range period. With the approach you are learning in this book, a swing entry is only made once the conditions are in place for a reversal, and the entry is made on a minor swing in a lower time frame to reduce the initial capital exposure.

Let's take a look at a swing entry strategy. Figure 6.11 is 60m S&P mini (ES) futures contract. The low on the chart is a potential Wave-5 low. To keep the chart uncluttered, I am not showing the time and price targets near the low, which suggest EOW-5 time and price support. The higher time frame daily momentum (not shown) is bear OS, a position to consider a long trade following a smaller time frame 60m momentum bullish reversal. A momentum bear OS position implies the downside should be limited and a bullish reversal is probable following the next lower time frame momentum bullish reversal. The last bar on the chart is the last 60m bar for November 27 for the pit hours session. Non-pit-hours session data is not considered since the volume is so low. The 60m ES has made the momentum bullish reversal. The swing entry for the following day is one tick above the prior swing high. If the entry is executed, the initial protective sell-stop is one tick below the swing low made prior to entry.

We don't know if the market is going to continue to advance and take out the swing high. For all we know it could continue to decline or chop sideways. What we do know is as of November 26, the ES is in a position to complete a Wave-5 low and a trade above the swing high should confirm a Wave-5 low is complete. If the ES takes out the swing high, it would void any logical bear pattern and be a reason to be long. We call this a *pattern reversal signal*. If this is the case, the ES should rally for at least two to three weeks

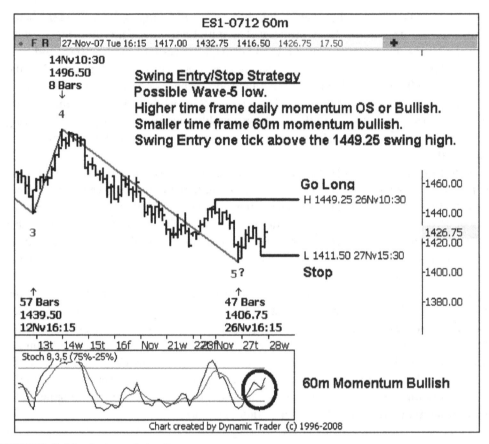

FIGURE 6.11 Go-Long Swing Entry

since the bear trend lasted over five weeks from the early October high (not shown) to the November 26 low.

The initial capital exposure would be significant if the trade is executed, so this particular setup may not be appropriate for a leveraged futures trade for a relatively small account. It would be a great setup for an unleveraged or margined SPY (S&P ETF) or S&P index mutual fund position. The beauty of this daily/60m setup is the trader can use the 60m intraday data to identify the setup and swing entry strategy but doesn't have to be watching the market during the day. The buy-stop at 1449.50 to go long can be put in after regular trading hours. If executed the following day, the protective sell-stop is automatically entered at 1411.25. Most trading platforms have an "if this happens, then do this" contingent option. If a buy-stop is executed, a sell-stop is immediately entered. If the ES does not trade above the swing high the following day and the buy-stop is not executed, the following evening the trader can see if the conditions are still in place for the swing entry and enter the appropriate buy-stop for the next day.

If the trader is available to monitor the market the following day, the next smaller time frame 15m data may be used for the swing entry setup. This doesn't mean you have to be glued to the screen all day. Set an alert to notify you when a 15m momentum bullish reversal is made. Then you can identify the swing high or low and place the buy-stop to execute the trade.

Figure 6.12 is the ES 15m data for just the period from the November 26 high shown on the 60m chart. The last 15m bar on the chart was made late afternoon November 27 with a 15m momentum bullish reversal. Both the daily and 60m momentum were already bullish for a three-time-frame momentum setup. The ES had made a decline to the 78.6% retracement. We don't know if the ES is going to advance and take out the 15m swing high at 1431.50 or not. What we do know is with the November 26 low in a probable position to make a Wave-5 low, which should last at least 2-3 weeks, and with the daily and 60m momentum bullish, taking out a 15m swing high is a good sign the trend is reversing to bullish. If a swing entry long trade is elected on the 15m data, the initial capital exposure would be much less than if only the 60m data and November 26 high were used.

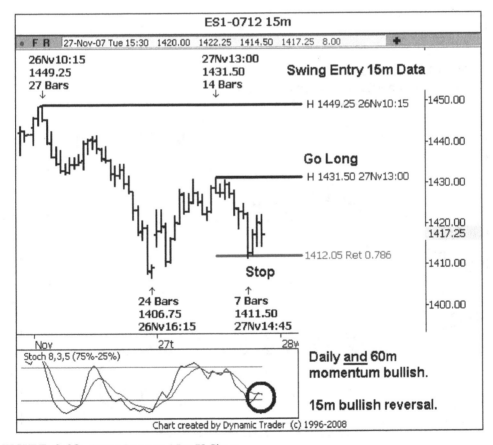

FIGURE 6.12 Swing Entry on 15m ES Chart

To identify the setup and determine the SE entry and stop price on the 15m data would require the trader to be able to monitor the market during the day. Again, that does not mean sitting in front of the computer all day. The final condition to place the trade is a 15m momentum bullish reversal. Set a momentum reversal alert on your trading software, turn up the computer's volume, and go about your business during the day (within earshot of the computer's alert). If the alert is made (15m momentum bullish reversal), take a look at the chart to identify the swing high for the swing entry buy-stop price and swing low for the initial protective sell-stop. Place the buy-stop order and contingent sell-stop order and go about your business. No need to stay glued to the computer. You already have all the specific information needed to place the order. The market will either execute the buy-stop or it won't.

Figure 6.13 is IBM weekly data into the October 2007 high. IBM has made five distinct sections up from the July 2006 low for a possible five-wave trend. We don't know if October 2007 has made a Wave-5 high to complete the bull trend, but if time and price factors indicate this could be the case, we would look for market action to either exit

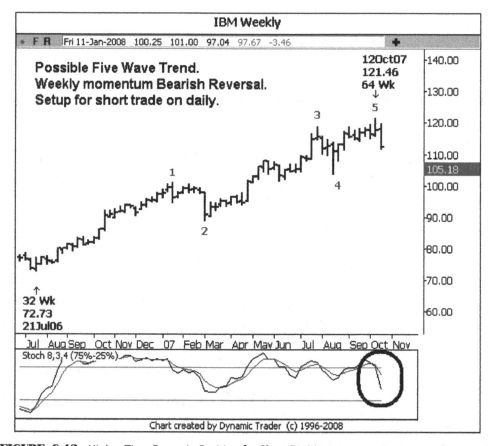

FIGURE 6.13 Higher Time Frame in Position for Short Position

longs or initiate shorts, because a decline lasting at least several months should follow if a five-wave trend is complete. As of the last weekly bar on the chart, the weekly Stoch momentum has made a bearish reversal for a swing entry short setup on the daily data.

Figure 6.14 is IBM daily data around the October 2007 high shown on the weekly chart. The weekly momentum made a bearish reversal the week ending October 19. It wasn't until October 31 that IBM made a daily Stoch momentum bearish reversal. IBM had tagged the 50% retracement at the 100% time retracement (seven trading days down, seven up). The pattern up from the October 22 low appears to be corrective with overlapping sections. If IBM takes out a swing low, the odds are a Wave-5 high is complete and the bear trend will continue for weeks if not months.

Most people who trade stocks have regular day jobs and don't sit in front of the computer watching ticks all day. Weekly and daily data are all you need to position trade stocks, or any other market for that matter, for probable trends of several weeks to several months. In this IBM weekly/daily example, if a five-wave trend is complete at the October high, the minimum to expect is a corrective decline greater in time and price

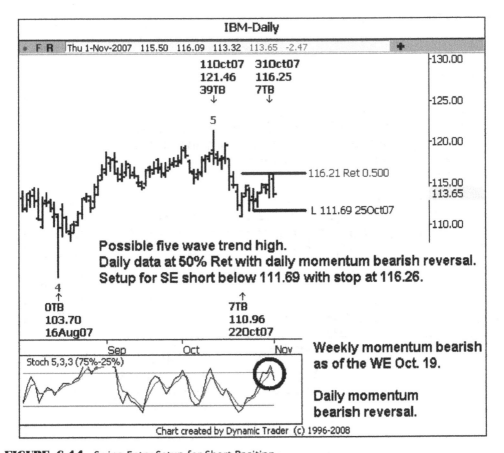

FIGURE 6.14 Swing Entry Setup for Short Position

than any since the October 2006 low, which was the beginning of the potential five-wave trend into the October 2007 high. It would definitely be a time to not be long IBM and a good time to consider a short position. If you have an aversion to short positions, get a job because you definitely can't consider yourself a trader. Markets trend up and markets trend down. Take advantage of both potential trends.

How about very short-term setups, including day traders? The exact same strategies are used. Figure 6.15 is the 15m, ES data for January 17 through the 11:15 bar. The next higher time frame 60m momentum was bearish going into this day. Only short trades should be considered on smaller time frame bearish reversal setups. The 15m momentum made two bearish reversals prior to the 11:15 bar, one just above the OS zone and one in the OS zone. Neither was in the position to initiate a short trade. By the 11:15 bar, the ES 15m momentum had reached the overbought zone, a setup for a short position on the smaller time frame 5m momentum. I recommend for day trades to have two higher time frames momentum in the direction of the smaller time frame momentum for the best opportunities for a successful trade. In this case, the 60m momentum was

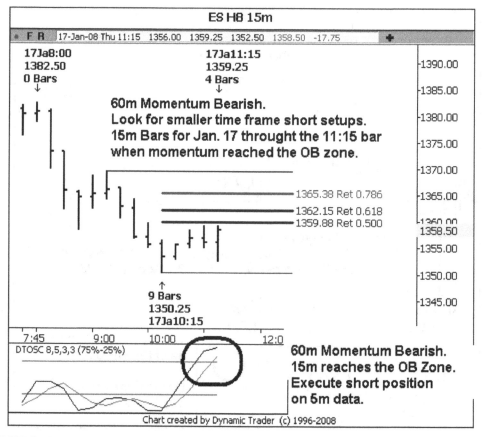

FIGURE 6.15 15m Setup for Day Trade on 5m Data

bearish and the 15m OB, so a 5m bearish reversal would put three intraday time frames in the same bearish momentum position.

Figure 6.16 is the 5m data for January 17, the same day as the 15m data shown on the previous chart. The date-time marker along the top of the chart points to the 5m 11:15 bar when the 15m momentum became overbought. A few 5m bars later, 5m momentum made a bearish reversal for a swing entry short trade setup below the minor swing low at 1356.25. A short position was elected on the next bar with an initial protective buy-stop one tick above the swing high made before entry at 1362.75.

In this example, the ES made a consistent bear trend throughout the day with just two minor corrections through the data shown. However, the short-term 15m and 5m position only set up for a short trade on the second correction. It can be aggravating to start the day with a bearish bias because of larger time frame factors such as the 60m bearish momentum, but unless the conditions are complete on the smaller time frame for a high probability multiple time frame setup, a trade should not be initiated. It is always easy to be an after-the-fact trader and "know" what the market was going to do. But the trade decision is made from the last bar on the chart when you never know what is going

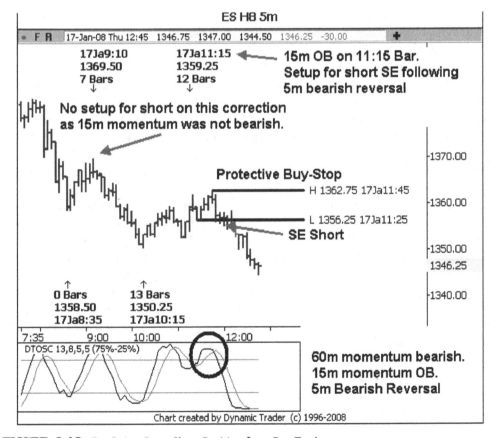

FIGURE 6.16 5m Swing Entry Short Position for a Day Trade

to happen. If you do not have the patience and discipline to wait for conditions with a high probability outcome according to your trade plan, you are not a trader. You are a game player with no respect for rules that should keep you safe, and you will eventually contribute your trading account to the pros who have patience and follow the rules. Get smart. Have a plan and trade the plan. Give yourself the edge you must have to put the odds for success in your favor.

The swing entry strategy is the second of two entry strategies that may be used for any market, any time frame, and any condition. Never buy or sell at a target price. Always require the market to move in the direction of the anticipated trend to execute a trade, and I'm sure you will find your results improve substantially.

POSITION SIZE

Capital preservation is a key to long-term successful trading. Almost everyone has seen the numbers of how much percentage gain it takes to make up a loss. A 20% drawdown takes a 25% gain just to get back to breakeven. A 50% drawdown takes a 100% gain to get back to even. It takes a lot to make up a significant loss.

Too many traders swing for the fences with visions of big profits from big positions. That's a pipe dream. Big positions can result in big losses that are very difficult to recover. There will come a time when you think you've got the market wired. Every technical position from short- to long-term points to one thing: a major trend. You break every commonsense risk rule and commit your account to the position with a wide stop "to give it room." The market moves against you and you think it is a buying opportunity to add even more positions at a better price. You know the end of this story. The market doesn't stop moving against you and you either exit with a major loss or are taken out by the broker when you run out of capital for margin.

A major loss is very difficult to recover from, both emotionally and financially. *Successful traders always have a relatively close stop.* If stopped out for a loss, it is an acceptable loss. *It is absolutely critical to minimize losses and preserve capital.* It is that simple. Assume any trade you place could be a loser, and never risk more than a small amount of capital on any one trade or any group of open trades.

The best professional traders rarely have a greater than 50% win record. That's right. Long-term successful traders usually have more losers than winners. Most amateur traders simply don't accept this reality, which is why they are not ruthless about limiting the potential loss on any one trade. Listen up, reader. If you have better than a 50% winning trade percentage over time, you are among the trader elite. If you get good at trading, you will have around a 30 to 40% win percentage. *That is why it is absolutely, positively, unquestionably critical that the losses on losing trades are relatively small and profits on winning trades are relatively large.* There is no other way to trading success.

Up to this point in the book, you have learned to identify conditions for trade setups and objective entry strategies with a defined entry and initial protective stop price so you know exactly what the capital exposure is per trading unit before the trade is executed. Now it is time for you to learn what is the *maximum* capital exposure (risk) that is acceptable for any trade and all open trades.

I use the term *capital exposure* to define the dollar amount that may be lost on a losing trade. Most trading educators call this *risk*. Risk is the probability of an event happening and has nothing to do with a dollar amount. Risk is not a proper term for the dollars that may be lost. Capital exposure is a much better term. However, since risk has become a term associated with the amount of capital that could be lost, I'll occasionally use the term since it has become a convention.

Let's get down to brass tacks and learn what every successful trader puts into practice. The maximum capital exposure for any trade must be relatively small and the maximum capital exposure per trade unit will determine maximum position size.

There are many complicated methods to determine position size but the simplest is the best. When I first started trading in the mid-1980s, the teachings of W. D. Gann were my main guide. One of Gann's rules was to never risk more than 10% of your account capital on a position. That rule is often repeated. Over the years, I have had many expensive lessons that 10% is way too much to risk on any one trade. Professional traders only risk a very small amount of capital on any one trade and a small maximum amount on all open trades. *Three percent maximum* capital exposure on any one trade and *6% maximum* exposure on all open trades is the accepted standard, and it is a good one.

The maximum exposure should be a percentage of the account equity available. If your available equity is $20,000, the maximum capital exposure on a trade should be $600 ($20,000 × 3 percent). The maximum capital exposure on all open trades should be $1,200 ($20,000 × 6 percent). It's that simple. If you go over these limits, you are stacking the odds of success against you and you are not conducting your business of trading in a responsible manner.

Most traders also have a maximum loss that is acceptable for any one month. If that maximum is reached, they stop trading for the month. A maximum monthly loss must be no more than 10 percent. If closed trades have resulted in a 10% drawdown to the account in less than a month, stop trading for the balance of the month. Either you or your trading plan needs a time out. There will always be opportunities next month. Take a breather.

Maximum position size is a function of maximum initial capital exposure per trade unit. First, calculate the *maximum trade capital exposure* of 3% of available account balance. Then calculate the *capital exposure per unit* based on the objective entry price and initial protective stop. The unit could be a futures contract or per share. Finally, divide the maximum account capital exposure by the trade unit capital exposure to arrive at the maximum position size for the trade.

Figure 6.17 is 15m ES. Let's assume the S&P has made the conditions to consider a long trade as of the last bar on the chart. If the Tr-1BH entry strategy is used following

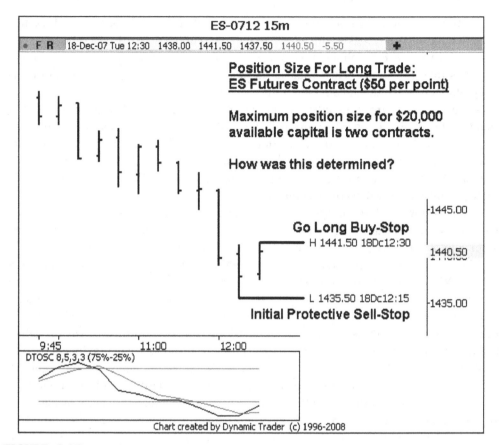

FIGURE 6.17   Calculate the Position Size

the 15m bullish reversal, a buy-stop to enter a long trade is at 1441.75, one tick above the high of the last completed bar. If the ES advances and the buy-stop is executed, the initial protective sell-stop is at 1435.25, one tick below the low. We know the objective entry and stop price before the trade is executed. We don't know if it will be executed, but if it is, we know at what price the entry will be made and what price the stop will be placed. I realize markets can gap above buy and below sell stops and you don't always get filled at the order price; it doesn't happen often in high volume, active markets and we have no control over it.

The trade capital exposure per contract is 6.5 points (1441.75 − 1435.25) or $325 (6.5 × $50). If you have a $20,000 account, what is the maximum position size? Three percent of $20,000 equals $600. Dividing $600 by $325, and rounding up, your answer is two contracts. You can have a *maximum* of two contracts for this trade. If you were to put in a buy-stop order to enter a long trade for more than two contracts, you have no business with a trading account. You don't understand one of the most important principles of the business of trading: capital preservation. One part of capital preservation is to limit the potential loss on any one position to a relatively small amount. The maximum

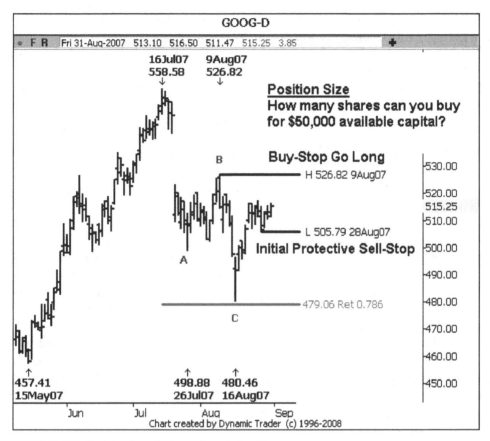

FIGURE 6.18 Position Size for Long Google Position

position size is the maximum capital exposure allowed for the available account capital divided by the per unit capital exposure.

Figure 6.18 is Google daily data. Let's say you've been following Google for a couple of years. You missed buying it at $200, missed again at $300, and missed again at $400. Each time it rallied $100, $200, and more in a matter of weeks or months. Not only are you not going to miss buying Google again after it completes its next correction, but you are going to load up for a big gain to make up for the earlier missed opportunities and to set yourself up for early retirement! As of the last bar on the Google daily chart, if Google just takes out the potential Wave-B swing high, an ABC correction should be complete and off goes Google for another quick $100 to $200 gain. If you have $50,000 of available capital, what is the maximum number of Google shares you can buy with the swing entry strategy to enter above the potential Wave-B swing high with an initial protective sell-stop one tick below the minor swing low at 505.79?

The maximum number of shares you can buy is 72! The maximum capital exposure for any one trade is $1,500 ($50,000 × 3 percent). The trade unit capital exposure is $21.05 ($526.83 − $505.78). The maximum number of shares you can buy is $1,500 divided by

$21.05, or 72 shares. If you buy 73 shares, please, close out your account right now. Even if you get lucky with Google, you will eventually lose most or all of your account because you have broken an inviolate rule of capital preservation. You lack the discipline to make logical and sound trading decisions and are playing at something other than real-world, professional trading. You have risked more capital than allowed by any logical trading plan.

How to Calculate Maximum Position Size:

$$\frac{\text{Available Capital} \times 3\%}{\text{Capital Exposure per Unit}} = \text{Maximum Position Size}$$

If this math confuses you, stop trading right now. I mean it. You need to be able to understand simple concepts and mathematics to be a successful trader. And this is as simple as it gets.

Years ago, I set up a simple spreadsheet to calculate maximum position size. All I have to do is enter the entry and stop price, value of each tick, and the account balance, and it gives you the maximum position size. You can set up a simple spreadsheet yourself or you can download one in MS Excel from www.highprobabilitytradingstrategies.com. In most cases, you won't need a spreadsheet or even a calculator to quickly figure out the maximum position size. It is not very complicated.

The maximum capital exposure for all open positions should be 6% of available capital. Never get beyond this limit. Always remember, capital preservation is critical to success. All successful traders limit the potential loss on any one trade to a relatively small amount. Limited capital exposure on any one trade does not guarantee success, but it will give you the opportunity for success.

CONCLUSION

In this chapter, you have learned two objective entry strategies that can be used with any market, any conditions, and any time frame. Both entry strategies require the market to move in the anticipated direction before a trade is executed. That is a key concept that every entry strategy should have. With an objective entry strategy, there is no decision to be made for the entry price and initial protective stop-loss once the high probability trade conditions have been identified. Those two prices are determined by the market position and entry strategy, and you will know the maximum trade unit capital exposure before any trade is executed.

You have also learned that limiting losses on any one trade to a relatively small amount is critical to long-term success. You also learned how to quickly calculate the maximum position size for any trade.

Now that we know how to identify optimal trade conditions and objective strategies to enter the trade and protect capital, it is time to complete the trading plan and learn about trade management and exit strategies.

CHAPTER 7

Exit Strategies and Trade Management

Sound and logical trade management and exit strategies are the key to maximizing the return on each and every trade. In this chapter you will learn how to manage the trade from entry to exit, including how to adjust the stop-loss and exit the trade.

U p to this point, you've learned how to identify the optimal conditions for a trade setup and the objective entry strategies, including the exact entry price and initial protective stop-loss price. Identifying good entry setups is only one part of a complete trading plan. But you can't make a single dollar with the best entry strategies. You only make money on a closed trade. There can be an enormous difference in your net success depending on how well you manage the trade and your ability to consistently stay with a trend until the market conditions suggest the trend is at its conclusion.

The maximum return you can gain from any trend is entirely dependent on the market. That's right. You don't have control of how far or long a market will trend. You do have control over how long you stay with a position, so the best you can gain from a market trend is to be able to stay in a position for the majority of the trend. I would like to be able say I'm going to teach you how to stay in every market position from the early stages of a trend to the later stages. I can't do that, because no matter how good your technical analysis and trade management, the market will often give information that gets you in late or out early. Welcome to the business of trading.

What I *can* teach you is to recognize the market information that will help you identify conditions that are *usually* present near the end of the trend so you can protect open positions or prepare to reverse positions. Many times you'll have a brilliant campaign and maximize the possible gain from a trend from start to finish. Often you will exit well before the trend ends, and the conditions will not be ideal to reenter.

There is an old market axiom, "You can't go wrong taking a profit." It is absolute nonsense. It encourages taking a profit quickly and possibly missing out on the larger time frame trend. Taking a profit too quickly on a full position can greatly limit your potential return. After all the hard work of identifying an optimal trade and low capital exposure entry strategy, taking a quick profit in the initial stages of a trend is not maximizing the potential of your position. There is nothing more aggravating than exiting a trade for a small profit only to see the market continue to trend much longer and further. The objective is to understand the *probable* position of the trend from the information at hand and maintain an open position for the majority of the trend. That's what this chapter is all about.

MULTIPLE-UNIT TRADING

Multiple-unit trading should increase your trading success significantly. It made a big difference when I incorporated it into my trade plan years ago. It's nothing new. Successful traders have been using multiple-unit trade strategies as long as there has been trading.

What do I mean by multiple-unit trading? *Every* position has at least two units. A unit may be just one futures contract or it could be 10 contracts. It may be 100 shares of stocks or it may be 1,000 shares. A unit can be any amount, but for every trade, there must be at least two units. If the trade entry is successful and the market moves in the anticipated direction, one unit is usually exited relatively quickly for a relatively small profit. The second unit is held with the intention of capturing the longer-term trend. Whether you are a day trader or position trader or any time frame in between, a multiple-unit trade strategy should be a key part of your trading plan.

Concepts are important. Concepts are the basis of how we make decisions. The concept for the first unit strategy is to assume you are incorrect about the larger time frame trend and exit the unit as if the market is only making a minor correction. The idea is to capture a relatively small profit even if your analysis and expectations are incorrect and a trend does not develop as anticipated. If a trend develops as anticipated, the second unit is held to maximize the return for the larger time frame trend. Jaime Johnson, who is the chief technical analyst for our DT Daily Reports for futures, stock/ETF, and Forex has done several tutorials over the years about how to be dead wrong on the market position but still end up with a profit by using a two-unit trading strategy. We like to remind traders over and over again that a multiple-unit trade strategy is a very important part of any trading plan.

For the examples in this chapter, all positions will be taken with two units which we'll call the short- and long-term units. You will learn the specific two-unit strategies with the trade management examples. I know if you incorporate two-unit positions with every trade, you will be very pleased with the results.

TWO-UNIT TRADE CONCEPT

1. Assume you are incorrect about the trend position and the market is only making a minor correction, not a new trend. Exit one unit once the conditions are in place to complete a minor correction.

2. Maintain the second unit to take advantage if a trend develops as anticipated.

RISK/REWARD RATIOS

Some trading educators make a big deal about so-called risk/reward ratios and may even base trading decisions on them. What do we mean by a risk/reward ratio and why is it basically a bogus idea? Risk/reward is supposed to compare the initial capital exposure (risk) to the potential reward (profit) as a ratio. Traders are often taught to only take a trade with a 3:1 risk/reward ratio. Right off the bat, we've got some confusing information. A 3:1 risk/reward ratio would mean there is three times the risk to the potential reward. What they really mean is a reward/risk ratio of 3:1. Okay, I'm being picky. But being picky and precise with how we think about and express ideas is critical to success.

I'll use the word *risk* for this discussion to mean the more appropriate term, *initial capital exposure*. The dollar amount of risk for any trade can be defined in advance. If the entry price is $40 and the initial protective sell-stop is $35, we know the risk is $5 if stopped out (baring a gap through the stop price). The risk for any trade is a function of the entry price less the stop price and is known before a trade is taken.

But what about the reward? How do we determine what is the probable reward for any potential trade? We guess. That's right. The reward part of the equation is just a best guess of the minimum price objective we believe the market will make for the trade we are considering. The potential reward is never known. I've seen all kinds of ways put forth to calculate the potential reward, some logical and useful, some nothing but the trader's or educator's excuse to come up with a number. The potential reward can be based on any of a number of factors. Market structure such as typical E-wave price targets, prior support or resistance, the probability of a market exceeding a swing high or low, and price percentage change are just a few reward targets taught.

The potential reward estimate should be based on the same factors used to make a trade decision, not on some factor not related to the same conditions used to execute the trade. If you believe a market is in a position to complete a correction, the minimum expectation is the market will resume the trend direction prior to the correction and make a new extreme beyond the high or low where the correction began. That extreme should be the minimum reward for the trade. The 100% alternate price projection is another logical reward target. Whether a market is in a trend or countertrend, the next section will often reach the 100% alternate price projection. Not always, but we assume that should be the case and the 100% APP can be the reward target.

In every case, the reward is a best guess. Usually, it is an optimistic guess by the trader to justify the trade. Some market educators make the so-called risk/reward ratio a key trading strategy and never consider a trade unless the ratio is a minimum such as 3:1 (reward/risk). Most professional traders don't pay much attention to a risk/reward ratio. They focus on identifying optimal trade setups, good trade execution, and good trade management through the trade exit. If the focus is on these positive factors, closed profitable trades will usually be several times the initial capital exposure. I don't make too much of a risk/reward ratio because I know it is only a best guess. I suggest you don't get too hung up on it yourself and avoid any trading educators who claim they teach you how to only take trades with some minimum risk/reward (reward/risk) ratio. It is a somewhat meaningless buzzword that can often hook you into expensive and often irrelevant trading education programs.

In the trade management examples in this chapter, you will see how we quickly determine if there seems to be enough profit potential in a trade to initiate the trade. You will see how it is a quick and commonsense decision.

RISK/REWARD RATIO

Forget about it. It's only a best guess. Focus on positive and logical trade management and the risk/reward will take care of itself. Get hung up on so-called risk/reward ratios before taking a trade and there is a good chance you have caught the dreaded paralysis of analysis disease!

EXIT STRATEGIES

Once again, concepts are important. Start with a logical concept and devise a strategy based on the concept. There are four important concepts for exit strategies. The first: Always let the market take you out by moving against the position. Do not exit at a predetermined price target. A market will often blow right through a price target, sometimes by a substantial amount. If you exit at the price target, you may miss maximizing the profit potential of a trade if the trend continues beyond expectations. Price targets or other conditions may be a reason to adjust the protective stop closer to the current market position, as you will learn in this chapter, but they are *never* a reason to exit the trade at a specific price. What you give back by letting the market move against the position a small amount before exiting should be more than made up by those times a market trends right through a price target.

I guess you should never say "never." One situation where you might use a specific price objective to exit would be if you were about to leave for vacation and would not be able to update your data each night to assess the current position and make decisions. In that case, you will have two open orders in the market: the protective stop and the take-profits, exit-price order

The second important exit strategy concept is that the exit strategy should be based on the same market conditions that determined the conditions to identify the trade entry in the first place. If the dual time frame momentum position was a key factor to enter a trade in the direction of the larger time frame trend, a dual time frame momentum position should be a key factor in the exit strategy. The factors of momentum, pattern, price, and time that are keys to identify a trade entry are the same factors used to identify the exit strategy.

The third important concept is to determine the general exit strategy and trade management of both units before the trade is entered. That doesn't mean pick a target price and exit the trade if the target price is reached. It does mean to identify the trade objective and what conditions will require a stop-loss adjustment and exit strategy for each unit, before the trade is entered. Specific actions are taken if the conditions are manifested.

Fourth and very important, the trade management and exit strategy may change as the market provides more information. As each new bar is made, whether a weekly or intraday time frame, new information is available. As the market structure (pattern) develops, it may provide important clues to the position of the trend and where a stop should be adjusted. Price targets will often be adjusted depending on the pivot highs and lows made as a trend develops. Changes will probably be made to the trade management plan for any specific trade as the market provides new information.

I wish there was one fixed rule-based exit strategy that could be used with all markets, all conditions, and all time frames. There isn't, if you want to maximize the potential return for any position. It is easy to make up a completely objective rule based on price or momentum and call it an exit strategy. But no rule-based exit strategy will maximize the potential reward for a trade. As I've stated over and over again throughout this book, trading is a business like every other business. You have to gain knowledge and experience and constantly make decisions. You can never eliminate the decision-making process by rules, systems or any software if you want to succeed in the business, any more than you can eliminate the decision-making process from any other business and succeed.

However, it is very important that any changes to the trade management and exit strategies as a trade progresses are logical decisions based on the same factors that the trade decision was based on in the first place. As you will see in the comprehensive trade campaign examples in this chapter and the next, each decision should be a very logical conclusion to the information available at the time.

EXIT STRATEGY CONCEPTS

1. Let the market take you out of the trade with a trailing stop by moving against the trade direction. Never exit at a predetermined price target.

2. The trade management and exit strategy should be based on the same factors and market conditions that the entry strategy was based on.

3. Determine the general exit strategy of both units before the trade is entered. What is the objective of the trade?

4. The trade management and exit strategy may change as the market provides more information. Any changes should be a logical consequence of the new market information.

TRADE MANAGEMENT

Trade management is the all-inclusive term for how the trade is managed from entry to exit, including the entry strategy, multiple-unit position, adjusting the stop-loss on each unit, possibly pyramiding the position, and the exit strategy for each unit. Most of the preceding comments about exit strategies also pertain to trade management.

Whenever a trade is considered, there must be a trade management plan before the trade is executed. That doesn't mean you take a lot of time to devise a different management plan for each trade. The trade management plan should not necessarily be a list of specific rules or actions taken for each trade. But it will include the guidelines for taking action based on the trade objective, including what action should be taken as a market provides new information.

In a static medium like this book, it is difficult to illustrate all of the relevant factors of a trade campaign from entry to exit with screen shots and commentary. There will be quite a bit of commentary for each example in this chapter as I explain the rationale for each position and trade management decision. Plus there will be several charts for each trade campaign to illustrate the major milestones and waypoints along the way. But a more effective way to teach the decision-making process is to be able to advance bar by bar, which is exactly what I do in the CD that accompanies this book. However, as I've said repeatedly, don't even think about watching the CD until you have finished the book. The CD assumes you have read the entire book and are familiar with all the terms and strategies. It is a continuation of the learning material and a bar-by-bar practical application of what you have learned.

The trade examples that follow are obviously after the fact. The most important objective is to teach you how to think in a progressive and logical manner to make decisions based on the information provided by the market, bar by bar. Once you have learned how to think and make logical decisions, you are prepared to trade any market, any time frame, and any condition. This is why I include a great deal of commentary with these examples. I describe the decisions made and the reasons they were made, so that you can learn the decision-making process.

Okay, it's time to get started and see how we manage a trade from entry to exit.

Weekly-Daily Setup for a Position Trade

Figure 7.1 is XAU weekly data. The XAU is a gold and silver mining stock index. The ETF GDX closely tracks the XAU. A trader interested in trading shares of any mining stock should also chart this sector index for the general trend of the mining stock shares. As of the last bar on the chart, the week ending (WE) August 17, 2007, the XAU has made a sharp decline after being in a broad trading range for over a year. A trading range like this is usually a consolidation period or a complex correction. From a longer-term point

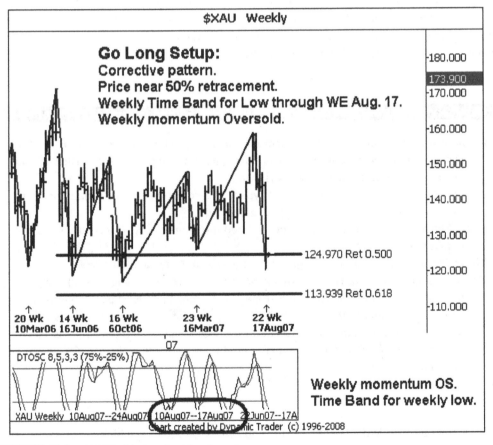

FIGURE 7.1 XAU Weekly in a Position for a Low

of view, it is likely the XAU will eventually break up, not down, from the trading range in a new bull trend to a new high.

With a complex correction, there is no high probability pattern we can count on to identify the last decline in the correction. Any low may be the final low of the correction. The objective is to identify conditions that should result in a weekly low in order to position long for a potential bull trend breakout to a new high. This would have been the same strategy for about a year as the XAU made several weekly lows, followed by advances lasting several weeks but never breaking away to a new high.

As of the last bar on the weekly chart in Figure 7.1, the XAU has tested the 50% retracement area of the May 2005 to May 2006 bull trend for the fourth time. Based on the weekly cycles of the past 18 months or so, the Time Band for a weekly low is a narrow two-week period of the WE August 10 through the WE August 17. The Time Band is based on the overlap of the low-low and high-low cycles, although only the low-low counts are shown on the chart. I choose an eight-week momentum lookback period where the DTosc reached the OB and OS levels at the weekly highs and lows for the past 18 months or so. If this momentum cycle continues, the next weekly momentum bullish reversal should be followed by a rally lasting at least several weeks. The weekly momentum is oversold. If the recent momentum rhythm continues, a momentum bullish reversal should be made in the next bar or two.

Summary of XAU Weekly Position as of the Week Ending August 17

Momentum: Oversold. A weekly momentum low is likely within the next bar or two followed by a rally lasting several weeks. At the least, the immediate downside should be very limited before a weekly low is made.

Pattern: Corrective. The trading range is typical of a corrective or consolidation pattern which is typically followed by a rally to a new high.

Price: The 50% retracement area has been tested three times. The XAU is currently back in that range.

Time: The WE August 10 to WE August 17 is the weekly Time Band for a low.

Trade Strategy: Go long. With weekly momentum, pattern, price, and time all in a position for a low, right now, the trade strategy is to consider a long position execution on the smaller time frame daily chart. The objective of the short-term unit is to exit on a retracement of the prior decline in the event only a corrective rally is made. The objective of the long-term unit is to hold for a probable bull trend advance to a new high.

Figure 7.2 is the XAU daily chart through Friday, August 17, which is the same date as the last weekly bar on the weekly chart in the previous figure. All of the relevant information is on the chart.

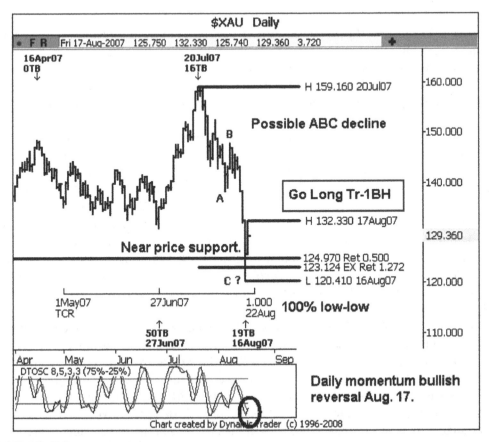

FIGURE 7.2 Long Trade Setup

Summary of XAU Daily Position as of August 17 and Trade Strategy

Momentum: Daily bullish reversal with weekly momentum oversold.

Pattern: Possible ABC decline.

Price: Just below the 50% internal retracement (May 2005 low to May 2006 high) and 127% Ex-Ret (June 27 low to July 20 high).

Time: Daily time factors in a position for a low. August 22 is the 100% L-L; August 13 is the 100% time retracement. See weekly Time Band for most compelling time factor at August 16 low.

Entry Strategy: Go long on the trailing one-bar-high with a stop one tick below the August 16 low.

The 1BH as of August 17 is 132.33 and the swing low is at 120.41 for an almost 12-point capital exposure. The proper position size based on the trade capital exposure and account size will risk no more than 3%. In these examples, I am not going to assume any particular account size. The maximum position size is an objective calculation you have learned to make and nothing additional will be learned by assuming any particular account size and going through the calculations for maximum position size for each trade example.

The expectation is the XAU should eventually break up from the prolonged trading range and eventually make a new high well above the July 2007 high. We don't need to make any fancy risk/reward calculations with this potential trade. If the XAU exceeds the July high, the potential reward will be well over three times the risk if the order is executed above the August 17 high. You engineers with paralysis of analysis can get your spreadsheets out. From my point of view, there is lots of upside potential compared to the minimal capital exposure and that's all I need to know to consider the trade.

I'm going to talk through the trade management and exit strategy and then list the plan. We've determined the XAU is in a good position to consider a long trade and the specific entry strategy. Before we enter the trade, we must identify the trade objectives and plan the trade management strategies. The first consideration is, what if we are dead wrong about a probable bull trend to a new high and the best we get is a minor corrective rally of the decline from the July high followed by a bear trend to a new low?

Trade management (short-term unit): Trail the stop at the 1BL if the XAU either reaches the 61.8% retracement or following the second daily momentum bearish reversal.

Why wait for two bearish reversals? Even if the XAU is only making a corrective rally, corrections usually have at least three sections (ABC) which will make two momentum bearish reversals, one at the Wave-A high and one at the Wave-C high. I used to trail the stop-loss on the short-term (ST) unit after the first smaller time frame momentum reversal against the weekly trend for a quick profit, but I found the market usually went higher (lower) to make a second momentum reversal even if I was wrong about a more extended trend developing. This is the basic short-term unit exit strategy for many trades.

Why trail the stop at the 1BL if the 61.8% correction is reached even if the daily momentum has not made two bearish reversals? If the XAU is only making a corrective rally and not a new bull trend as anticipated, most corrections are complete by the 61.8% retracement so I want to be out of the first unit around there—but only by using a Tr-1BL, not exiting at the 61.8% retracement price itself.

The objective of the long-term (LT) unit is to maintain the position with a relatively wide stop in the event the XAU makes a bull trend to a new high as anticipated.

Trade management (LT unit): If the weekly momentum reaches the overbought zone, the bull trend should be in the final stages and the stop will be adjusted relatively close to the current market position. We'll define the specific exit strategy for the LT unit if the bull trend progresses and the market provides more information to make a specific decision.

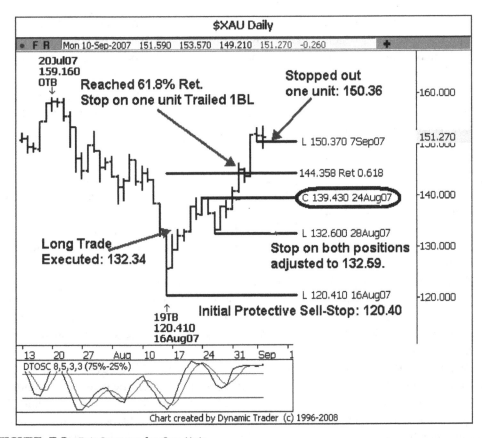

FIGURE 7.3 Exit Strategy for One Unit

Figure 7.3 is the daily chart with data through September 10. It has a lot of information on the chart, so following is a list of the significant events and trade management through September 10:

1. A long trade was executed on the TR-1BH on Monday, August 20 at 132.34, one day after the daily momentum bullish reversal was made. The initial protective sell-stop is at 120.40, one tick below the August 16 low, for an 11.94 capital exposure.

2. Over the next nine trading days after the trade was entered, the XAU continued to rally, making a daily momentum bearish, then bullish reversal and a trade above the August 24 minor swing high. The stop on both positions is adjusted to 132.59, one tick below the minor swing low made on the momentum bullish reversal. This wasn't a specific action called for in the trade management plan, but it is a logical one. Once the August 24 minor swing high was taken out, if the XAU declined to take out the August 28 minor swing low, it would void any logical bullish pattern and suggest a three-swing corrective rally could be over. There would be no reason to remain

in a long position. Note that the stop-loss was adjusted only after the minor swing high was taken out, which signaled the minor swing low should be complete. If the XAU immediately declined and hit the new protective sell-stop, at least a small profit would be made.

3. On September 4, the XAU reached the 61.8% retracement before making a second daily momentum bearish reversal. The stop on the ST unit is now trailed at the 1BL. No change to the stop on the second unit.

Trade result (ST unit): On September 9, the XAU took out the trailing 1BL and, at 150.36, stopped out the ST unit, which had been entered at 132.34. Profit on half the position: 18.02 (150.37 – 132.34).

As of September 9, the XAU has reached the 100% alternate price projection of the first swing up projected from the August 24 minor swing low. The 100% APP is not shown on the chart.

Trade management (LT unit): The stop on the second unit is adjusted to a close at 139.42 or below, which is the potential Wave-1 or A closing high. Should the XAU decline and close below the potential Wave-1 or A closing high (see August 24 horizontal line) for an overlap, it would void any probable bullish pattern and be a definite reason to exit the second unit.

Figure 7.4 adds the daily data through October 9. The XAU continued in a strong bull trend to a new high as anticipated. On Friday, September 21, the weekly momentum reached the overbought zone. The September 21 date is marked on the daily chart. If you look back at the weekly chart, at least in the past 18 months or so, a weekly momentum bullish reversal has been made within a couple weeks of each time the weekly momentum reached the OB zone. The XAU upside should be relatively limited.

A tactical decision during this period was when and to where to adjust the stop on the long-term unit. From early September through September 21, the XAU did not make so much as a two-day correction. The daily momentum hung in the OB zone and did not make a momentum cycle to a bullish reversal to give a logical place to adjust the stop, at least based on the daily momentum cycles.

Trade Management (LT Unit): Following the wide range up day on September 18, the stop was adjusted to the September 5 low.

Why here? No firm reason except it was a bit below the 61.8% retracement as of the September 18 high (retracement not shown on the chart) and the low of a narrow range day prior to another wide range up day. Few traders would keep such a wide stop on a position with an open and unrealized profit, but the objective is to remain in the trade until there is some market condition that suggests the bull trend is near completion. Most trends make at least five waves or sections, as you learned in Chapter 3. As of September 18 only a possible Waves 1 and 2 were complete. A Wave-3 high and Wave-4 correction followed by a new high should be made before the pattern conditions have met the minimum structure for a trend. A Wave-4 retracement is typically 38.2% to 50% of Wave-3, so the stop is kept away from any typical retracement likely for a Wave-4.

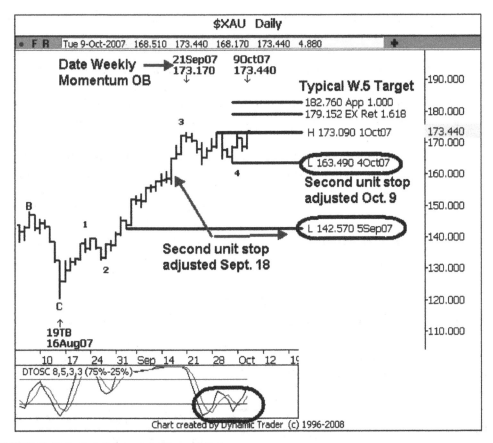

FIGURE 7.4 Exit Strategy for Second Unit

The majority of traders are unsuccessful or, at best, do not maximize returns from a trend. One of the major reasons for this lack of success is trailing a stop too close to the market and getting stopped out of a trade well before any conditions have manifested to complete the trend. Two of the most important conditions to be aware of are the higher time frame momentum position and the pattern or structure of the trend. Unless the higher time frame momentum has reached the position typical for a momentum reversal, the assumption is the trend is not in a position to end. Unless the minimum pattern conditions for a trend have been made (five sections), the assumption is the trend has further to go.

Trends may end before the higher time frame reaches an extreme or a particular pattern is made. Anything can happen. But *you must make logical decisions based on the information through the last bar*. In the case of the XAU as of mid-September, no conditions were in place to suggest the trend was at or near completion.

As of October 9, the last day on the chart in Figure 7.4, the XAU had made a three section, potential Wave-4 correction with a new high above the potential Wave-3.

Trade management (LT unit): Adjust the stop on the second unit to 163.48, one tick below the potential Wave-4 low.

The 179.15–182.76 price zone includes the 162% Ex-Ret of Wave-4 and the 100% APP of Wave-1. Both are typical targets for a Wave-5. Plus the weekly momentum is overbought. The immediate upside is probably limited to this price zone.

Trade management (LT unit): If the XAU trades to 179.15 *or* the daily momentum makes a bearish reversal, trail the stop on the remaining unit one tick below the daily 1BL.

Figure 7.5 adds the data through the date the second position was stopped out on October 15. On October 11, the XAU reached 179.15. The following day, the stop on the long-term unit was adjusted to the low of the prior day and trailed at the one bar low.

Trade results (LT unit): The long position was stopped out just three days after the XAU reached the price target, for a 46.11 profit (178.45 – 132.34).

You should reread this commentary and study each chart. Be aware that each trade management decision to adjust the stop on both units was based on the information

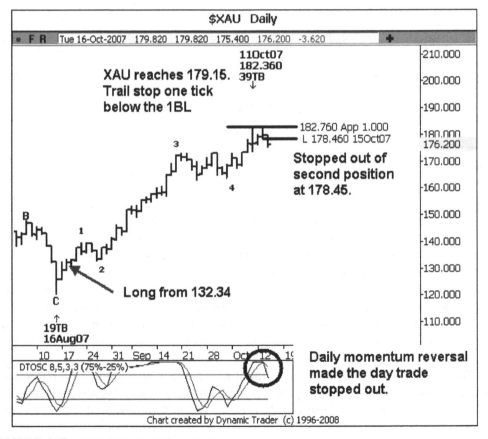

FIGURE 7.5 Second Unit Exited on Tr-1 BL

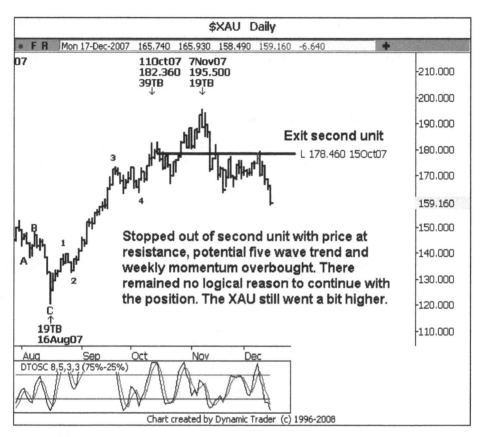

FIGURE 7.6 XAU Continued Higher after Trade Exit

at hand and what you have learned in the chapters on momentum, pattern, price, and time position. None of the decisions was arbitrary. Stops were never adjusted just because there was a certain amount of unrealized gain. Stops were never adjusted at a fixed and arbitrary amount from the current market price. There was always a logical reason and purpose for each trade management decision. If you use a logical thinking process throughout a trade and make logical tactical decisions based on the actual market activity as a trend develops, you will usually capture most of the trend.

Was October 11 a Wave-5 high for a perfect trade campaign that was entered within points of the low and exited within points of the high? Figure 7.6 adds two months of data from October 11 when the long-term unit was stopped out. October 11 only began a minor one-week correction, followed by a new high into early November, before beginning a more substantial correction to the entire bull trend that began months earlier on August 16. But as of mid-October, conditions were in place to complete the bull trend, including overbought weekly momentum, and it was an appropriate time to trail the stop on the long position very close to the market.

Every trade should be reviewed for what you did right and what you did wrong. The most important question to ask yourself during the review is, did I make logical trade management decisions based on the current information when the decision was made?

Weekly-Daily-60m Setup for Long Trade

The next trade example is the S&P. We'll use the weekly and daily data for the setup conditions and the 60m data for trade execution and management. With every trade, you must be aware of at least the next higher time frame position, particularly because the higher time frame momentum position determines the trade direction. For an even higher probability trade position, the two higher time frames' momentum should be in the same position. Using two higher time frames will always result in fewer trades but also should result in a higher percentage of successful trades.

Figure 7.7 is the S&P daily continuous data through November 22. All of the critical information is right on the chart.

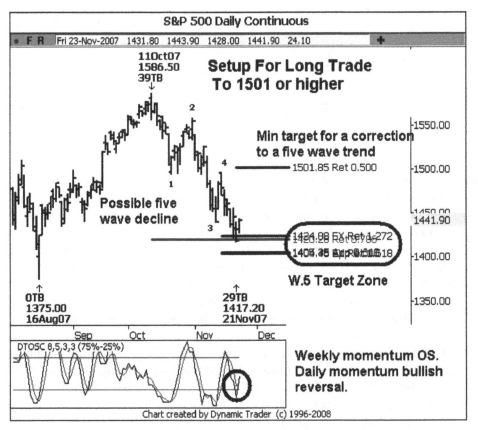

FIGURE 7.7   S&P in a Position for a Wave-5 Low

Summary of S&P Position as of Friday, November 23

Momentum: While a weekly chart is not shown, the weekly momentum has been over-sold for two weeks, which suggests the downside should be very limited if the S&P continues to decline, and a daily momentum bullish reversal should coincide with a weekly momentum bullish reversal. The S&P is at or near a position to make an advance lasting several weeks. The daily momentum made a bullish reversal Friday, November 23.

Pattern: Potential five-wave trend low. Trends frequently end with five distinct waves or sections. Whenever a trend has completed four waves without violating the five-wave trend guidelines, the trend may be at or near its end.

Price: The November 21 low reached the probable Wave-5 target zone, which includes the 127% and 162% Ex-Rets of Wave-4, where Wave-5 is the 100% APP of Wave-1, the 61.8% APP of waves 1 to 3, and the 78.6% retracement of the August low to October high. This target zone includes all the typical Wave-5 targets.

Time: The November 21 low is just two bars past the 62% time retracement of the August low to October high (not shown). The potential waves 1 and 3 took seven and eight trading days. The November 21 low is five trading days from the potential Wave-4 high. If Nov 21 did not complete a Wave-5 low, it should be complete within the next two or three trading days.

Trade Strategy: Go long. Weekly-daily momentum, pattern, price, and time are at or near a position to complete a five-wave bear trend that has lasted about six weeks. If this is the case, the minimum expectation is for a corrective rally to the 50% retracement at 1501.75. The objective of the short-term unit is to exit on a retracement of the decline from the potential Wave-4 high in the event the S&P only makes a minor correction of the last section down. The objective of the long-term unit is to hold for a probable 50% or more correction of the entire five-wave decline from the October high.

Let's go to the 60m chart of the S&P mini (ES) for the trade execution setup. Figure 7.8 is the 60m data beginning from the November 14, probable Wave-4 high shown on the previous daily chart through midday of Tuesday, November 27. On Monday, the S&P made a slight new high and declined to a new low. Wave-5 itself looks like a five-wave decline. The daily momentum is still bullish as of Monday's close. Monday's low reached the lower end of the probable Wave-5 price target zone. A 60m momentum bullish reversal was made as of the last 60m bar on the chart. The conditions are all in place to execute a long trade on a Tr-1BH.

Entry strategy (both units): 60m Tr-1BH.

The S&P may not be completing a five-wave trend from the October 11 high (see the daily chart). Maybe the S&P will only make a minor corrective rally of the last section down from the November 14, potential W.4 high.

Trade management (ST unit): If the S&P reaches the 61.8% retracement at 1462 of the last section down, *or* following the second 60m momentum bearish reversal, trail a stop at the 1BL.

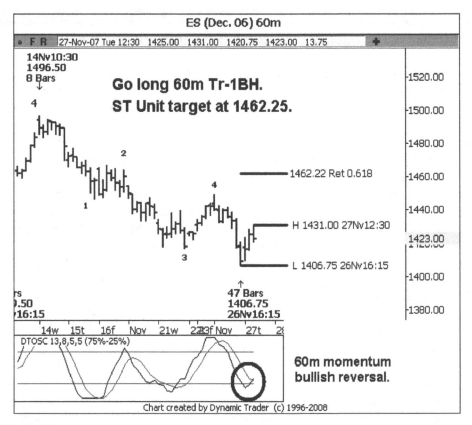

FIGURE 7.8 Entry Strategy for Long Trade

The objective is to hold the long-term unit with a wide stop until the weekly momentum is overbought or makes a bearish reversal. If the S&P has made a five-wave bear trend, at least a three-section corrective rally should follow, if not a new bull trend to a new high. We want to hold the long-term unit until at least three sections up have been made.

Trade management (LT unit): If the weekly momentum reaches the OB zone, trail the stop on the long-term unit at the daily 1BL following the *second* daily momentum bearish reversal following the weekly momentum OB position, *or* trail at the 1BL if the S&P reaches a probable Wave-C price target.

Figure 7.9 is the 60m data through early November 29. The long position was executed November 27 at 1431.25 with a stop at 1406.50 for a 24.75 point capital exposure per contract. If this is too large of capital exposure per futures contract for your trading plan, use the SPY ETF for the trade. On November 28, the S&P reached the 61.8% retracement and the stop on one unit was trailed at the 1BL per the ST unit trade management plan.

Trade results (ST unit): On the first bar of November 29, the protective sell-stop was executed at 1466.25 for the long position taken at 1431.25 for a short-term unit profit of 35 points.

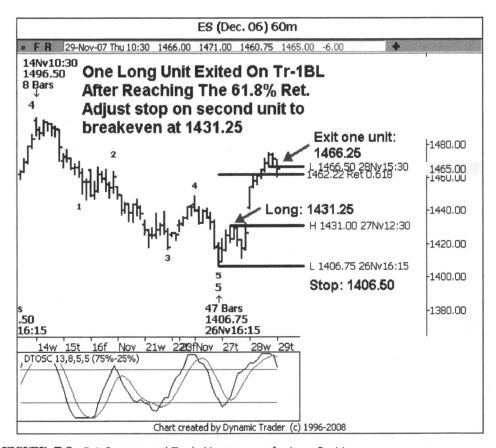

FIGURE 7.9   Exit Strategy and Trade Management for Long Position

Figure 7.10 adds the 60m data through early December 6. The S&P has made a probable Wave-B decline and traded above the probable Wave-A high. Adjust the stop to 1462.75, one tick below the Wave-B low.

If the S&P is making an ABC correction, the ideal Wave-C target is 1510.25 to 1518.00, which includes the 61.8% retracement of the five-wave decline, the 162% Ex-Ret of Wave-B, and the 61.8% APP of Wave-A. The weekly momentum has not reached the OB zone and the daily momentum is bullish but just below the OB zone. The immediate upside should be relatively limited. Most important, the 60m momentum is OB, the same position as when the Wave-A high was made. The objective of the long-term unit was to hold until either the weekly momentum was overbought or a Wave-C price target is reached.

Trade management (LT unit): Adjust the stop on the long-term unit to the Tr-1BL if either the S&P trades to 1510.25 *or* the 60m momentum makes a bearish reversal.

Figure 7.11 adds the 60m data through early December 7. On the last bar of December 6, the S&P reached 1510.25, the beginning of the ideal Wave-C price target zone and the stop on the long-term unit was trailed at the 1BL as planned.

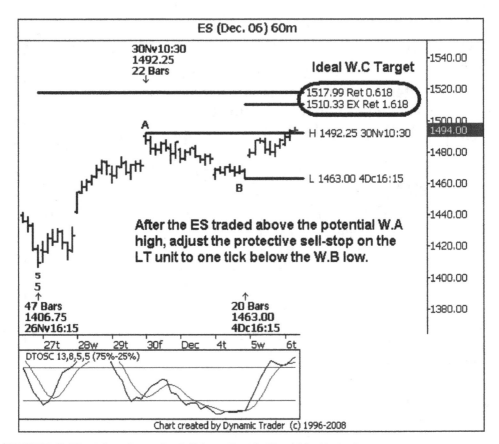

FIGURE 7.10   Adjust Protective Sell-Stop: Upside Should Be Limited

Trade results (LT unit): Stopped out at 1507.00 on the second 60m bar the morning of December 7 for the long position taken November 27 at 1431.75, for a profit of 75.25 points.

The S&P did continue higher the following day, eventually reaching 1527.00 on December 11, about 9 points above the 61.8% retracement, to complete a Wave-C high followed by a decline to below the November low. The daily momentum made a bearish reversal on December 11. Only the fast line of the weekly momentum reached the OB zone the WE December 21 with a bearish reversal the following week.

Let's review this trade campaign. The initial capital exposure per contract was relatively large at 24.25 points. The beauty of the objective maximum position size is capital exposure per unit is not relevant by itself. It is only relevant by the position size. *It's the total capital exposure of the position size relative to the account size that is relevant,* so no trade is taken if the capital exposure of the total position is greater than 3%. It doesn't matter if you have a small or a large position. The risk will never be more than 3% as long as you follow the maximum risk per trade rule. The objective is to identify conditions with a high probability outcome and take advantage of those conditions.

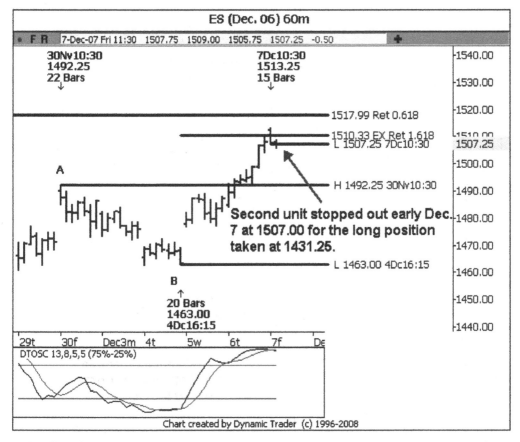

FIGURE 7.11 Second Unit Stopped Out Near 61.8% Retracement on Tr-1 BH

In this case, the initial capital exposure per futures contract would be $1,212.50 (24.25 × 50). Two contracts (units) totaled $2,425. You would have to have $80,800 available capital to take a two-unit *futures* trade ($2,425 divided by.03). If this is larger than your account, no worries. Take the position with the SPY (S&P ETF) which trades tick for tick with the S&P. On an unleveraged SPY position, the first unit returned approximately 2% in two days. The second unit returned approximately 5.3% in less than two weeks. The initial capital exposure was less than 1.8%. If these returns don't impress you, you shouldn't be trading because they are impressive returns over a very short period of time on a very low-risk, low capital exposure trade.

If you are a futures trader you are no doubt freaking out about the wide stop, probably because you are focusing on the capital exposure per contract instead of the far more important maximum capital exposure per trade. No worries. You have a solution to take advantage of the probable Wave-5 reversal on November 26. Move down to the 15m data for trade execution. More than likely, you will have an execution setup with much less capital exposure. Figure 7.12 is the 15m data for November 26 and 27. The 60m

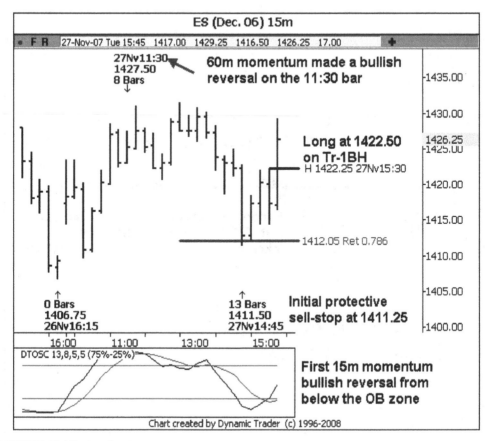

FIGURE 7.12   Smaller Time Frame 15m Entry Strategy

momentum bullish reversal was made on the 11:30 bar, which is marked on the chart. Later in the day, a 15m momentum bullish reversal was made on the 15:30 bar. The Tr-1BH entry was made at 1422.50 (one tick above the 1422.50 bar high) with a stop at 1411.25 (one tick below the swing low) for an initial capital exposure per contract of just 11.25 points versus the 24.25 points on the 60m data.

Ratcheting down to a lower time frame won't always result in lower capital exposure, but it often will if you are able to give your attention to the screen during the trading day.

The short-term unit was taken off very quickly for a small profit at a minor retracement and the stop on the long-term unit was adjusted to breakeven. This ensured at least a small profit if the outlook was not correct and the S&P did not complete a five-wave bear trend and the rally was only a minor correction. I know, if the first unit was managed like the second unit, the net profit would have been substantially greater. But we never *know* in advance what the market will do. Many times a market will only make a minor correction even though all factors point to a larger time frame trend. Always trade two units and take the first unit off at a minor correction target. I'm sure you will find your net results over time will be much greater with this logical, two-unit strategy for all trades.

The stop on the second unit was kept at breakeven until the S&P had completed two sections for a potential ABC correction. Only then was it advanced to the potential Wave-B low. The stop was then trailed very close to the market at the 60m 1BL once the 60m momentum was OB and price had reached the probable Wave-C target zone.

Each trade management decision was a logical choice based on the market position *as new bars were added*. I wish there was a fixed formula for price targets or momentum position for an exit strategy so we didn't have to think about how to manage a trade as it progresses. I know some trading educators claim they have discovered the secret. They haven't. Trading is like every other business. You have to make decisions based on the available information. Every market, every day provides new information. It is your job to understand and apply that information to logical decisions. A market can do just about anything. Momentum reversals aren't always made at the OB or OS zones. Price targets are not always reached. Wide range reversal bars can result in a significant price movement before a momentum reversal signal is made. Highs and lows are sometimes made outside of any typical time factors. Anything can happen but you must make a decision based on the probable position with the information you have as of the last bar on any chart.

Stock Setup

Figure 7.13 is the daily data for OIH, the oil services ETF. The February 20 low was in an ideal position to complete an ABC correction.

Summary Position of OIH as of February 21

Momentum: Weekly momentum is bullish. Daily momentum made a bullish reversal February 21.

Pattern: Probable ABC low, which implies a continuation of the bull trend to above the December high.

Price: February 20 low made at the extreme probable target for a Wave-C low including the 61.8% retracement and 162% APP of Wave-A.

Time: February 13–21 is the daily Time Band for low. February 20 is in the 38% to 62% time retracement zone.

Trade Strategy: Long on the Tr-1BH following the February 21 daily momentum bullish reversal. Strategy for the ST unit is a Wave-C target at 145.59–146.70, which includes the 100% APP and 78.6% retracement. The general objective for the long-term unit is a continuation of the bull trend to above the December high. Specific objectives will be made if the trend progresses.

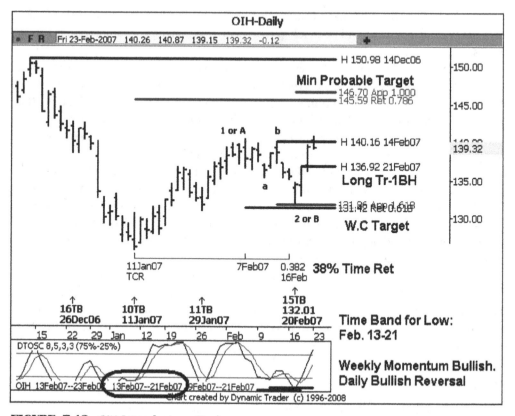

FIGURE 7.13 OIH Setup for Long Trade

OIH looks like a great setup for a long position. If we are not correct about a continuation of the bull trend to a new high, the strategy is to take off the ST unit if an ABC correction up to the probable Wave-C target beginning at 145.59 is made. The short-term unit target is at the 100% alternate price projection of what is labeled the Wave-1 or A range, projected from the February 20 probable Wave-2 or B low. If OIH is not continuing the bull trend to a new high as anticipated, this would be the ideal target for a three-section correction.

Trade entry: A long position was executed on February 23 at 136.93, one tick above the Tr-1BH. The stop is placed at 132.00, one tick below the potential February 20 Wave-C (of Wave-2 or B) low for an initial capital exposure of 4.93.

Figure 7.14 adds about 10 days of data to the OIH daily chart. OIH declined and the long position was stopped out on March 5.

Trade result (both units): 4.93 loss. The initial protective sell-stop was not adjusted.

The weekly momentum was still bullish although the fast line had reached the OB zone. Daily momentum made another bullish reversal on March 6. Is this another setup for a long trade?

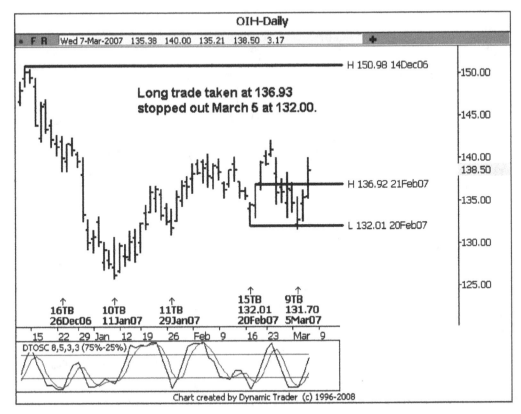

FIGURE 7.14 Stopped Out of Long Position for Small Loss

With the new high after February 20 and sharp reversal to take out the swing low on March 5, which stopped out the long trade, the pattern cannot be considered bullish. It definitely has the overlapping characteristics of a correction. The current pattern position knocks OIH out of the high probability setups to try another long trade.

How did it turn out? About two weeks later, OIH broke to new highs and didn't look back for several months, continuing the bull trend to $200! The weekly momentum soon reached the OB zone but hung there for several months, not giving another bullish reversal below the OB zone until August for another stab at a long position. Did we miss a major trend that we should have participated in? No. The information did not reflect the high probability conditions to consider another long trade.

Weekly-Daily-60m Setup for Short-Term or Position Trade

W. D. Gann taught over and over in all his publications, including his very expensive commodity and stock courses published in the 1930s and 1940s, "The big money is made with the big trends." No truer words have ever been said. You can trade for ticks and, if you're good at it, pay the overhead with a little left over. Or you can trade for points and

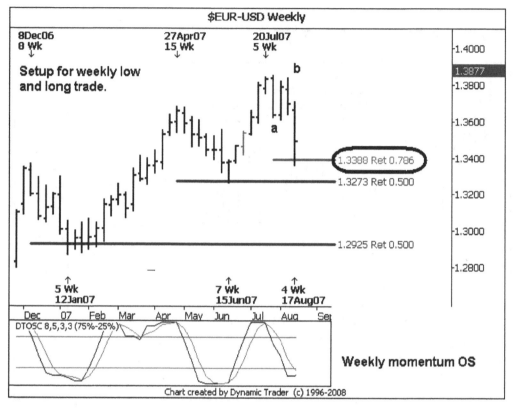

FIGURE 7.15   Setup for Weekly Low

potentially make some real money. I'll have more to say regarding trading time frames in the last chapter.

Even short-term traders should be aware of the higher time frame position. Figure 7.15 is the EUR/USD weekly data through the week ending August 2007. The EUR/USD had been in a consistent bull trend since November 2005, making higher highs and higher lows with no pattern factor that suggested the bull trend was over. There are no compelling time factors at the WE August 17 low. However, pattern, price, and momentum suggested that the EUR/USD was making another correction and the WE August 17 was in a position to be a corrective low. The EUR/USD had reached the 78.6% retracement with the weekly momentum oversold on a potential ABC correction. The EUR/USD was in an almost ideal position for a long trade.

Figure 7.16 is the daily data through Fri., August 17. The EUR/USD is in an ideal position to complete a Wave-C low. The daily momentum has made a bullish reversal. If the Tr-1BH entry strategy is used, the stop would be very wide because of the very wide range day on August 17. If the EUR/USD is only making a correction instead of a new bull trend section to a new high, it should only reach around the 61.8% retracement at 1.3657, which would be the target to exit the short-term unit. We don't need a calculator to see

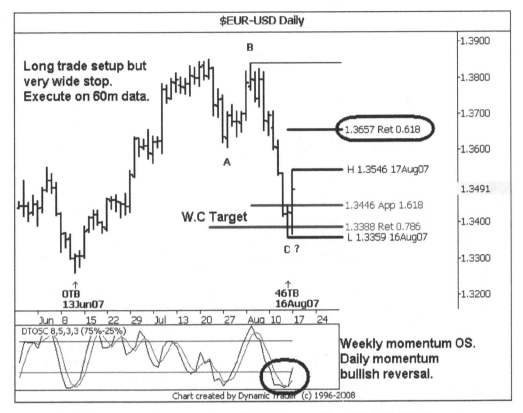

FIGURE 7.16 Long Trade Setup with Weekly Momentum OS and Daily Bullish Reversal

that the reward/risk on a Tr-1BH with such a wide stop would not be good, at least for the ST unit. The solution: Move down to the 60m data for trade execution for a potential setup with much less initial capital exposure.

I haven't made a summary position list as I did for the previous trades. While this is a good exercise to go through, all of the relevant information may also be noted on a chart, as I've also done on the 60m chart in Figure 7.17. I strongly recommend you do this and print each chart as a trade progresses so you have a record of your trades that can be reviewed at a later time.

Figure 7.17 is the 60m data from the August 16 low through early August 22. To reduce the number of charts needed to track this trade, this chart includes two 60m go-long setups.

Entry strategy (both units): Long Tr-1BH following a 60m momentum bullish reversal.

A long taken on the 60m reversal for a potential ABC at the 50% retracement on August 20 (labeled 1) would have been stopped out the next day for a very small 21 pip loss.

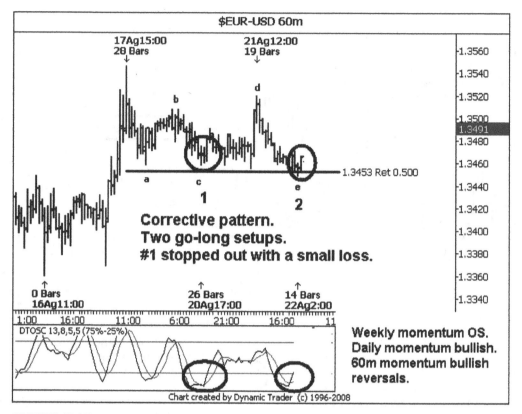

FIGURE 7.17 Long Setups with Two Higher Time Frame Bullish Momentum

First entry strategy results (both units): Long 1.3479. Stopped out at 1.3458 for a 21 pip loss.

Two days later, another 60m bullish reversal was made (labeled 2). A long taken on the Tr-1BH was entered at 1.3469 with a stop at 1.3451 or an 18 pip capital exposure. I'll track this trade by pips since a pip can be worth different amounts depending on the lot size chosen by the trader. The important point here is the initial capital exposure is *very small*.

Trade entry (both units): Long at 1.3469 with a stop at 1.3451 for an 18 pip capital exposure.

Figure 7.18 continues the 60m data. The EUR/USD traded above the Wave-1 or A high on August 22.

Trade management (both units): Adjust the stop on both units to 1.3465, one tick below the minor swing low shown on the chart.

If the EUR/USD is only making an ABC correction, not a continuation of the bull trend to a new high as anticipated, the ideal Wave-C target zone is 1.3636–1.3656, where a Wave-C would be 100% of Wave-A and the minor 61.8% retracement shown on the earlier chart.

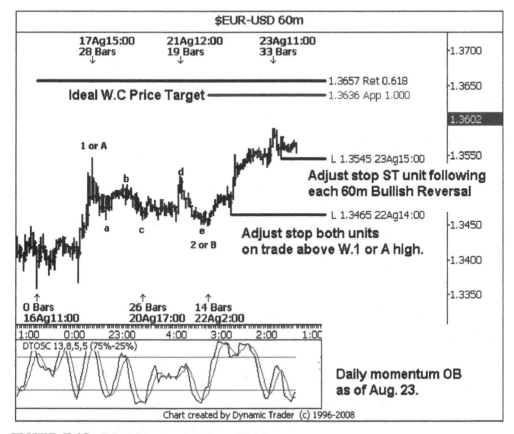

FIGURE 7.18 Stop Adjustments on Long Position

Trade management (ST unit): If the EUR/USD reaches 1.3636, trail the stop on the short-term unit at the 60m 1BL.

As of August 23, the daily momentum has reached the OB zone. This implies the immediate upside should only have a day or two to go. Once a higher time frame momentum reaches the overbought zone, the lower time frame momentum usually has only one or two reversals to go before the higher time frame makes a reversal. We want to keep the stop on the ST unit relatively close to the market. A logical strategy is to adjust the stop to one tick below the swing low made prior to any smaller time frame momentum bullish reversal. That is exactly what to do with the ST unit

Trade management (ST unit): Adjust the stop on the short-term unit to one tick below the low made prior to each 60m bullish reversal. As of the last bar on this chart, that would be 1.3544.

Trade management (ST unit): Tr-1BL if the EUR/USD reaches 1.3636, the beginning of a Wave-C target zone.

The stop on the long-term unit is kept very far from the current market position until the market provides a reason to make an adjustment. In this case, the next adjustment should not be made until the daily momentum makes another *bullish reversal*. That should be several days away as the daily momentum has only now reached the overbought zone. Do not lose sight of the objective. The market information implies the EUR/USD should go to a new high above the July high at 1.3852. If the recent bull sections are a guide, it will go much higher. The ST unit is already in a position for a reasonable profit if stopped out. The LT unit would make at least a small profit if stopped out. Do not risk taking a small profit too soon when a large profit is probable. Do not lose sight of the trade objective.

Figure 7.19 extends the 60m data through August 25. On August 24, the 1.3636 Wave-C target was reached, the Tr-1BL exit strategy was initiated, and the short-term unit was stopped out a couple bars later at 1.3625, one tick below the trailing 1BL.

Trade results (ST unit): Long at 1.3469. Stopped out at 1.3625 for a 156 pip profit.

The short-term unit ended up with a pretty substantial profit of 156 pips on an 18 pip capital exposure. Each action, from entry to stop adjustment to exit, was made in a logical manner based on the information the market provided. Don't lose sight of the

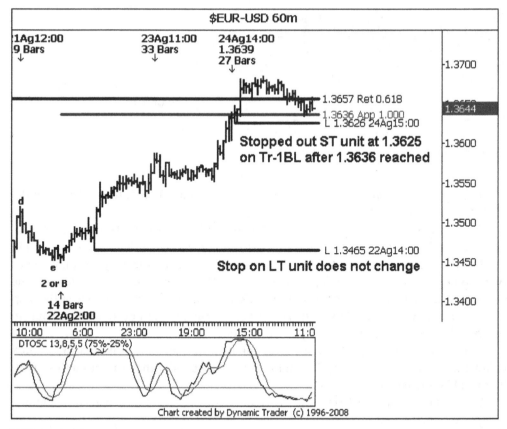

FIGURE 7.19 Short-Term Unit Stopped Out

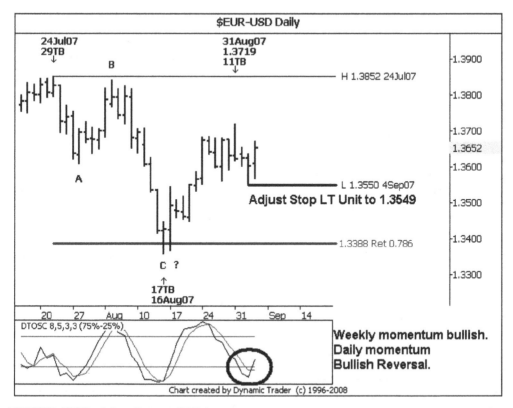

FIGURE 7.20 Adjust Stop on LT Unit

fact that this was only the short-term unit that was exited relatively quickly in the event the EUR/USD was only making a corrective rally and not a continuation of the bull trend to much higher levels. We have no more use for the 60m data. We'll mange the LT unit with the weekly-daily data.

Figure 7.20 is the daily data through September 5, the day the daily momentum made a bullish reversal.

Trade management (LT unit): Adjust the stop to one tick below the low made prior to the daily momentum bullish reversal. The LT unit stop is adjusted to 1.3549. Until the weekly momentum reaches the OB zone, adjust the stop to one tick below the swing low made prior to any subsequent daily momentum bullish reversals.

Most new and unsuccessful traders focus on a very small time frame. They trade for ticks or pips instead of trading the larger trends for points. The objective of this trade was to trade the larger time frame weekly-daily trend for a probable bull section that would exceed the July 07 high. The intraday data was used to trade the short-term unit for a trade that may only last a few days in the event we were incorrect about another bull trend and the EUR/USD was only making a correction to the recent decline followed

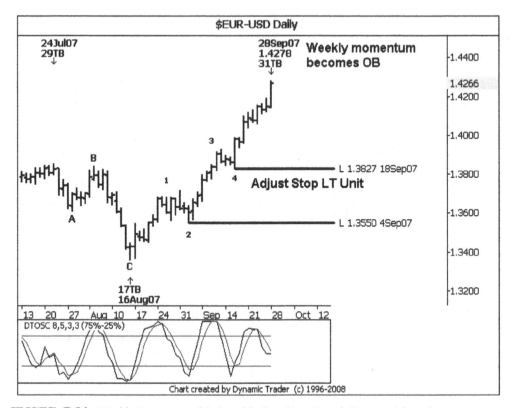

FIGURE 7.21   Weekly Momentum OB, Possible Five-Wave Trend: Time to Adjust Stop

by a bear trend to a new low. Now we'll just focus on the weekly and daily position for the probable larger time frame trend.

Figure 7.21 is the daily chart with data added through Friday, September 28, when the weekly momentum became overbought. The daily momentum made another bullish reversal during this period and the stop on the LT unit was adjusted to the swing low made prior to the daily momentum reversal, as shown on the chart. Once the weekly momentum reached the OB zone, a weekly high is probable within a couple of weekly bars. The upside should be relatively limited before a weekly high is made. Plus, as of September 28, the EUR/USD has completed four sections. A possible five-wave bull trend may be near completion—a pattern structure that also suggests the upside should be relatively limited.

Note on Figure 7.21 that the daily momentum made a bearish reversal during the week ending September 28, the same week the weekly momentum became OB. The next daily momentum bearish reversal is likely to coincide closely with a weekly momentum bearish reversal. So we have a logical exit strategy.

Trade management (LT unit): Adjust the stop to one tick below the swing low following the next daily momentum bullish reversal. Following the next daily momentum bearish reversal, trail the stop one tick below the daily 1BL.

A daily momentum bearish reversal after the higher time frame weekly momentum reaches the OB zone often coincides with a weekly high. The stop should be trailed very close to the market once this dual time frame momentum position has been made for a probable larger time frame high.

Figure 7.22 extends the daily data through Tuesday, October 9. The EUR/USD made a daily bullish reversal on October 5. The stop on the LT unit was adjusted to 1.4030, the low made prior to the daily bullish reversal. On Tuesday, October 9, the LT unit was stopped out as the EUR/USD traded below the 1.4031 swing low.

Trade results (LT unit): Long at 1.3469. Stopped out at 1.4030 for a 561 pip profit.

The LT unit had a large profit of 561 pips! The daily momentum never reached the OB zone or made a bearish reversal before the trade was stopped out. The trade management strategy was logical throughout the trade, with stops adjusted according to the information the market provided.

The long-term unit trade lasted almost six weeks and resulted in an enormous profit. That success was a result of keeping the stop relatively far from the market in the early

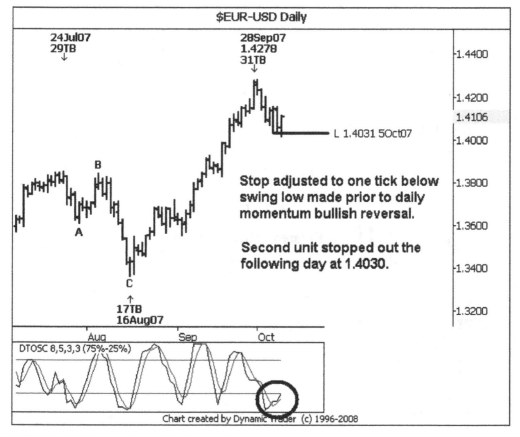

FIGURE 7.22   Long-Term Unit Stopped Out

stages of the trend. Once the short-term unit was exited, there was no need to even look at intraday data. To effectively manage the trade would only take literally a couple of minutes a day. Most days there was no change to the trade management plan. Only on a few occasions during the six-week period was new information provided by the market position that called for a change in the immediate trade management plan.

It appears we had a brilliant campaign and took out what could be close to the maximum profit from the bull trend, entering very close to the low of a correction and exiting very close to a high made with the weekly momentum overbought. Let's take a look at what happened in the weeks following our trade exit.

Figure 7.23 is the EUR/USD weekly data. A weekly momentum bearish reversal was made the week the LT unit was exited. The following week, the EUR/USD began to rally again and the weekly momentum did not make a bullish reversal until three weeks later. The EUR/USD rallied another six weeks following the exit of the long position into a high in November We ended up exiting near the low of a correction and just prior to the continuation of the bull trend!

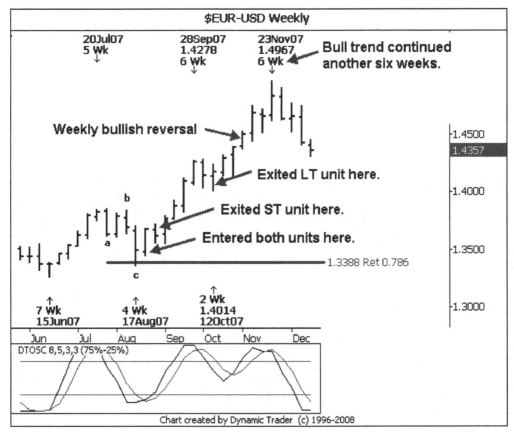

FIGURE 7.23 EUR/USD Bull Trend Continues

Did we do something wrong exiting the long position when we could have more than doubled the already major profit by holding the position another six weeks? Was the October two-week correction which stopped us out of the long position really a buying opportunity? Based on the dual time frame momentum position we use as the first filter to identify a trade setup, we did exactly the right thing. The weekly momentum made a bearish reversal from the OB zone, which is typically followed by a sideways to down trend for several weeks, which is not a time to hold a long position. Unless the weekly momentum either reached the oversold zone or made a bullish reversal, long trades could not be considered if we are going to follow our trading plan.

Never lose sight of the objective of trading: to identify conditions with a high probability outcome, not to capture every trend. That is exactly what we did with the EUR/USD trade, and we exited in a logical manner based on the trading plan. That is the best you can do.

TRADE ONLY THE HIGH PROBABILITY, OPTIMUM SETUPS

These four trade campaigns have not only taught you specific trade management strategies from entry to exit, but also how to make decisions based on the momentum, pattern, price, and time information as a market progresses. Each decision should be a logical consequence of the market position. If you know how to make decisions, you will know how to manage any trade, in any market and any time frame. The same process is applicable to every time frame, from short-term day trades with intraday data to position trades with weekly and daily data.

I have done more than just show you a few cherry-picked, after-the-fact entry and exit strategies. You have learned how to identify high probability conditions to consider a trade, objective entry strategies with a defined entry and initial protective stop prices, and how to adjust the stop in a logical manner through the trade exit. You now have the tools to apply to any market and any time frame for your own real-time trading.

The CD that accompanies this book goes through different trade examples of different time frames, bar by bar, so you will gain more confidence in the strategies you have learned in the book. But don't get ahead of yourself. Finish the book before you view the CD. There is lots more important information for you that the CD assumes you know.

After you've finished the book, you might also want to visit the book web site at www.HighProbabilityTradingStrategies.com which includes more current trade examples from entry to exit for book readers.

In the next chapter, you will learn from trades made by several traders from around the world who follow the high probability trading strategies taught in this book. Their trade examples include many different markets and time frames. You will learn how a successful trader thinks and makes decisions as a market progresses and provides you with new information.

PART TWO

Trading the Plan

CHAPTER 8

Real Traders, Real Time

In this chapter, you will learn from real-time trade examples from a variety of traders who apply the High Probability Trading Strategies you have learned in this book. The strategies are applied to a variety of markets and time frames by traders who use a logical decision making process to manage each trade from entry to exit.

I have taught the high probability trading strategies you have learned in this book for years to traders all over the world. I asked some of my students and Dynamic Trader software owners if they would like to submit their own trade examples for a chapter of this book. I've included examples from several students from around the world who trade a wide variety of markets and time frames.

Some of the examples submitted included detailed commentary about the trade from entry to exit. Others were just chart screen captures with comments right on the chart. For some examples, I've included the comments just as submitted by the trader. For those examples that only included brief comments on their charts, I've expanded on the comments with the trade description. In every case, I've recaptured each chart with chart notes to make as clear as possible the market position and trade decisions made by each trader.

While each trader does not have the same trade plan, there is a consistency in approach to recognizing a high probability setup to managing the trade. You will also learn that a trade management plan may be changed as a trade progresses and as new market information appears that may change the probable position of the market from what was originally anticipated when the trade was entered.

ADAM SOWINSKI (SLORZEWO, POLAND)

EUR/USD Long Trade
Higher time frame: Daily
Lower time frame: 60m

Adam is Polish, and English is not his native language. The comments that follow are his, but I have added a few explanatory comments of my own in italics, in parentheses. I have also re-created the charts he sent and included chart comments so you can more easily follow the trade. This was an ideal ABC setup and Adam used all of the factors taught in this book, which he learned from prior Dynamic Traders Group educational material.

The EUR/USD Setup

Major trend bullish
Possible ABC correction
Possible long trade

My assumption was that a corrective ABC should unfold. In my trading methodology, I trade on hourly time frame in the direction of the higher daily time frame. I use DT Oscillator (momentum) position to help me get in the trade. What I saw on the chart was a three legs down move or a potential ABC. Wave-C divided into a nice five-wave pattern with subdivision of waves 3 and 5. I have made all necessary price projections, which give me a narrow zone of 1.4299 to 1.4308 *(for support)*. (See Figure 8.1.)

This price zone included:

1.4303: 78.6% retracement of the October 22 to November 23 rally
1.4305: W.C = 100% APP W.A
1.4299: W.5:C (Wave-5 of C) = 162% APP W.1:C (Wave 1 of C)
1.4208: W.5.5:C (Wave 5 of 5 of C) = 162% APP W.1.5:C (Wave 1 of 5 of C)

The EUR/USD hit that zone on December 20 at 1 P.M. Central European Time (CET). This low was one bar after the 62% ATP of Wave-A *(not shown on chart)*. The 8 daily DTosc was deep in the OS zone. It was a very strong candidate for a Wave-C low.

The Trade Plan

My trading plan for this set up was to trade two units. I would enter the trade with the one bar high strategy *(60m trailing 1BH)* following the next *(60m)* 34 hourly DTosc *(momentum)* bullish reversal. In case I am wrong, I would trail my first unit with one-bar-low *(trailing 60m 1BL)* exit strategy at 50% retracement *(if price reaches the 50% retracement)* of the December 18–20 decline. (See Figure 8.2.) I will adjust my stop-loss

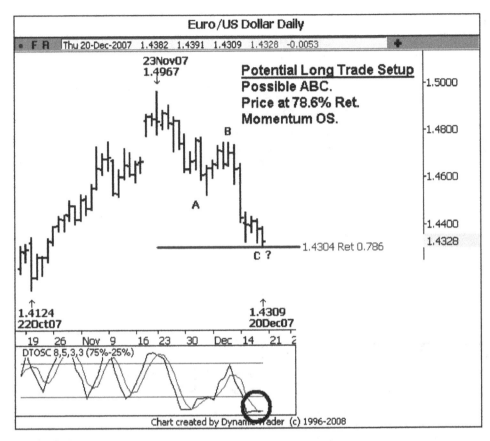

FIGURE 8.1 Long Trade Setup

for the second unit one tick below the low prior to each *(60m)* 34 hourly DTosc bullish reversal until stopped out.

Trade Management

The two-unit long trade was triggered on December 21 at 2 A.M. CET at 1.4341 with 35 pips stop-loss at 1.4306. My minimal profit objective *(50% retracement)* was hit on December 20 at 7 A.M. I started to employ my first unit exit strategy *(60m trailing 1BL)*, which exited at 1.4387. From now on, I was in a small profit no matter what happens next. I stayed with my second unit and according to my plan, my stop-losses were adjusted every time *(60m)* 34 hourly DTosc made a bullish reversal. (See Figures 8.3 and 8.4.)

Trade Result: 292 pips profit
Unit 1: 46 pips profit
Unit 2: 246 pips profit

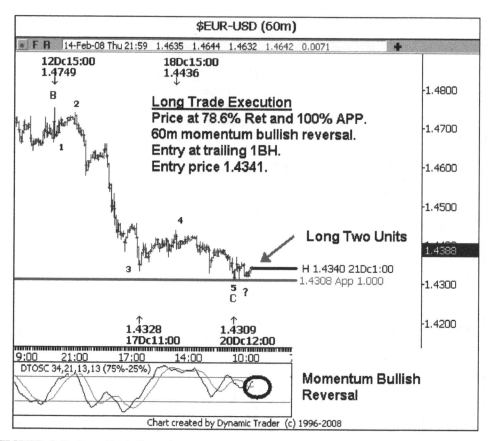

FIGURE 8.2   Long Trade Execution

What I Have Learned

Although I could have gained more from the second unit, I followed my trading plan which I have learned from Dynamic Trading Workshop. I am very successful with this approach and the most important thing I have learned so far is to do your homework, make all price and time projections, and wait. I waited for this trade to the point where I had all the conditions in place. I think this is why this trade was so profitable.

Trading is not an easy business. You must work hard and wait for the best opportunity. I discovered that patience and hard work is the key to success. Patience is also necessary for proper money management and not to overtrade so in case of multiple losses in a row, you can be there for tomorrow.

Robert's Follow-Up

Adam had the patience and discipline to wait for an ideal setup. All of the factors were in place December 20 for a potential ABC corrective low. Most important, Adam had a

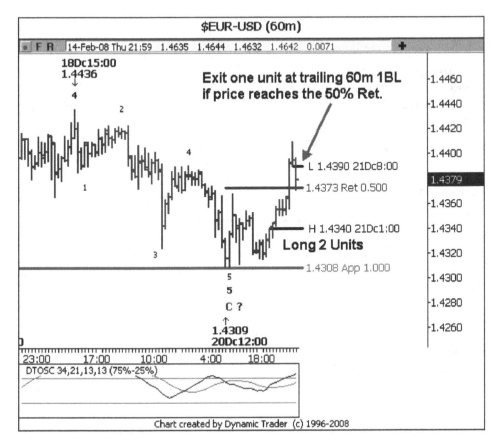

FIGURE 8.3 Unit One Exit

specific trade management plan for both units before the trade was even executed. Once the EUR/USD reached the first price target zone for a Wave-C low, Adam used the trailing one-bar-high entry strategy following the 60m momentum bullish reversal.

Adam was quick to take a relatively small profit on one unit. Once price reached the minor 50% retracement, Adam trailed the stop at the 60m 1BL, taking a relatively small 46 pip profit. At this point, even if the EUR/USD did not make an ABC correction at the December 20 low and reversed to make a new low, stopping out the second unit, he would still have made a net profit of a few pips on the two-unit trade.

Adam held the second unit for the potential of a longer-term trend, which he anticipated from an ABC corrective low. A key feature of his success is he kept the stop on the second unit relatively far from the market, only adjusting the stop following a 60m momentum bullish reversal, a very logical strategy. Unsuccessful traders often trail the stop much too close to the market and get stopped out for a relatively small profit when they could have held for a much larger profit.

The EUR/USD continued higher a few days after Adam was stopped out but this did not concern him. He is more concerned having the patience to wait for a high probability

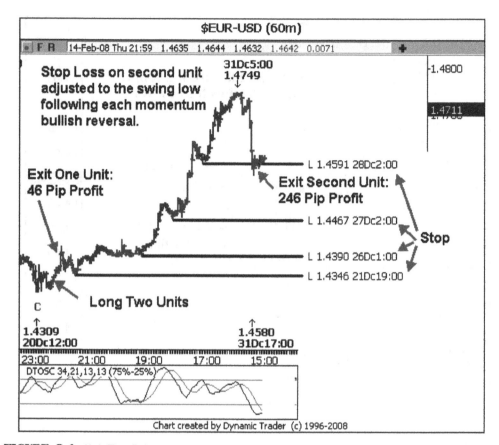

FIGURE 8.4 Unit Two Exit

setup and following his trading plan than being an overactive trader and buying low tick and selling top tick. These are characteristics of an accomplished trader.

Adam had a total of 296 pips profit in six trading days on this trade, thanks to his patience and discipline to wait for a high probability setup and trade management plan.

JAGIR SINGH (LONDON, UNITED KINGDOM)

GBP and JPY Short Trades
Higher time frame: Weekly, daily
Lower time frame: 60m

Jagir submitted five examples with as many as 11 chart screen captures for each example. This entire chapter could have been just his examples! The trades he submitted included big winners and small losers with a good variety of trade situations.

Jagir had traded for less than a year when he sent me these examples. He had flown from the United Kingdom to attend a live one-day workshop I offered in Denver in February 2007. He was a new trader at the time and had had some trading instruction in the United Kingdom but didn't start trading on a regular basis until the spring of 2007, following the workshop in Denver.

I think an important reason for his success is that he was new to trading and didn't have a lot of bad habits and ego to overcome when he began trading. He was the ideal student. He treated trading as a business right from the start. As you will see from the two examples I include here, he followed the high probability trading plan taught in this book to a T and has found great success.

Jagir did not send any text commentary with his examples. All of the comments and key information were right on the charts, which makes it easy for him to keep a record of his trades. I've recaptured the relevant charts with comments and written the text commentary to describe the trade as he described it in his brief chart notes. He gave a few examples with large profits, but I've chosen to show a couple of trades with fairly small profits where a less experienced trader may have had losses, given the market reversals made during the trades. Jagir made at least small profits on these trades by applying good trading strategies and good trade management.

GBP/USD Short Trade Setup

Weekly and daily momentum overbought
Possible ABC corrective high

As of September 24, 2007, the British pound (GBP) weekly momentum had turned bearish and the daily momentum was overbought. The GBP had poked above the 78.6% retracement for a possible ABC corrective high. The Time Band for a high was September 26 to October 1, but the high-high band began on September 21. The higher time frame weekly and daily positions were ideal for a possible ABC high and a short trade setup. (See Figure 8.5.)

Trade Execution   The 60m chart shows the possible ABC count into the September 24 high. Jagir showed that the Wave-C had probably subdivided into five waves. Jagir's chart showed several price targets clustered around the September 24 high, including a 78.6% retracement, 100% APP of Wave-A, 162% Ext-Ret of Wave-C, and more. I've only shown the 162% Ext Ret on the 60m chart to keep the chart from being cluttered. (See Figure 8.6.)

Trade Management   Once the 60m DTosc made a bearish reversal, Jagir trailed a stop to go short two units at the 60m trailing 1BL. The short position was executed at 2.0254 and the initial protective buy-stop was one tick above the September 24 high at 2.0322. The objective to cover half of the position (one unit) was at the minor 50% retracement at 2.0200.

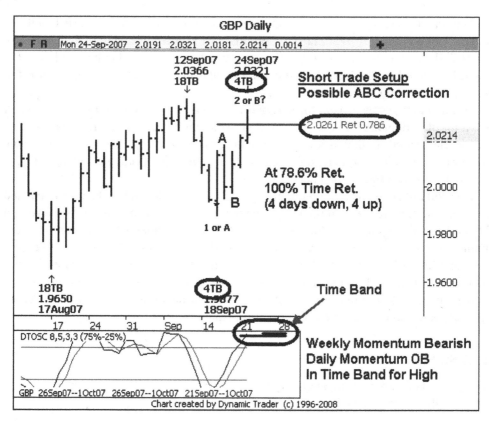

FIGURE 8.5 Short Trade Setup, GBP

The GBP declined sharply, hesitating for some time at the 50% retracement, where Jagir exited half of his position at 2.0217 for a small profit of 37 pips. (See Figure 8.7.)

Once the GBP reached the 61.8% retracement and the momentum was oversold, Jagir moved the stop on the second unit to one pip above the minor swing high at 2.0230, ensuring at least a small profit on the second unit. (See Figure 8.8.)

The GBP advanced off the 61.8% retracement, made a swing high below the protective buy-stop level, and then declined in what appeared to be a minor ABC. Rather than hold the short for a continued decline as originally planned, Jagir exited the second unit once it was clear it should be a minor ABC correction which should be followed by a continued advance. The second unit was exited at 2.0172 for an 82 pip profit. It turned out to be a wise move to exit the second short unit because the GBP eventually continued much higher.

Trade Result: 119 pips profit
Unit 1: 37 pips
Unit 2: 82 pips

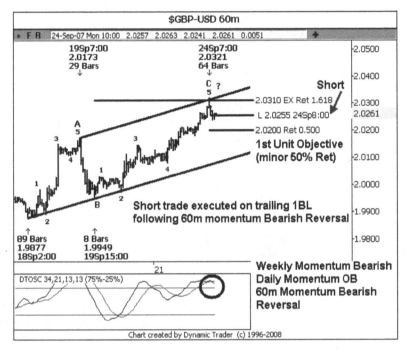

FIGURE 8.6 Short Time Frame Details of Short Trade Setup

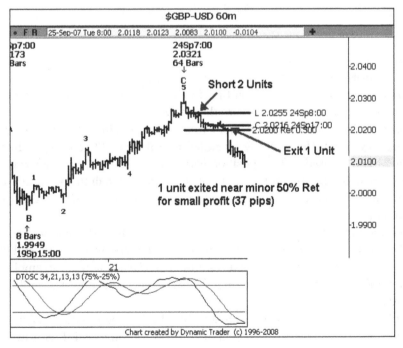

FIGURE 8.7 First Unit Trade Management

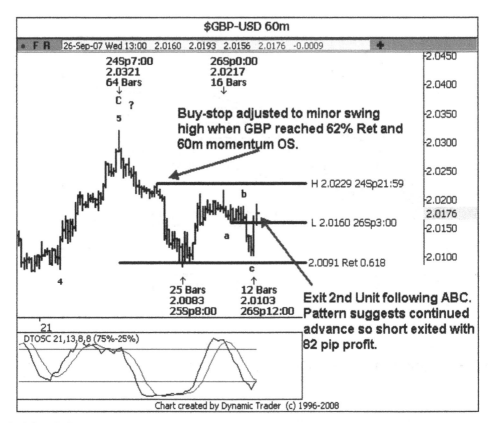

FIGURE 8.8 Second Unit Trade Management

Robert's Follow-Up This trade is a great example of how you can make a profit even when dead wrong about the larger time frame trend by using two units and making decisions based on the market position as the trend develops.

With the bearish weekly and daily momentum, Jagir anticipated a short trade should have a long way to go. He correctly identified a probable ABC corrective high as of September 24 and entered a short position very close to the extreme high on the 60m trailing 1BL entry strategy. He took a quick but small profit on half the position at a minor retracement in the event the decline was only a minor correction and not the beginning of a bear trend.

He did not adjust the stop on the second unit until the GBP had declined to the major 61.8 percent retracement and the 60m momentum was oversold. He still kept the stop fairly far from the market at a minor swing high. This is another example of how successful traders keep the stop wide on most trades and don't adjust it until there is a technical reason to do so.

On September 27, Jagir changed strategy. The GBP had made a potential minor ABC decline and traded back above the potential W.A low. A confirmed three-wave decline implies a correction, which implies the advance should continue. Rather than hold the second unit short position, Jagir exited just after the GBP traded above the minor W.a low, for another small profit of 82 pips on the second unit.

As it turned out, this was a very smart move as the GBP eventually continued to advance to a new high.

JPY Short Trade Setup: Possible ABC Corrective High

As of September 21, the last bar on the daily Japanese yen (JPY) chart, the weekly momentum was OB and daily momentum had made a bearish reversal for a dual time frame momentum short setup. The JPY had reached a minor 78.6% price retracement and 62% time retracement. Everything was in place for a possible irregular ABC corrective high. With a typical ABC, the Wave-C exceeds the extreme of the Wave-A. In this case, the potential Wave-C was below the Wave-A high, but with momentum, price, and time in place for a high, Jagir considered the correction could be an irregular ABC and a good short setup. (See Figure 8.9.)

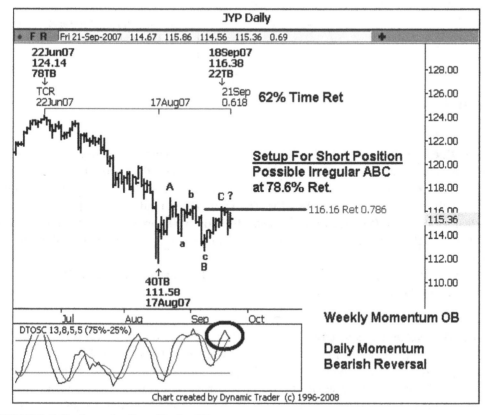

FIGURE 8.9 Setup for Short Trade, JPY

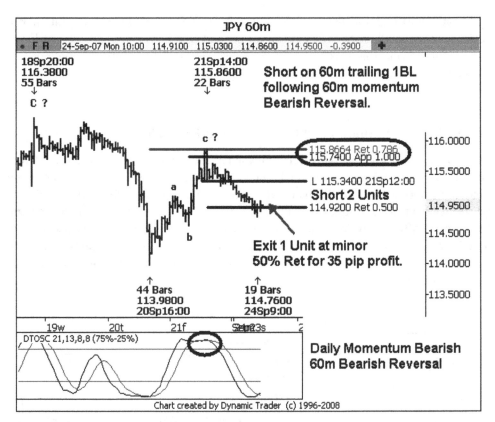

FIGURE 8.10   Short Entry Strategy

Trade Execution   The 60m chart shows the data following the September 18 possible Wave-C high that was shown on the daily chart. The JPY declined and made a possible minor ABC advance into the September 21 high. The high was right in the zone of the 78.6% retracement and 100% APP. The 60m DTosc made a bearish reversal for an ideal short setup. (See Figure 8.10.) Jagir trailed a go-short stop one pip below the 60m trailing 1BL. A two-unit short position was taken at 115.33, not far from the minor W.c high.

Jagir took a 35 pip profit on one unit when the JPY reached the minor 50% retracement and the 60m momentum was OS.

Trade Management 2nd Unit   As of the last 60m bar on Figure 8.11, the JPY declined to the September 20 low and had made what may be a minor ABC correction. Jagir adjusted the stop on the second unit to the minor swing high at 115.16 after a 60m momentum bearish reversal. Jagir also put in an order to add to the short position one tick below the minor W.b low at 114.40. The JPY was in a good position for another short position with the daily momentum bearish and the 60m momentum overbought.

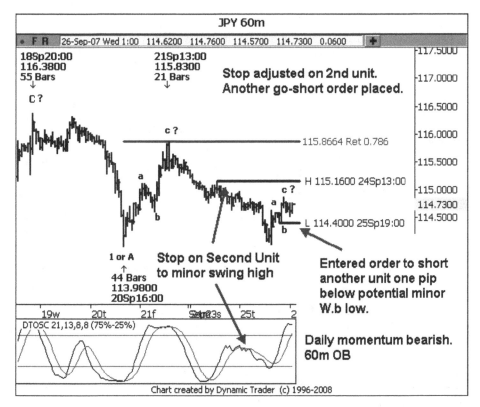

FIGURE 8.11 Second Unit Trade Management

The JPY did not decline as anticipated but advanced sharply and stopped out the second unit for a 26 pip profit. (See Figure 8.12.)

Trade Result: 61 pips profit
Unit 1: 35 pip profit
Unit 2: 26 pip profit

Robert's Follow-Up   This is another great example of how a profit may be made even when the market does not do what is anticipated—in this case, make a decline to a new low. Good trade management not only avoided a loss, but locked in a profit.

All of the conditions of dual time frame momentum, price, time, and pattern were in place for a corrective high followed by a decline to a new low. Jagir took profits on half the position at the minor 50% retracement, then adjusted the stop to a minor swing high on the second unit following the next 60m momentum bearish reversal. Even if stopped out, at least a small profit would be made on the second unit.

Jagir made a good choice to add to the short position following a possible minor ABC correction. It turned out it was not a minor ABC correction and the JPY advanced

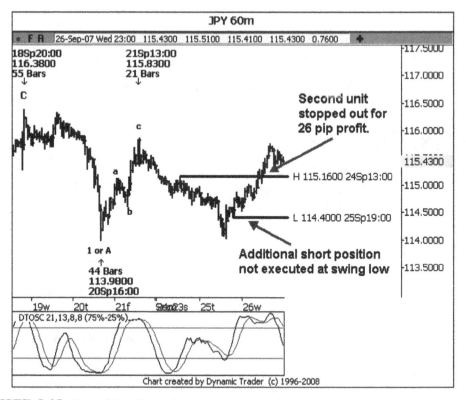

FIGURE 8.12 Second Unit Stopped Out

sharply, eventually to a new high. The additional short position was never executed at the minor swing low.

Jagir waited for optimal conditions to enter the trade, took a small profit on half the position fairly quickly, kept his stop wide on the second half position, and adjusted the stop in a logical manner. Good lessons can be learned from Jagir's trade management in both of these examples.

CEES VAN HASSELT (BREDA, THE NETHERLANDS)

Gold Long Trade
Higher time frame: Monthly, weekly
Lower time frame: Daily

Cees is a longtime Dynamic Trader software user and proponent of the type of trading strategies taught in this book. While I've re-created the charts Cees sent, similar charts and most comments shown for this gold trade were on his web site at www.traderplaza.nl beginning in December 2007, with periodic follow-up charts as the bull trend progressed.

All of the text comments belong to Cees, with my comments in the "Robert's Comments" and "Robert's Follow-Up" sections, as well as some in italics in parentheses within his comments. Cees did not provide specific trade strategies for his gold setup. The gold analysis was information he provided his web site visitors for probable gold trend, price, and time targets. Even though this is not a specific trade with specific trade management strategies from entry to exit, I thought it would be instructive to include this example.

Gold Long Trade Setup: Breakout of Irregular Correction to Continue the Bull Trend

December 13, 2007: Gold is still strong and doesn't correct very much. A break above 825.50 *(February 2008 futures contract)* is a first possible long entry. (See Figure 8.13.) But gold can make first a retrace to the 808–800 area *(807–797 continuous daily data)*. There is still an annoying point that silver is still not breaking out. An outbreak of silver above the first minor resistance of 1485 would give some more power to the upside on gold as well as silver.

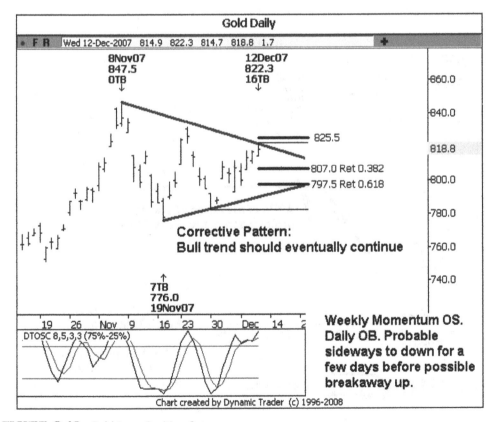

FIGURE 8.13 Gold Long Position Setup

Robert's Comments   The key factor is that Cees recognized that the pattern of trade off the November 8 high was probably a correction and gold should eventually continue the bull trend. The weekly momentum (not shown) was oversold but the daily momentum was overbought, so a minor correction ("retrace" in Cees's words) was probable before the bull trend would continue.

Cees's Follow-Up Comments   The breakout did occur on December 26. This breakout confirmed that we were in Wave-3. Gold broke out of the triangle and filled the small gap of November 27. (See Figure 8.14.)

Now that we are in the trade, we are going to predict the probable time and price targets for the Wave-5 high. We try to make a high probability guess where and when the top in gold will be made.

Time Projection for Gold High

A Dynamic Time Projection gives us two probable dates for a top: around February 18 or around March 10, 2008. (*The Dynamic Time Projection routine makes the type of time projections taught in Chapter 5 and displays the results as histogram bars in the indicator window as shown in Figure 8.14.*)

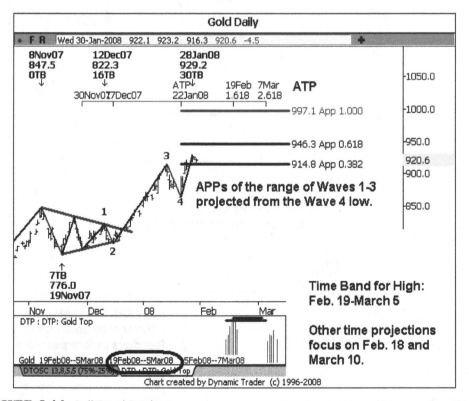

FIGURE 8.14   Bull Trend Breakout

I made two Time Bands, a short-term and an intermediate-term. (*Only the interme-diate term is shown on this chart.*) This gives us a time range of February 19 to March 5 for a probable high.

An alternate time projection from the waves 1 and 2 lows projected from the Wave-4 low gives us February 19 and March 7.

We now have two time zones to watch for a high: February 18–27 and March 7–10 with possible extension to March 15. (*These time targets were based on both the short- and intermediate-term Time Bands and several time projections not shown on this daily chart.*)

Price Projection for Gold High

The price projections for a Wave-5 high shown on the daily chart are 955 and finally 1005 (*for a February futures contract*). (*The numbers are 946 and 997 based on the continuous contract shown in the daily chart.*) The longer-term monthly wave count gives a most likely high target of 1038. This would all mean that we are in the final Wave-5 of 5 of a longer-term wave that should end in the coming months, and that most likely we have to take our profit somewhere around the $1,000 level. (See Figure 8.15.)

We still think we are in the final phase of the gold bull trend.

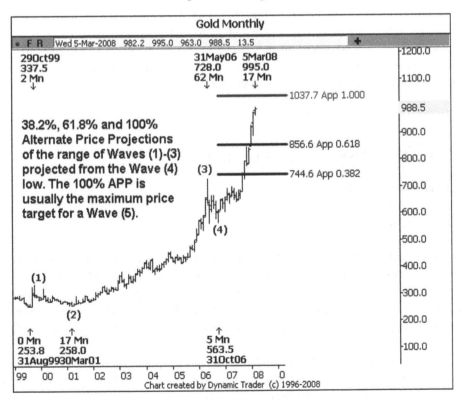

FIGURE 8.15 Price Targets for Gold High

Robert's Follow-Up

Cees was right-on about the breakout to a new high in his mid-December comments and chart. The maximum price targets around 997 to 1038 (gold continuous data) were both 100% alternate price projections of the range of waves 1 to 3, projected from a Wave-4 low for the Wave-5 of 5 shown on the daily chart and the higher time frame wave (5) shown on the monthly chart. The 100% APP of the range of waves 1 to 3 is typically the maximum target for a Wave-5.

This example is being included in the book in early March, 2008. Gold has reached $995, the beginning of the maximum price targets Cees predicted weeks earlier. According to Cees's time projections, gold should complete a final top by mid-March. At the least, according to Cees's charts and comments, we should be in the final phase of the gold bull trend. Readers can check their gold data to see how it worked out.

Additional Follow-up

As I make the final proof for this chapter for the book in late May 2008, I though it would be instructive for a final follow-up. Gold made a top March 17 at 1038.6 (continuous contract data). Cees's latest time target to complete a major high was March 15. The actual gold high was made March 17 with the daily closing high made March 14. Cees projected the maximum price target probable at 1038. The actual high on March 17 was 1038.6! Talk about a dead-center hit time and price target bulls-eye. Cees didn't use any secret strategies not taught in this book. If this doesn't convince you the strategies taught in this book will be valuable to you, close your account and get a job.

KERRY SZYMANSKI (TUCSON, ARIZONA)

Long S&P Swing Trade
Higher time frame: Daily
Lower time frame: 60m

Kerry has traded stocks and futures for over 10 years, beginning when he was still working as a real estate broker and investor. For several years, he has offered an intraday alert service for day and swing traders for the S&P, Euro, and 10-year note futures at www.harmoinicedge.com. Like all of the examples in this chapter, the following trade is not after the fact, but is one specifically recommended to his subscribers and updated until the trade was closed out.

Kerry sent me a series of six charts with trade strategy and trade management comments right on the chart. I've reproduced the critical information from the charts and added text commentary based on Kerry's chart comments.

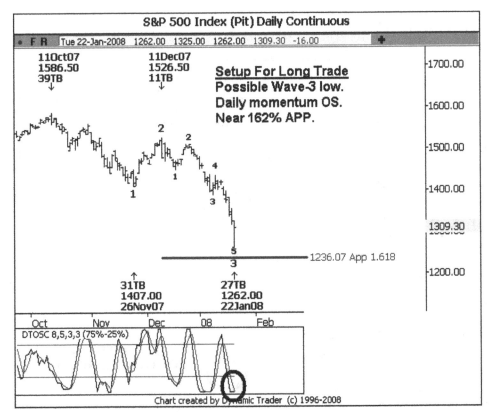

FIGURE 8.16 ES Long Trade Setup

S&P Long Trade Setup: Possible Wave-3 Low with Daily Momentum Oversold

As of January 22, 2008, the S&P was potentially at a Wave-3 low just above the 162% APP with the daily momentum oversold, a great setup for a long trade. Notice that the Wave-3 appears to have clearly subdivided into five waves. (See Figure 8.16.)

Entry Strategy

The 60m data shows a probable minor ABC decline to the 78.6% retracement on January 23, the day after the extreme low shown on the daily chart. A 60m DTosc momentum bullish reversal was made. Kerry's entry strategy was to go long one tick above the minor swing high at 1311.00 with a stop one tick below the minor swing low at 1269. (See Figure 8.17.) This is a very wide stop for a futures trade, so Kerry suggested traders might want to use the SPY ETF stock to limit the initial capital exposure.

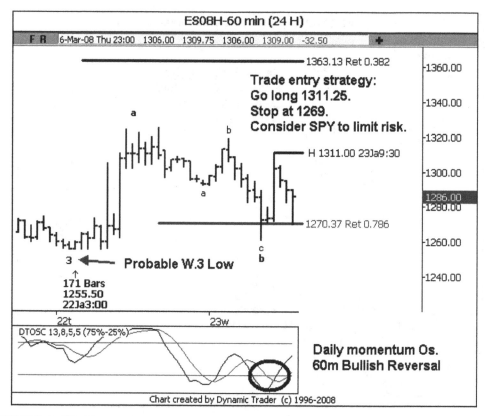

FIGURE 8.17 ES Entry Strategy

Trade Management

Kerry's initial strategy was to exit one unit if the ES reached 1360 (just below the 38.2% retracement) and exit the second unit at 1390 (just below the 50% retracement). Stops were adjusted as follows, as the trend progressed.

A two-unit long trade was executed at the 1311.25 buy-stop above the minor swing high with an initial protective sell-stop at 1269. (See Figure 8.18.) This is a wide stop for a futures trade, and Kerry recommended considering the SPY ETF stop for a much lower-risk trade for this setup. All futures traders should be prepared to trade a corresponding ETF for high probability trade setups that may have more initial capital exposure with a futures trade than is acceptable for your trading plan. Why waste all the hard work to identify trade setups just because the capital exposure may be too great for a highly leveraged trade?

Early the day after entry, Kerry recommended trailing the stop 10 points below the recent high, which placed the trade in at least a small profit if stopped out. Kerry recommended exiting one unit at 1360, which was reached near the end of the day. One unit was exited the following day at 1360 for a 38.75 point profit.

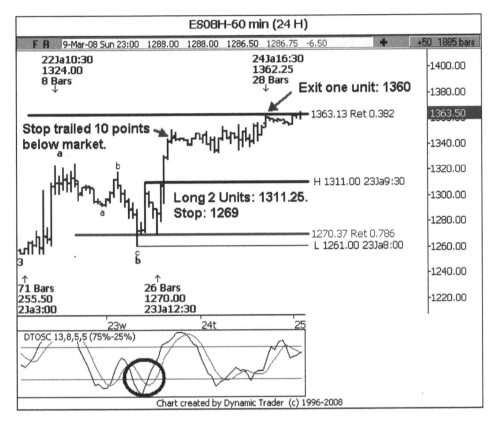

FIGURE 8.18 First Unit Trade Management

The morning of January 25, Kerry recommended moving the stop on the second unit up to 1356.25, one tick below a minor swing low. The ES did not immediately continue to advance to the 50% retracement, and the second unit was stopped out later in the morning for a 45 point profit. (See Figure 8.19.)

Trade Result: 83.75 points
Unit 1: 38.75 points ($1,937.50 per futures contract or 3.0 percent SPY)
Unit 2: 45 points ($2,250 per futures contract or 3.4 percent SPY)

Robert's Follow-Up

Kerry uses the 24-hour data. I generally only look at pit session data because the volume is so low overnight and there are often quick but meaningless swings and volatility overnight.

Kerry's initial target to exit one unit was the 38.2% retracement of Wave-3. Usually, the minimum expected retracement for a correction is 50% *except for a possible Wave-4* where the probable retracement is in the 38.2-50% Wave-3 retracement range. That is why

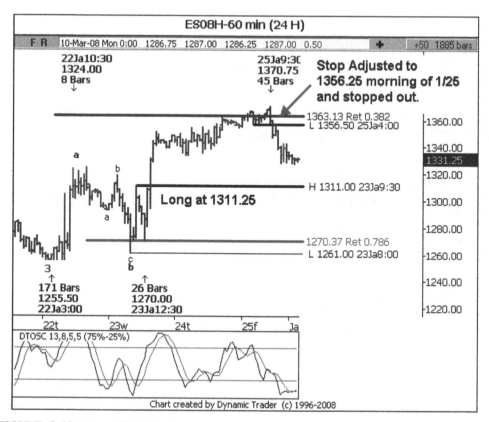

FIGURE 8.19 Second Unit Exit Strategy

Kerry prepared to exit one unit near the 38.2% retracement and the second unit near the 50% retracement.

While there was a relatively large capital exposure following trade entry, the stop was quickly adjusted to lock in at least a small profit as the ES shot up by the end of the day of entry. The stop on the second unit was brought close to the market to ensure a reasonable profit if stopped out.

The second unit was stopped out on the second day after the trade was entered, for a total of 83.75 points profit on the two units. Unit 1 made an unleveraged profit of 3.0% and unit 2 made 3.4 percent, for an average for a full position of 3.2%. Not bad for a two-day unleveraged trade.

DERRIK HOBBS (WARSAW, INDIANA)

Long Soybean Trade
Higher time frame: Weekly
Lower time frame: Daily

I first met Derrik around 2002 when I lived in Tucson, Arizona, and he was visiting our mutual friend, Larry Pesavento. Derrik had been a longtime Dynamic Trader software owner and subscriber to the DT Reports. Derrik later published his own trading book, *Fibonacci for the Active Trader* (TradingMarkets Publishing Group, 2004).

Derrik trades for his own account and advises on risk management and hedging strategies for farmers. I've re-created the charts he sent to me. The trade description and commentary are all his except my comments in parenthesis italics and in the "Robert's Comments" and "Robert's Follow-Up" sections.

The Setup for Long Soybean Trade: Possible ABC at Price and Momentum Support

In addition to my own trading, I work with many farming operations to develop risk management strategies and assist with hedging decisions for their crops. My analysis and recommendations are centered around the Dynamic Trading high probability strategies. My analysis considers five areas:

1. Wave analysis.
2. Two standard deviation regression channels.
3. Fibonacci price zones (where multiple extensions and retracement levels converge to form a support or resistance zone).
4. Candlestick charts.
5. DT Oscillator for momentum.

In the middle of April 2007, the November soybean contract was in the midst of a significant decline after spending much of the winter in a strong uptrend. Many producers/farmers began to get concerned that the ride was over, and fear was beginning to set in. I was receiving daily phone calls regarding the idea of just "... taking our profits and getting out before it gets real ugly."

After running my analysis, it was clear to me we were probably in a classic three-wave correction (A,B,C). I am especially partial to these corrections when Wave-C lands on the bottom of my uptrending regression channel. It looked like that may be the case with November 2007 soybeans as of mid-April. I also found a large number of Fibonacci price retracements and extensions that came together between $7.60 and $7.30. These support zones were right on the bottom of the regression channel. (See Figure 8.20.)

Robert's Comments   I've only included some of the key price projections Derrik provided on this chart, including the 61.8% and 78.6% internal retracements, 127% and 162% external retracements and the 100% alternate price projection of Wave-A from the Wave-B high. The most probable Wave-C target should be around 7.60, which includes one projection from each set, including the 61.8% internal retracement and 100% alternate price projection.

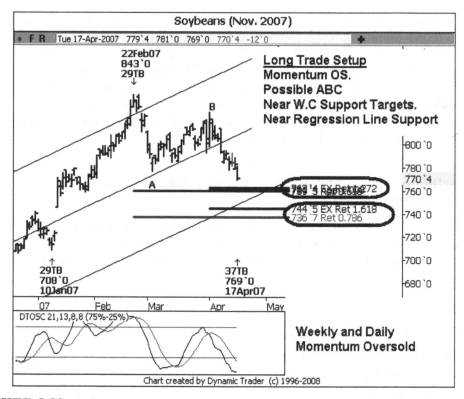

FIGURE 8.20   Soybean Long Position Trade Setup

As of April 17, the last daily bar on this chart, the weekly and daily momentum is oversold and price is not far above the regression support channel line. Regression channels are a key factor in Derrik's decision-making process, and you will see how well they may be included with the strategies taught in this book.

Trade Entry

In speaking with my farmers, I communicated that I would not be selling at these levels, but that I would be looking for an opportunity to buy and, in a farmer's case, simply hold off on any kind of hedging decisions. To confirm my analysis, I was looking for a DT Oscillator momentum bullish reversal. Once this occurred, I would go long even though my producers were nervously holding on to soybeans in their bins, praying that my analysis would be accurate.

On April 20 I got my entry signal with the DT Oscillator bullish reversal, only to find the market push down deeper into my Fibonacci support zone. *(Derrik went long at 767'25 on April 20 with an initial protective sell-stop at 743'75, which was a bit below the regression support channel line and several minor price projections he had made on his chart that I do not show on this one.)*

If I did not have the DT tools and education, I could have been shaken out of this trade, but I knew that price could play around in my Fib price support zone and regression support area and still be a valid setup, so I held tight.

My next round of phone calls came as the market decided to bounce up, as I had hoped. These new calls centered around one question "When do we sell?" My objective in a strong trending market is to take half the profits at the median of the regression channel and to take the rest of the profits at the top of the regression channel, which, as you will see, worked out very well for myself and the farmers I advise.

Trade Management

Beans bounced up out of the support zone and on May 8 made a swing low at 765, then three days later gapped up. I adjusted the stop to breakeven. I use structure like this to adjust stops. So now, barring any kind of gap-down event, I've gotten myself to breakeven on the position. (See Figure 8.21.)

The next spot I had an opportunity to move my stop was on May 30 when there was a two-day sell-off followed by a strong reversal so I moved my stop to the low on May 30

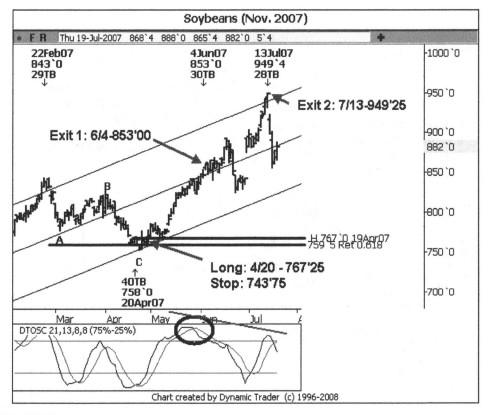

FIGURE 8.21 Trade Management

at 823. (*Note*: I require at least a two-day sell-off to consider a swing point low/structure point to move my stop.)

On June 4 I sold half of my position when it hit the regression median line, but still kept my stop on the other half down at 823, the last structural point.

As I said in my earlier comments, the regression median line is my first objective on these trades when I look to exit part of the position.

Once this objective is reached, I give the position a lot of breathing room because it tends to get bumpy/choppy around the median of a two standard deviation channel—and sure enough, that's what happened on this trade. From June 18 to June 22 we had a 68 cent sell-off, but I had left my stop down at the May 30 low and was within pennies of being stopped out of the trade. A gap up June 29 relieved those concerns.

When beans gapped up so hard on June 29 and consolidated for six days... it was my desire to place a stop below that six-day consolidation low if we got a break out to the upside. In this case, I got my wish and beans broke up from the six-day consolidation, so I moved my stop to the low of June 29 at 875.

Finally, four sessions after breaking out of that consolidation, beans hit my final objective at the top of the regression channel on July 13. As soon as we touched the two standard deviation ceiling I cashed in the position—and none too soon! (See Figure 8.22.)

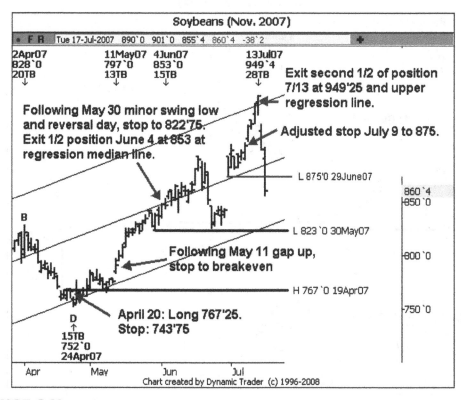

FIGURE 8.22 Trade Management Details

This was just one of those perfect trades where it seemed like nothing could go wrong, and my trailing stop methods of placing a stop below price structure worked like a charm. Many times when volatility picks up, the market will set up this structure only to take it out and stop my positions out. But staying consistent to this money management principle allows me to capture runaway market conditions like this—and I end up yielding small profits or small losses in choppy conditions with this stop strategy.

Trade Result:
Unit 1: $4,287.50 per contract
Unit 2: $9,100.50 per contract

Robert's Follow-Up

I don't think you can get a better example of "The big money is made with the big trends." This is another great example of how successful traders keep the stop far from the market and only make adjustments when specific market action warrants. Derrik uses market structure to make stop adjustments. What does he mean by *market structure*? He makes logical decisions based on the market activity including following gaps, minor swing lows, and consolidation breakouts. You can never know in advance what the market structure will be, so the specific trade management strategy may be changed as the trade progresses. A part of the trade management plan that is very objective is to take off part of the position at the regression median line and another part at the extreme of the regression channel.

Derrik was very candid that this was an ideal, trend trade where everything worked out nicely, but he often gets stopped out with less trending and more volatile and choppy markets for small profits or small losses. His objective is to be in and stay in a trade when a market makes a major trend. The same approach he uses for position trades can also be applied for shorter-term trades with intraday data.

CAROLYN BORODEN (SCOTTSDALE, ARIZONA)

ES (S&P Mini) Short Trade
Higher time frame: 15m
Lower time frame: 3m

Carolyn is a longtime friend who has her own intraday trade and chat room at www.FibonacciQueen.com and is the author of *Fibonacci Trading*. She has worked in the trading industry her entire adult life, starting as a phone clerk on the Chicago Mercantile Exchange as a teenager and including a short stint working for me in Tucson, AZ. in the early 90's.

She focuses on index futures markets and very short-term day trades where a 15m chart is long-term! Carolyn sent me a few charts of intraday trades for the day I contacted her. Her text description was brief, so I've recaptured the charts and added the text description that follows for the ES short trade for March 10, 2008.

The Setup for a Short Trade

Figure 8.23 is a three-minute chart of ES for Friday, March 7, through the morning of Monday, March 10. The ES had reached a major resistance area for a possible ABC high. Carolyn calls this a *two-step* pattern setup. The resistance area included three minor 100% APPs, the 127% Ext-Ret of the Wave-B, the 50% retracement from the March 7 high, and the 78.6% retracement from the March 10 early morning high. Carolyn calls these *symmetry setups* when several 100% alternate price projections make a very narrow-range zone.

Carolyn generally uses two types of entry triggers. One is a decline below a minor swing low, or a trailing one-bar-low, as you've learned in this book. Another is to enter on a Commodity Channel Index (CCI) indicator setup—in this case, when the 3m 14 CCI

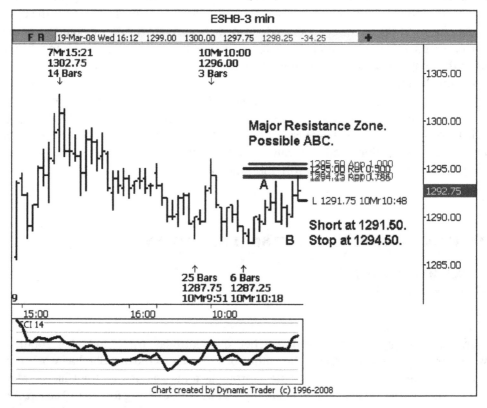

FIGURE 8.23 Day Trade Setup

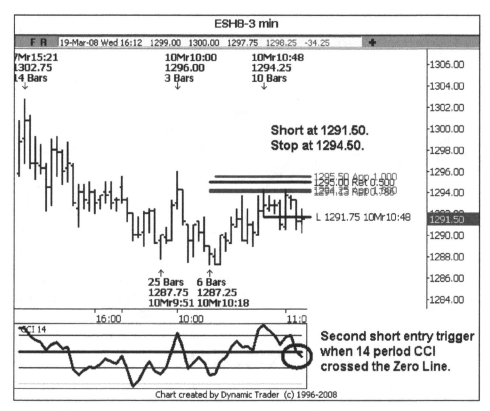

FIGURE 8.24 Day Trade Execution

crosses below the zero line. Carolyn uses the CCI indicator a great deal for entry/exit conditions. I have not described the CCI indicator in this book, but it is a common indicator and lots of information about it is available online or in other trading materials. Carolyn describes her CCI setups and triggers in detail in her book, *Fibonancci Trading: How To Master The Time and Price Advantage.*

Trade Execution and Exit Strategy

Figure 8.24 adds several more 3m bars of data through the trade entry. The 1291.75 one bar low was taken out to execute the short trade with a stop at 1294.50, one tick above the recent high. The ES later advanced to trade at the 1294.25 swing high but did not reach the stop, and later declined. The 3m CCI 14 soon crossed the zero line for the alternate entry two ticks below the 1291.50 trailing one-bar-low entry.

Figure 8.25 shows the data through the trade exit. The ES almost immediately declined sharply and reached the 100% alternate price projection about an hour later. The exit buy-stop was placed one tick above the one-bar-high at 1281.75 and stopped out on

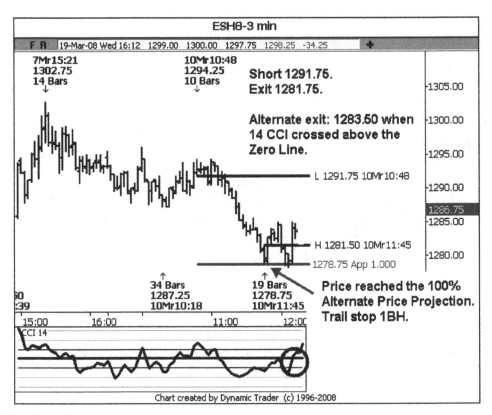

FIGURE 8.25 Day Trade Exit Strategy

the next bar. The alternate exit was when the 3m CCI 14 crossed above the zero line a few bars later.

Trade Result
No multiple unit exits
10 points or $500 per contract

Any Market, Any Time Frame

Carolyn did not provide a strategy for multiple unit exits with her example. She also admitted that not all of her intraday trades are in a 10-point profit position in less than an hour! However, you do often get fast moves once an intraday corrective high or low is complete, especially on the short side. Carolyn relies mostly on just time and price targets to identify highs and lows for entry and exit setups with the CCI often the trigger to execute the trade. It is important to note that the general trade plan is the same whether trading a larger time frame weekly/daily data or very short-term day trades like this example.

USD/CAD Short Trade
Higher time frame: Daily
Lower time frame: 60m

Jaime Johnson splits his time between Bogata, Columbia, and Encinitas, California. He has been trading for about eight years. The past few years his trading has focused on Forex swing trades. He is well grounded in the high probability trade strategies taught in this book, as he is also the chief technical analyst for our DT Reports. Jaime rarely looks at a time frame less than 60 minutes for his Forex trades. Jaime has also produced a comprehensive Forex trading course called *No BS Forex Trading*, available from Dynamic Traders Group.

The trade description is Jaime's with my comments in parenthesis italics and in the "Robert's Follow-Up" section.

The Setup: Higher Time Frame Daily Trend Bearish, Short Trade on 60m Bearish Momentum Reversal

The higher-degree time frame (13) daily DTosc *(momentum)* was bearish and the January 22 high was in the position to be a multiday corrective high.

The January 22 low was in the position to be a minor Wave-1 or A low and the January 23 high was in the position to be a minor Wave-2 or B high. (See Figure 8.26.) In either case, at least a short-term decline for a day or two was likely. Following the (34) 60-minute DTosc bearish reversal, I entered a two-unit short position at 1.0233 on January 24. The protective buy-stop was placed at the pip spread plus five pips above the January 23 Wave-2 or B high at 1.0328.

When the 100% APP of the January 22, Wave-1 or A decline was reached *(1.0145)*, the typical Wave-C price target, I trailed the protective buy-stop for one of the short units 10 pips above the market. I also adjusted the protective buy-stop for the second unit to breakeven. The first unit was stopped out at 1.0119 for a profit. *(First unit trade result: 114 pip profit.)*

Second Unit Trade Management

As the USD/CAD continued to decline, the pattern had more impulsive *(trend)* characteristics than corrective. More than likely the decline was not just an ABC correction but a bear trend that typically has at least five sections. Once the January 24 Wave-3 low was taken out, the protective buy-stop for the remaining short unit was adjusted to a few pips above the January 28 Wave-4 high. (See Figure 8.27.)

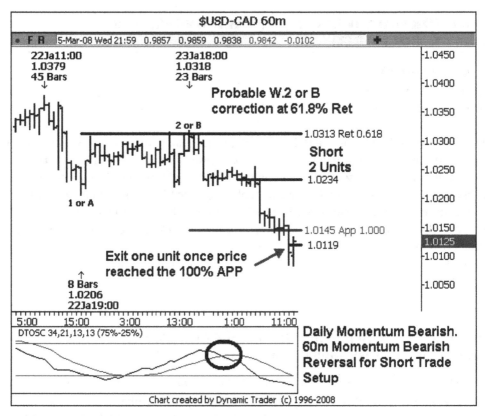

FIGURE 8.26 USD/CAD Short Trade Setup and First Unit Exit Strategy

Stop-Loss Adjustment

Once Wave-5 appeared to be subdividing in a five-wave pattern, the protective buy-stop continued to be adjusted to a few pips above a minor swing high. Once the January 30 low was in the pattern position to be a Wave-5:5 (Wave 5 of 5) low and the higher degree (13) daily DTosc was bear OS, I adjusted the protective buy-stop to a few pips above the 0.9972 prior minor swing high and the second short unit was eventually stopped out at 0.9980 for a 245 pip profit. (See Figure 8.28.)

Trade Result: 359 pips profit
Unit 1: 114 pips profit
Unit 2: 245 pips profit

Robert's Follow-Up

The first chart in this example labeled the first two swings off the January 22 high as a Wave-1 or A and Wave-2 or B. Jaime did not have an opinion if the CAD/USD was making

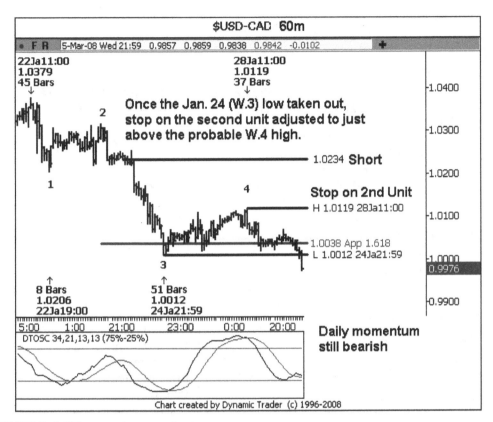

FIGURE 8.27 Second Unit Trade Management

an ABC (or other type) of correction or beginning a bear trend. In either case, the setup was for a probable continued decline to complete a Wave-C or a Wave-3. Jaime took profit quickly on one unit, just after the market reached the 100% alternate price projection. If the CAD/USD was only making an ABC or other type of correction, this would be a typical price target. The stop on the second unit was also moved to breakeven when the short-term unit was stopped out. Even if the market reversed up sharply, at least a small profit would be secure for the two-unit trade.

The CAD/USD continued sharply lower and didn't make a short-term low until reaching the 162% alternate price projection, which is a typical Wave-3 target. The daily momentum was still bearish and not OS, so more than likely the trend would continue lower. Jaime did not adjust the stop closer to the market until the January 22 potential Wave-3 low was taken out. This is another example of the difference between experienced and inexperienced traders. The stop-loss was kept relatively far from the market activity until there was a logical technical reason to adjust the stop.

As the CAD/USD continued to decline from the January 28, probable Wave-4 high, Jaime then adjusted the stop-loss more frequently to just above each minor swing high. On January 30, the CAD/USD reached a major retracement (78.6%) and minor Wave-5:5

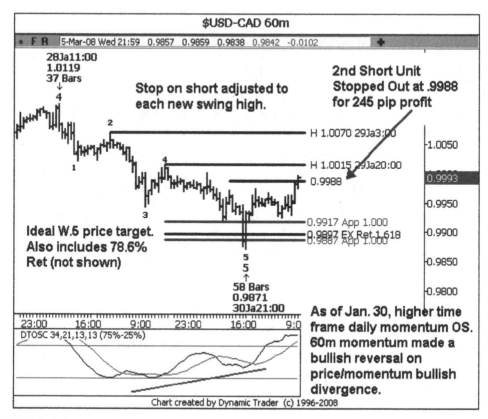

FIGURE 8.28 Second Unit Exit

price target, plus the higher time frame daily momentum was oversold. The CAD/USD was in a position to complete a five-wave trend, and Jaime then trailed the protective buy-stop on the second short unit closer to the market. The trade was stopped out on January 31 for a 245 pip profit on the second unit.

Each trade management action was taken as a logical consequence to the price, pattern, and momentum position of the market as it unfolded. During this period, the CAD/USD appeared to be making textbook E-wave structures, which were helpful to identify the trend position. This is not always the case and is not necessary to make trading decisions, but it is helpful to recognize the probable pattern position if one is being made.

CHAPTER SUMMARY

In this chapter, you've seen trades from a variety of markets and time frames by traders from around the world who have learned the high probability trading strategies taught in this book. The traders varied from relatively new to those with years of experience.

Some of the traders used technical indicators not described in this book. Each had a bit different trade plan, but all of the trade management strategies were based on a logical application of the strategies taught in this book.

Many other trade examples were submitted that unfortunately could not be included because of space limitations. Check our web site periodically at www.highprobability tradingstrategies.com for more student and current trade examples for an ongoing trading education.

CHAPTER 9

The Business of Trading and Other Matters

Trading is a business like any other business.

To be successful at any business or profession takes knowledge and experience. Like every other business, traders must have a plan of how they will use information to make decisions and mange their business.

Trading is no different than any other business. I'm always amazed and frustrated that so many new traders who have taken the time to master and become successful at another business or profession think that trading is different. They throw out all the rules of success and believe they can quickly and easily learn to trade and it will be the path to riches. Trading takes time to learn and master like any other business. You must gain the knowledge and experience, develop a trading plan, test, evaluate and review to constantly improve, just like any other business. The beauty of trading is you can gain the knowledge and experience without much capital risk. You have the opportunity to trade unleveraged markets with a small account and small risk as you learn to trade. Few other businesses offer this opportunity.

Give yourself the opportunity for success. Treat trading like any other business.

ROUTINES AND TRADING RECORDS

How much time you have to spend each day for your trading business depends on your trading time frame and how many markets you consider trading. If you are a day trader, you may be sitting in front of the monitor(s) five or six hours a day making quick decisions. If you're a swing trader (doing trades that typically last a few days) making decisions based on intraday data, you should only have your attention on the markets once they meet the minimal conditions for a trade. You may only have to put in an hour or two a day in front of the monitor. If you're a position trader making decisions based on monthly, weekly, and daily data, you should only have to spend 30 minutes or so each evening scanning the data and charts for potential setups, or a bit more time if you are a stock/ETF trader and following a lot of markets.

Whatever time frame you trade, the routine is the same. The day begins with a list of markets that are at or near the initial trade conditions. Once the initial conditions are met, entry orders are placed. If a trade is executed and you're not stopped out at the initial stop, the trade is monitored according to your trade plan and stop-loss decisions are made as the trade progresses. The routine is the same regardless of whether you are day-trading off 15- and 5-minute bars or position-trading off weekly and daily bars.

A very important key routine, even if you are a day trader, is to do most of your analysis and preliminary decision making outside of market hours. There are few decisions that a swing or position trader makes on a daily basis for any one market because there is not that much new information each day for trades lasting a few days to a few weeks. But even day traders should start the day with a plan by identifying which markets have the best potential for trade setups that day.

Every consistently successful trader keeps records of all trades with at least brief notes of why the trade was considered, how it was executed, and the trade management plan. The record keeping may be as brief or as detailed as suits you, but you must track your trade activities. The monthly brokerage statement of trades is not enough. This statement only lists trades but doesn't provide any information about why and how you got in and out.

I used to keep a very detailed journal with a form I made up in Excel to list all the details of the market conditions for considering the trade, the entry strategy, and how the trade was managed, including notes on every stop-loss adjustment. Each form included a copy of the chart when the trade was entered and at least one additional chart with data through the trade exit. This journal has evolved to a simpler format, partly because my trade plan and the information I need to make a trading decision has become much simpler over the years.

My trade plan has evolved from very detailed and complex Gann, Elliott, chart geometry, time, and price strategies to much more simple strategies as outlined in this book. Today, I make notes right on the chart and print a copy when a trade is made. I may make additional handwritten notes right on the chart printout. If I'm not stopped out at the initial protective stop, I may make another one or two chart prints as the trade progresses, to note significant decision-making periods. I put the charts with notes in a three-ring binder and have a complete log to review each trade.

It is fast and easy to record trades this way. Fast and easy means it will get done, and all of the relevant information is recorded. Detailed and complex means it probably won't get done on a regular basis. I strongly suggest you develop a trade recording process that suits your temperament. By that I mean one that you will do in a timely manner on a consistent basis that includes all the relevant information needed to review the trade at a later date.

If you are a very short-term day or swing trader, you may need only a single chart with appropriate notes that you print when the trade is complete. Your trading software should have the ability to make notes right on the chart or have a dropdown note function. All you have to do is hit the print button when the trade is made, maybe make a few quick notes on the printed chart, and at the end of the day you have a complete trade record.

There are some software programs available for trade record keeping. You might check them out to see if they are suitable for you. I've found that printing a chart with notes right on the chart printout is suitable for me, but you may want an even more organized and detailed record that a trade record software may provide.

You should periodically review your trading activity. This is simply good successful business practice. A short-term trader will review at least once a week. A swing or position trader may only make a comprehensive review once a month. Whatever method you devise to track and record your trades, you should be able at a later time, even years later, to pull up the information and know why and how the trade was entered and the trade management strategy from entry to exit for all of the trades.

One of the key differences between a successful and unsuccessful trader is that *every* successful trader has a trade record-keeping system to track and record trades with comments, and most unsuccessful traders do not. You don't have a choice in this matter. Record, review, and evaluate. Good trade record keeping does not ensure success, but I believe a lack of it does ensure failure. If you want to have the chance of being successful, keep good records.

> *All consistently successful traders have a trade record keeping system with enough information to review a trade from entry to exit at any time.*

WHY TRADERS WIN OR LOSE

I believe there is one primary reason traders are not successful: They lack a trade plan. *All consistently successful traders have a written trade plan. Most unsuccessful traders do not have a written trade plan.* A trade plan does not guarantee success, but lack of one guarantees failure.

A trade plan outlines the process and information needed to make a decision. Without a trade plan, decisions are not made on a consistent basis based on a consistent approach to act on relevant information. A trade plan does not have to be a long list of detailed rules that each market must abide by before a trade is placed. But your trade plan should include at least the minimum conditions that must be met before a trade is considered, objective entry strategies, and narrow guidelines as to how the trade will be managed through trade exit.

Throughout this book, you have learned all of these factors to develop a trade plan. You have learned that dual time frame momentum setups are one way to identify the minimum conditions to consider a trade. You have learned specific, objective entry strategies once the minimum conditions to consider a trade have been met. You have learned how to identify time, price, pattern, and momentum conditions to adjust stops to manage the trade through the exit. As a trade progresses, you will have to make decisions, but the decisions should be made in the context of the market position, not some arbitrary fear or greed factor that is not related to the original reasons the trade was made.

Some readers will be asking, "Why don't you just give us a trade plan?" There are a couple of reasons. First, you probably wouldn't follow it. You would second-guess the objective rules and make unwarranted assumptions when decisions needed to be made.

It is very difficult to follow someone else's plan. A few years ago, I trained for and participated in several adventure races over a two-year period. The adventure races were mostly nonstop 24 hours and included mountain biking, trail hiking/running, kayaking, rappelling, and land navigation. They were brutal. I read several books on endurance training and understood the key training principles. I hired an endurance trainer over several months to make a training plan for each day to work on developing my biking and running endurance. Each weekend I received an e-mail with the next week's training plan. Did I follow the plan exactly every day? No. The plan was a good guideline of what to work on, but many days I varied the plan to suit my current condition. The training plan kept me focused. I worked within the principles of the plan but some days made variations depending on how I felt that day. The trainer's plan was a key to improving my performance, but I think I progressed more or at least kept more motivated and interested in the training by making some changes. In other words, I used the trainers plan as a guide to develop my own plan. It is very difficult to follow another person's plan.

Second, you may want to begin with a more rigid and objective plan than a plan I would suggest. A more objective plan may result in fewer setups that meet your more objective rules and guidelines but may also result in a higher rate of successful trades. This is usually the trade-off with more rules: Fewer trades are entered, but often the fewer number of trades have a higher rate of success. As you gain more experience, you may broaden the rules and guidelines to allow you to apply your added knowledge to the decision-making process.

Prior chapters have given you all the information you need to develop a trade plan and make decisions when necessary. Let's review the major elements of every trade plan to guide you to making your own specific plan.

Key Trade Plan Elements

1. *Objective minimum trade setup conditions.* What are the objective minimum conditions that must be met to consider a trade? I believe the dual time frame momentum setups you learned in this book are the best objective conditions to identify potential trades that should be a part of your trade plan. The key is that the dual time frame setups are logical and objective. They work. The dual time frame momentum conditions are the best trade filter I've discovered in over 20 years.

2. *Nonobjective setup conditions.* Pattern, price, and time position should be considered for a trade setup. These can be objective or subjective conditions. Have the minimum pattern conditions been made to imply that a correction or trend could be complete? Has the market reached a typical price and/or time target for a correction or trend reversal to be made? There are decisions to be made, but the decisions are within very narrow guidelines, as you have learned in previous chapters.

3. *Objective entry strategy.* I have a very firm belief that once the conditions for a trade setup have been made, the entry strategy should be objective. In other words, there are no more decisions to be made as to how and at what price to execute the trade and place the initial protective stop. You have learned two objective entry strategies in this book, the momentum reversal and the swing breakout. They are all you need.

4. *Trade management/exit strategy.* How are you going to manage the trade through the exit? Here is where most of your trade decisions will be made. You could make this part of your plan highly objective, such as trail the stop on one unit at the trailing 1BL/H following the first smaller time frame momentum reversal against the larger time frame trend. Or trail the stop on one unit if the market reaches the 100% alternate price projection. These would be objective exit strategies that will serve you well.

   However, to maximize your knowledge and experience, you should consider the price, time, and pattern position as part of your trade management strategy. This is where decisions will have to be made depending on specific conditions as a market progresses. You have learned from the trade examples in prior chapters, including those of the traders featured in Chapter 8, that the trade management plan may change as a trend progresses and a market provides new information.

   A very important part of trade management is to always trade at least two units, exiting one unit on short-term conditions and holding a second unit for higher time frame conditions. Consider an objective exit strategy for the short-term unit, and a strategy based on decisions made according to the market position as the trade progresses for the larger time frame unit.

These are the four elements to any trade plan. In the trade examples in previous chapters, you have learned all you need to know to develop your own trade plan and make decisions based on these four elements. The CD examples will demonstrate more trades from entry to exit based on a trade plan following these four principles.

Don't be fooled into believing that you can buy success, that you can follow another person's trade plan step-by-step, or buy a trade system and be successful. You will only be successful if you gain the knowledge and experience and develop your own trade plan that includes these four elements just described.

Every successful trader has a written trade plan. Most unsuccessful traders do not.

TECHNOLOGY, TRADING TIME FRAMES, MARKETS TO TRADE, AND LEVERAGE

What time frame has the best potential for trading profits? Which markets are the best to trade?

The trend in the past 10 years or so is for shorter-term trading, particularly day-trading with high leverage. Not many years ago the trading time frame for most traders, including highly leveraged futures traders, was from a few days to a few weeks or months. Today we would call that *swing* or *position* trading. Until at least the early 1990s, real-time data was very expensive, commissions were relatively high, computers were expensive, and there were very few real-time trading software programs available. All that changed rapidly by the mid-1990s.

When I began trading in the early 1980s, very few traders had software charting programs. Most of us made our charts on grid paper that we bought from blueprint shops, or updated a charting service booklet of markets that we received each week or two by mail. I also remember sitting at the brokerage office and making 15-minute charts each day by updating my intraday chart booklet every 15 minutes.

Trades were not placed with an online trading platform with instant fills. We called the broker with the order, the broker called his representative, the order eventually got filled, and we got a call back with the fill price. The fill price was often a few ticks away from the market at the time of the trade decision due to the lag between dialing the broker and the order being filled. We got all of this great service for as much as $100 per futures contract!

We now have very inexpensive real-time data with one-minute charts if we like, with all kinds of choices of fabulous trading software and instant order execution for about $3.00 a trade for a futures contract and a penny a share for stocks. We can make dozens of trades a day if we want. We can leverage up to 100:1 with some Forex accounts. How times have changed with the wondrous technology advancements. Are a higher percentage of traders successful today than in the pre-online trading days? Probably not. I suspect even a lower percentage are successful than in the old, hand-charting days!

You are probably aware of the statistics that 70% or more (by some accounts it's closer to 90 percent-plus) of traders lose most or all of their trading capital within months. I don't have any hard statistics, but after more than 20 years of teaching trading and talking with brokers, that percentage has probably not gotten any better in recent years. I've talked with brokers who (confidentially) say more than 95% of their accounts lose money and are closed out within six months. The new technology, software, and real-time data services have not resulted in more successful traders. The new technology only provides more information faster. Traders must still learn how to use that information to make decisions.

Leverage has both very positive and very negative ramifications. If you're on the right side of the market, leverage will multiply profits greatly. If you're on the wrong side of the market, it can clean you out very quickly. For every yin, there is a yang.

Read this very carefully: *If you can't make money with unleveraged trades, you'll never make money with leveraged trades.* If you are not a consistently profitable trader in your leveraged futures, Forex, or stock account, why not learn to trade with unleveraged markets where the cost to gain the experience and to develop a trading plan should be very minimal? There are ETFs and mutual funds that track most of the major financial markets, including all the major stock indexes, bonds, gold and currencies, and even some commodities. You can take small positions as you gain experience and develop a trading plan. Once you develop a plan and gain experience and become profitable with the unleveraged trades, you can then apply your knowledge, experience, and trading plan to leveraged futures, Forex, and margined stocks.

You don't have to have a large account or take large risks to learn how to trade and develop a trading plan. It's true, you are not going to make a lot of money with a small account and unleveraged trades. You are also not going to lose a lot as you learn. The learning process can be costly with leveraged trades. Until you have developed a consistently successful trading plan that is profitable on a regular basis, your objective is not to make money but to *learn to trade.* That may sound odd, saying that your objective is not to make money, but that's the way it is. Once you have learned to trade, the money follows. There is absolutely no reason to take big risks until you have learned to trade successfully.

Are you interested in trading futures stock indexes like the ES Mini (S&P mini futures contract)? Trade the SPY ETF until you are consistently profitable, and then move on to the leveraged futures contract. Want to trade Forex? Forget 100:1 leverage until you have learned how to trade. Most of the major currency pairs have an ETF you can trade until you have learned how to trade successfully. *If you can't make money trading unleveraged, you will never make money trading leveraged.* It is that simple. This is a clear distinction between someone who is serious about learning how to trade and someone who thinks trading is a get rich quick activity.

I realize that day-trading has become very appealing in recent years, with all the new inexpensive technology: Get in and out quickly. Take your profit or loss quickly. Don't hold a position overnight. Minimize your exposure. It sounds enticing, but I believe the odds of being successful are stacked much higher against the day trader than the swing or position trader, at least until you have learned to trade. Something alters your discipline, beliefs, organization, and decision-making ability when you are watching a screen all day with the intraday bars building tick by tick. It is extremely difficult to remain disciplined, stick to a trading plan, and make logical, sound decisions with very short-term day trades.

I strongly encourage traders who are interested in day-trading to first develop a trading plan and experience with swing and position trading, preferably with unleveraged trades, before attempting to day-trade.

If you can't make money with unleveraged intermediate-term trades using weekly and daily data, you are going to get cleaned out fast making short-term trades with highly leveraged markets.

TRADE FOR POINTS, NOT FOR TICKS

One of the big drawbacks to day-trading is the profit potential is limited. Day traders trade for ticks, not for points. There is only so much movement in one day which means there is only so much profit potential. To make enough money to cover your trading expenses (software, data, education, etc.) by day-trading, you have to trade size. It is hardly worth your time and expense day-trading just two or three futures contracts, even if you have a very high win rate.

I believe day-trading provides the least return for your time and investment of any time frame of trading. At the least, even if you are a successful day trader, also consider longer-term positions that last from a few days to a few weeks to capture the longer-term trends with a potential for greater rewards. Put your knowledge and experience to work for greater profit potential. W. D. Gann taught, "The big money is made in the big trends." New traders should consider this truth carefully. Trade for points, not for ticks.

YOU CAN'T BUY SUCCESS

Sometimes I'm almost ashamed to be associated with the business of educating traders and developing trading software because the business is rife with outright scammers making promises and insinuating you can quickly and easily learn to get rich fast trading. You've seen the ads: Learn the "secrets" of Wall Street or the professional traders, and make a killing. You've seen the charts in ads with the little buy and sell arrows where every trade is a big profit; or the ads that claim hundreds of percent return if only you follow their system or subscribe to their advisory report; or the trading software (usually very expensive) that will supposedly give you the buy and sell signals for consistently profitable results. If you subscribe to any trading publication or surf some of the trading sites on the Web, I know you've seen a lot of these outlandish promises. You've probably taken the bait on a few of them and spent a lot of money with little or no results. You're not the only one. I've been a sucker myself, especially in the early years. I guess it's part of the learning process we all go through when we're learning something new and actually think there are some secrets we can quickly learn to put us on the road to riches.

Beware of any promoter making unrealistic claims. It's just common sense, which unfortunately our fear and greed drives out of our consciousness now and then. There are a lot of good trading educators. Some have been around for years and have a lot of experience trading and teaching traders. The legitimate trading educators never make unrealistic claims. In fact, I don't believe I've ever seen an ad or promotion by a legitimate trading educator that make a results-based claim. They know the best they can do is teach you whatever they have become good at. How and if you apply the knowledge is up to you.

The more knowledge and experience you gain, the quicker you will be able to discern what should be legitimate and useful information as opposed to having your chain pulled.

I've said it several times throughout this book and I'll say it again just to be sure you get the point: *You can't buy success.* You've got to earn it through education and experience.

YOU *CAN* BE A SUCCESSFUL TRADER

You know the odds are stacked against you being a successful trader. You've read the statistics from many sources about how a very high percentage of traders drop out or go bust after just a few months. But you do not have to be one of them.

If you apply yourself to learn to trade, you can be successful. Go about it in a businesslike manner. Study, evaluate, review, develop a trading plan and gain experience. Don't make the mistake of most new traders and overtrade with too large a risk for your account size. Consider trading unleveraged markets until you have developed a trading plan and tested it out in real time. While I can't make any promises or guarantees, if you apply the strategies you've learned in this book I believe you will have great success.

If you are already an experienced, successful trader, incorporate the strategies taught in this book into your trading plan and your results should improve, maybe dramatically.

Visit www.highprobabilitytradingstrategies.com for free updated trade examples and to learn more about the trade strategies taught in this book.

Best wishes and successful trading,

Robert Miner

More Bar-by-Bar Entry to Exit Trade Examples

T here were many more trade examples I wanted to include in the book and video CD but couldn't due to space limitations. Use passwords found in this book referred to on our web site to access ongoing education for book owners only including:

More trade examples by Robert, his students and book readers
Online tutorials and trade commentary
More strategies not taught in the book
Book owner forum and message boards
And lots more

For this and much more reader-only content, visit the book companion site, www.HighProbabilityTradingStrategies.com. Would you like a free month of one of our DT Daily Reports? Join us to register.

Glossary

The Glossary is in two sections. The first section is arranged alphabetically. The second section is arranged by chapter. Both sections include the same definitions.

GLOSSARY—ALPHABETICALLY

ABC (simple) correction A frequent correction pattern of three swings where the third swing (Wave-C) exceeds the extreme of the first swing (Wave-A). Also called a zigzag. A three-swing correction may also be an irregular ABC where the Wave-C does not exceed the extreme of the Wave-A. The time and price targets to complete a three-section ABC correction are very predictive. The assumption is always that a correction will make at least three sections.

alternate price projection (APP) Compares the price range of swings in the same direction. The most frequently used percentage alternate price projections are 62 percent, 100 percent, and 162 percent. Sometimes called *price extensions* by other authors and in some software programs. The principle is that the price range of a section is often one of the key APP ratios of recent sections. An APP is made from three pivot points. The price range between two pivots is measured and projected from a third pivot.

alternate time projection (ATP) Compares the time range of swings in the same direction. The most frequently used percentage alternate time projections are 62 percent, 100 percent, and 162 percent. The principle is that the time range of a section is often one of the key ATP ratios of recent sections. An ATP is made from three pivot points. The time range between two pivots is measured and projected from a third pivot.

bear, momentum When a momentum indicator is negative. In a two-line indicator, the fast line is below the slow line. A basic part of the high probability strategy is to trade in the direction of the momentum. Only short trades would be considered if the momentum is bearish unless the momentum is bear OS.

bear OS, momentum When an indicator is bearish and has reached the oversold (OS) zone. With a two-line indicator, the fast line is below the slow line and both lines have reached the oversold zone. In most cases, bear OS momentum warns that the downside should be limited before a momentum low and probable price low is made.

bearish reversal, momentum   When momentum changes from a bullish to a bearish trend. With two-line indicators, when the fast line crosses below the slow line. A momentum bearish reversal is often a setup for a short trade or to exit a long trade.

bull, momentum   When a momentum indicator is positive. In a two-line indicator, the fast line is above the slow line. A basic part of the high probability strategy is to trade in the direction of the momentum. Only long trades would be considered if the momentum is bullish unless the momentum is bull OB.

bull OB, momentum   When an indicator is bullish and has reached the overbought zone. With a two-line indicator, the fast line is above the slow line and both lines have reached the overbought zone. In most cases, bull OB momentum warns that the upside should be limited before a momentum high and probable price high is made.

bullish reversal, momentum   When momentum changes from a bearish to a bullish trend. With two-line indicators, when the fast line crosses above the slow line. A momentum bullish reversal is often a setup for a long trade or to exit a short trade.

capital exposure   The amount of capital (money) that may be lost if a trade moves against the initial position. In other words, the potential cost to find out if the trade decision will be profitable or not. Often called *risk*. The initial capital exposure per unit is the difference between the entry price and the initial protective stop price.

complex correction   Any correction with more than three sections (waves). The form of a complex correction cannot be predicted in advance. The time and price targets for a complex correction are not as easily identified in advance as for a simple ABC correction.

countertrend   A correction against the main trend. The assumption is always that a correction will make at least three sections. An important part of a trading plan is to identify the possible end of a correction in order to place a trade in the direction of the trend.

day trader   A very short-term trader who is usually glued to the monitor during market hours and enters and exits a trade during one trading day. The odds of success are very small unless the day trader has first perfected a consistently profitable trading plan for swing or position trades.

Dual Time Frame Momentum Strategy   See *Multiple Time Frame Momentum Strategy*.

dynamic ratios   A series of geometric and harmonic ratios used for Dynamic Time and Price Strategies, including .382, .50, .618, .786, 1.00, 1.272, 1.618, and 2.618. The uniqueness of the Dynamic Time and Price Strategies as taught in this book is that different ratios are used for time or price analysis. Plus the ratios are applied in unique ways depending on whether the market is making a trend or a correction.

E-wave   Elliott wave pattern analysis. See *Elliott wave*.

Elliott wave (E-wave)   Pattern analysis approach developed by R. N. Elliott. The idea is that trends and corrections are usually made in a limited number of patterns that conform to rules and guidelines that help distinguish if the section is part of a trend or correction. One of the most important values of Elliott wave pattern analysis is to help recognize if a market is in a position to complete a trend or correction. Trends are usually made in five distinct sections. Corrections should be at least three sections but may evolve into much more complex structures.

end-of-wave (EOW) price and time targets　A unique Dynamic Time and Price Strategy approach to project in advance the high probability time or price targets to complete a trend or correction. In this book, the EOW targets for a simple ABC and a five-wave trend are taught.

entry strategy　The strategy to determine the entry conditions and specific entry and initial stop-loss prices. The entry strategies recommended in this book are completely objective once the trade conditions have been met. The two recommended entry strategies in this book are the momentum reversal trailing one-bar-high (low) and the swing breakout.

exit strategy　The conditions to exit an open trade. The exit strategy must be determined before the trade is entered. The exit strategy may be completely objective, such as trailing the stop at the one-bar-high/low following a momentum reversal. Or the exit strategy may be more subjective and adjusted as a market progresses. Even if the exit strategy is more subjective, the objective of the trade and general conditions to consider exiting the trade should be defined in advance. See trade examples in Chapters 7 and 8 for how exit strategies are adjusted as a market progresses and provides new information.

Fibonnacci (Fib) ratios　See *dynamic ratios*.

impulse trend　An Elliott wave term for a five-section trend. Since many trends are complete with five waves, the trader should always be alert for the end of a trend if a market is making a fifth wave.

lookback period　The number of bars an indicator looks back to calculate the current indicator value. A relatively short lookback period will result in an indicator being relatively sensitive to recent price volatility and trends. A relatively long lookback period will result in the indicator being relatively slow to change.

momentum indicator　Most price-based indicators are also called momentum indicators. In most cases, the momentum indicator represents the rate-of-change over the lookback period. The rate-of-change may reflect whether the trend of the market is speeding up or slowing down compared with prior trends. Momentum does not always trend in the same direction as the price trend.

momentum reversal trailing one-bar-high/low entry strategy　Following a smaller time frame momentum reversal in the direction of the larger time frame momentum, the entry price is trailed one tick above/below the last completed bar. The entry price is adjusted with each new bar if the trade has not been executed, as long as the smaller time frame momentum has not made another reversal in the opposite direction. If the trade entry order is executed, the initial protective stop is placed one tick below/above the swing low/high made prior to entry. The principle is that the trade is only entered if the market takes out a bar high or low in the direction of the trade.

Multiple Time Frame Momentum Strategy　A strategy to place trades only when at least two time frames of momentum are in the same direction, such as weekly and daily or daily and 60m. The basic strategy is to trade in the direction of the larger time frame and execute the trade following a smaller time frame momentum reversal in the direction of the larger time frame momentum. Can use more than two time frames of momentum. (See Dual Time Frame Momentum Strategy Rules in text for bull OB and bear OS exceptions.)

multiple-unit trading   Every trade should be taken with at least two units. The exit strategy is different for each unit. One unit is considered short-term and is exited if the market reaches a minor corrective target. The second unit is considered long-term and is exited at a trend target. A multiple-unit trade plan should increase net profitability over time.

oscillator indicators   Usually used interchangeably with *momentum indicator*.

outlier   When determining the cycle ranges, an outlier is a time range that is much longer or shorter than the other ranges. The outlier ranges may be not be included when determining the cycle ranges.

overbalance (of time and/or price)   A term coined by W.D. Gann when the time and/or price of a correction is greater than the time and/or price of prior corrections. Warns that the larger time frame trend may be reversing for either a higher time frame correction or a new trend in the opposite direction.

overbought (OB)   An indicator level, usually expressed as a percentage of the minimum to maximum range of possible indicator values, that represents when an indicator is at a relatively high level, usually around 70 to 80 percent. For many indicators, if they reach an overbought level, the upside in price should be limited before a price high is made.

overlap guideline   If a market trades back into the range of the previous section, it has overlapped that section. This important guideline warns that the market should be making a correction and not a new trend.

oversold (OS)   An indicator level, usually expressed as a percentage of the minimum to maximum range of possible indicator values, that represents when an indicator is at a relatively low level, usually around 20 to 30 percent. For many indicators, if they reach an oversold level, the downside in price should be limited before a price low is made.

position size   The number of trading units (contracts, shares, lots) for the trade. The *maximum* position size should represent capital exposure of no more than 3 percent of the account. (See Chapter 6 for how to calculate maximum position size.)

position trader   Trades longer-term trends lasting from several days to several weeks. Trades for points, not for ticks. A successful position trader will probably make more money over time for the same capital and risk as a roomful of successful day traders—that is, if you could find enough successful day traders to fill a room. Most of the legendary traders of the past century have been position traders. "The big money is made in the big trends." (W. D. Gann) A position trader rarely if ever monitors the market during trading hours.

price/momentum bearish divergence   When price makes a new high but the momentum indicator makes a lower high. Warns that the advance is slowing down and a price high may soon be made, followed by a decline.

price/momentum bullish divergence   When price makes a new low but the momentum indicator makes a higher low. Warns that the decline is slowing down and a price low may soon be made, followed by an advance.

retracement, external price (Ex-Ret)   Retracements greater than 100 percent. The most frequently used percentage external retracements are 127 percent, 162 percent, and 262 percent. Mostly used to help identify the price target for the final section of a correction or trend such as a Wave-C of an ABC correction or a Wave-5 of a five-wave trend.

retracement, internal price (In-Ret)   Retracements less than 100 percent. The most frequently used percentage internal retracements are 38.2 percent, 50 percent, 61.8 percent, and 78.6 percent. Used to help identify the price target of a correction. Most corrections end at or very near one of the four key internal retracements. Chapter 4 teaches how to use other price techniques to qualify in advance which In-Ret is likely to be the end of a correction.

risk   In trading, usually refers to the amount of money that may be lost if a trade moves against the initial position. A more proper definition is the probability of an event occurring. Also see *capital exposure.*

risk/reward   The amount of money at risk versus the potential reward. Usually shown as a ratio such as 3:1, which is really the reward to risk, or $3 potential profit for $1 risk (capital exposure). The risk per unit can be defined by the difference between the entry price and initial protective stop price. The reward is always just a best guess of the probable minimum move the market is likely to make.

swing breakout entry strategy   Once the conditions for a trade are made, initiate a go-long or go-short entry at a price one tick above/below the recent swing high or low. Place the initial protective stop-loss one tick below/above the swing high or low made prior to entry. The principle is that the conditions for a reversal or trend continuation have been met and the trade is entered as the market moves above/below a swing high or low in the anticipated trend direction.

swing trader   Trades market swings that typically last two to three days or more. Has a much better chance for success than a day trader. Trades for points, not for ticks. May need to monitor the market during trading hours.

system, trading   A set of completely objective rules that determine the exact entry, stop-loss, and exit prices. Also called mechanical trading. "You can't buy success." To my knowledge, no trading system has been sold that has been consistently profitable in real-time trading over time. Instead of buying a system, give the system cost and your trading account to the charity of your choice. Put your money to good use rather than blowing it on a futile endeavor.

Time Band   In a bull trend, the overlap of the recent high-high cycle range and the recent low-high cycle range. If the recent time cycle rhythm continues, the assumption is the next high will be made in the Time Band (overlap) range. Outliers may be eliminated when measuring the L-L or L-H ranges. In a bear trend, the Time Band is the overlap of the recent low-low and high-low time ranges.

time retracement (TR)   Compares the time range of a corrective section to the prior trend section. The most frequently used TR ratios are 38.2 percent, 50 percent, 61.8 percent, 100 percent, and 162 percent. Simple ABC corrections are usually complete in the 38.2 to 61.8 percent time retracement range. Complex corrections are usually complete by the 100 percent time retracement of the prior trend section.

trade management   The general term for how each trade is managed from entry to exit.

trade plan   The plan as to how the business of trading will be conducted, including conditions for entry, entry to exit strategies, maximum capital exposure, and trade management. Every successful trader has a trade plan. See Chapter 9 for the four key elements of a trade plan.

trailing one-bar-high/low Once the conditions for entry have been met, including the smaller time frame momentum reversal, a go-long or go-short entry is trailed one tick above/below the high/low of the previous bar. Used on all time frames of data.

trend The main price direction. The side of the market you want to trade. Trends are often complete in five sections, also called an Elliott wave impulse trend.

GLOSSARY BY CHAPTER

The terms with no specific chapter reference are given first, followed by the terms specific to each chapter.

capital exposure The amount of capital (money) that may be lost if a trade moves against the initial position. In other words, the potential cost to find out if the trade decision will be profitable or not. Often called *risk*. The initial capital exposure per unit is the difference between the entry price and the initial protective stop price.

day trader A very short-term trader who is usually glued to the monitor during market hours and enters and exits a trade during one trading day. The odds of success are very small unless the day trader has first perfected a consistently profitable trading plan for swing or position trades.

Fibonnacci (Fib) ratios See *dynamic ratios* (Chapter 4).

overbalance (of time and/or price) A term coined by W. D. Gann when the time and/or price of a correction is greater than the time and/or price of prior corrections. Warns that the larger time frame trend may be reversing for either a higher time frame correction or a new trend in the opposite direction.

position trader Trades longer-term trends lasting from several days to several weeks. Trades for points, not for ticks. A successful position trader will probably make more money over time for the same capital and risk as a roomful of successful day traders—that is, if you could find enough successful day traders to fill a room. Most of the legendary traders of the past century have been position traders. "The big money is made in the big trends." (W. D. Gann). A position trader rarely if ever monitors the market during trading hours.

risk In trading, usually refers to the amount of money that may be lost if a trade moves against the initial position. A more proper definition is the probability of an event occurring. Also see *capital exposure*.

swing trader Trades market swings that typically last two to three days or more. Has a much better chance for success than a day trader. Trades for points, not for ticks. May need to monitor the market during trading hours.

Chapter 2 Multiple Time Frame Momentum Strategy

bear, momentum When a momentum indicator is negative. In a two-line indicator, the fast line is below the slow line. A basic part of the high probability strategy is to trade in the direction of the momentum. Only short trades would be considered if the momentum is bearish unless the momentum is bear OS.

bear OS, momentum   When an indicator is bearish and has reached the oversold (OS) zone. With a two-line indicator, the fast line is below the slow line and both lines have reached the oversold zone. In most cases, bear OS momentum warns that the downside should be limited before a momentum low and probable price low is made.

bearish reversal, momentum   When momentum changes from a bullish to a bearish trend. With two-line indicators, when the fast line crosses below the slow line. A momentum bearish reversal is often a setup for a short trade or to exit a long trade.

bull, momentum   When a momentum indicator is positive. In a two-line indicator, the fast line is above the slow line. A basic part of the high probability strategy is to trade in the direction of the momentum. Only long trades would be considered if the momentum is bullish unless the momentum is bull OB.

bull OB, momentum   When an indicator is bullish and has reached the overbought zone. With a two-line indicator, the fast line is above the slow line and both lines have reached the overbought zone. In most cases, bull OB momentum warns that the upside should be limited before a momentum high and probable price high is made.

bullish reversal, momentum   When momentum changes from a bearish to a bullish trend. With two-line indicators, when the fast line crosses above the slow line. A momentum bullish reversal is often a setup for a long trade or to exit a short trade.

Dual Time Frame Momentum Strategy   See *Multiple time Frame Momentum Strategy.*

lookback period   The number of bars an indicator looks back to calculatethe current indicator value. A relatively short lookback period will result in an indicator being relatively sensitive to recent price volatility and trends. A relatively long lookback period will result in the indicator being relatively slow to change.

Multiple Time Frame Momentum Strategy   A strategy to place trades only when at least two time frames of momentum are in the same direction, such as weekly and daily, or daily and 60-minute. The basic strategy is to trade in the direction of the larger time frame and execute the trade following a smaller time frame momentum reversal in the direction of the larger time frame momentum. Can use more than two time frames of momentum. (See Dual Time Frame Momentum Strategy Rules in text for bull OB and bear OS exceptions.)

momentum indicator   Most price-based indicators are also called momentum indicators. In most cases, the momentum indicator represents the rate-of-change over the lookback period. The rate-of-change may reflect whether the trend of the market is speeding up or slowing down compared with prior trends. Momentum does not always trend in the same direction as the price trend.

oscillator indicators   Usually used interchangeably with *momentum indicator.*

overbought (OB)   An indicator level, usually expressed as a percentage of the minimum to maximum range of possible indicator values, that represents when an indicator is at a relatively high level, usually around 70 to 80 percent. For many indicators, if they reach an overbought level, the upside in price should be limited before a price high is made.

oversold (OS)   An indicator level, usually expressed as a percentage of the minimum to maximum range of possible indicator values, that represents when an indicator is at a relatively low level, usually around 20 to 30 percent. For many indicators, if they reach an oversold level, the downside in price should be limited before a price low is made.

price/momentum bearish divergence When price makes a new high but the momentum indicator makes a lower high. Warns that the advance is slowing down and a price high may soon be made, followed by a decline.

price/momentum bullish divergence When price makes a new low but the momentum indicator makes a higher low. Warns that the decline is slowing down and a price low may soon be made, followed by an advance.

Chapter 3
Practical Pattern Recognition for Trends and Corrections

ABC (simple) correction A frequent correction pattern of three swings where the third swing (Wave-C) exceeds the extreme of the first swing (Wave-A). Also called a zigzag. A three-swing correction may also be an irregular ABC where the Wave-C does not exceed the extreme of the Wave-A. The time and price targets to complete a three-section ABC correction are very predictive. The assumption is always that a correction will make at least three sections.

complex correction Any correction with more than three sections (waves). The form of a complex correction cannot be predicted in advance. The time and price targets for a complex correction are not as easily identified in advance as for a simple ABC correction.

countertrend A correction against the main trend. The assumption is always that a correction will make at least three sections. An important part of a trading plan is to identify the possible end of a correction in order to place a trade in the direction of the trend.

E-wave Elliott wave pattern analysis. See *Elliott wave*.

Elliott wave (E-wave) Pattern analysis approach developed by R. N. Elliott. The idea is that trends and corrections are usually made in a limited number of patterns that conform to rules and guidelines that help distinguish if the section is part of a trend or correction. One of the most important values of Elliott wave pattern analysis is to help recognize if a market is in a position to complete a trend or correction. Trends are usually made in five distinct sections. Corrections should be at least three sections but may evolve into much more complex structures.

impulse trend An Elliott wave term for a five-section trend. Since many trends are complete with five waves, the trader should always be alert for the end of a trend if a market is making a fifth wave.

overlap guideline If a market trades back into the range of the last section, it has overlapped that section. This is a important guideline that warns the market should be making a correction and not a new trend.

trend The main price direction. The side of the market you want to trade. Trends are often complete in five sections, also called an Elliott wave impulse trend.

Chapter 4 Beyond Fib Retracements

alternate price projection (APP) Compares the price range of swings in the same direction. The most frequently used percentage alternate price projections are 62 percent, 100 percent, and 162 percent. Some times called *price extensions* by other authors and in some software programs. The principle is that the price range of sections is often one of the key APP ratios of recent sections. An APP is made from three pivot points. The price range between two pivots is measured and projected from a third pivot.

dynamic ratios A series of geometric and harmonic ratios used for Dynamic Time and Price Strategies, including .382, .50, .618, .786, 1.00, 1.272, 1.618, and 2.618. The uniqueness of the Dynamic Time and Price Strategies as taught in this book is that different ratios are used for time or price analysis. Plus the ratios are applied in unique ways depending on whether the market is making a trend or a correction.

end-of-wave (EOW) price and time targets A unique Dynamic Time and Price Strategy approach to project in advance the high probability time or price targets to complete a trend or correction. In this book, the EOW targets for a simple ABC and a five-wave trend are taught.

retracement, external price (Ex-Ret) Retracements greater than 100 percent. The most frequently used percentage external retracements are 127 percent, 162 percent, and 262 percent. Mostly used to help identify the price target for the final section of a correction or trend, such as a Wave-C of an ABC correction or a Wave-5 of a five-wave trend.

retracement, internal price (In-Ret) Retracements less than 100 percent. The most frequently used percentage internal retracements are 38.2 percent, 50 percent, 61.8 percent, and 78.6 percent. Used to help identify the price target of a correction. Most corrections end at or very near one of the four key internal retracements. Chapter 4 teaches how to use other price techniques to qualify in advance which In-Ret is likely to be the end of a correction.

Chapter 5 Beyond Traditional Cycles

alternate time projection (ATP) Compares the time range of swings in the same direction. The most frequently used percentage alternate time projections are 62 percent, 100 percent, and 162 percent. The principle is that the time range of sections is often one of the key ATP ratios of recent sections. An ATP is made from three pivot points. The time range between two pivots is measured and projected from a third pivot.

dynamic ratios A series of geometric and harmonic ratios used for Dynamic Time and Price Strategies, including .382, .50, .618, .786, 1.00, 1.272, 1.618, and 2.618. The uniqueness of the Dynamic Time and Price Strategies as taught in this book is that different ratios are used for time or price analysis. Plus the ratios are applied in unique ways depending on whether the market is making a trend or a correction.

end-of-wave (EOW) price and time targets A unique Dynamic Time and Price Strategy approach to project in advance the high probability time or price targets to complete a trend or correction. In this book, the EOW targets for a simple ABC and a five-wave trend are taught.

outlier When determining the cycle ranges, an outlier is a time range that is much longer or shorter than the other ranges. The outlier ranges may be not be included when determining the cycle ranges.

Time Band In a bull trend, the overlap of the recent high-high cycle range and the recent low-high cycle range. If the recent time cycle rhythm continues, the assumption is that the next high will be made in the Time Band (overlap) range. Outliers may be eliminated when measuring the L-L or L-H ranges. In a bear trend, the Time Band is the overlap of the recent low-low and high-low time ranges.

time retracement (TR) Compares the time range of a corrective section to the prior trend section. The most frequently used TR ratios are 38.2 percent, 50 percent, 61.8 percent, 100 percent, and 162 percent. Simple ABC corrections are usually complete in the 38.2 to 61.8 percent time retracement range. Complex corrections are usually complete by the 100 percent time retracement of the prior trend section.

Chapter 6 Entry Strategies and Position Size

entry strategy The strategy to determine the entry conditions and specific entry and initial stop-loss prices. The entry strategies recommended in this book are completely objective once the trade conditions have been met. The two recommended entry strategies in this book are the momentum reversal trailing one-bar-high (low) and the swing breakout.

momentum reversal trailing one-bar-high/low entry strategy Following a smaller time frame momentum reversal in the direction of the larger time frame momentum, the entry price is trailed one tick above/below the last completed bar. The entry price is adjusted with each new bar if the trade has not been executed, as long as the smaller time frame momentum has not made another reversal in the opposite direction. If the trade entry order is executed, the initial protective stop is placed one tick below/above the swing low/high made prior to entry. The principle is that the trade is only entered if the market takes out a bar high or low in the direction of the trade.

position size The number of trading units (contracts, shares, lots) for the trade. The *maximum* position size should represent capital exposure of no more than 3 percent of the account. (See Chapter 6 for how to calculate maximum position size.)

swing breakout entry strategy Once the conditions for a trade are made, initiate a go-long or go-short entry at a price one tick above/below the recent swing high or low. Place the initial protective stop-loss one tick below/above the swing high or low made prior to entry. The principle is that the conditions for a reversal or trend continuation have been met and the trade is entered as the market moves above/below a swing high or low in the anticipated trend direction.

trailing one-bar-high/low Once the conditions for entry have been met, including the smaller time frame momentum reversal, a go-long or go-short entry is trailed one tick above/below the high/low of the previous bar. Used on all time frames of data.

Chapter 7 Exit Strategies and Trade Management

exit strategy The conditions to exit an open trade. The exit strategy must be determined before the trade is entered. The exit strategy may be completely objective, such as trailing the stop at the one-bar-high/low following a momentum reversal. Or the exit strategy may be more subjective and adjusted as a market progresses. Even if the exit strategy is more subjective, the objective of the trade and general conditions to consider exiting the trade should be defined in advance. See trade examples in Chapters 7 and 8 for how exit strategies are adjusted as a market progresses and provides new information.

multiple-unit trading Every trade should be taken with at least two units. The exit strategy is different for each unit. One unit is considered short-term and is exited if the market reaches a minor corrective target. The second unit is considered long-term and is exited at a trend target. A multiple-unit trade plan should increase net profitability over time.

risk/reward The amount of money at risk versus the potential reward. Usually shown as a ratio such as 3:1, which is really the reward to risk or $3 potential profit for $1 risk (capital exposure). The risk per unit can be defined as the difference between the entry price and the initial protective stop price. The reward is always just a best guess of the probable minimum move the market is likely to make.

trade management The general term for how each trade is managed from entry to exit.

trade plan The plan as to how the business of trading will be conducted, including conditions for entry, entry to exit strategies, maximum capital exposure, and trade management. Every successful trader has a trade plan. See Chapter 9 for the four key elements of a trade plan.

Chapter 9 The Business of Trading and Other Matters

system, trading A set of completely objective rules that determine the exact entry, stop-loss, and exit prices. Also called mechanical trading. "You can't buy success." To my knowledge, no trading system has been sold that has been consistently profitable in real-time trading over time. Instead of buying a system, give the system cost and your trading account to the charity of your choice. Put your money to good use rather than blowing it on a futile endeavor.

trade plan The plan as to how the business of trading will be conducted, including conditions for entry, entry to exit strategies, maximum capital exposure, and trade management. Every successful trader has a trade plan. See Chapter 9 for the four key elements of a trade plan.

Bibliography

Armstrong, Martin A. *The Greatest Bull Market in History*, vol. 1 & 2 . Princeton Economics, 1986.

Belveal, L. Dee. *Charting Commodity Market Price Behavior*. Traders Press, 2000.

Boroden, Carolyn. *Fibonacci Trading: How to Master the Time and Price Advantage*, McGraw Hill, 2008.

Burnham, Terry. *Mean Markets and Lizard Brains*. John Wiley & Sons, 2005.

Chande, Tushar S., and Stanley Kroll. *The New Technical Trader*. John Wiley & Sons, 1994.

Elder, Dr. Alexander. *Come Into My Trading Room*. John Wiley & Sons, 2002.

———. *Entries and Exits: Visits to Sixteen Trading Rooms*. John Wiley & Sons, 2006.

Gann, W. D. *How to Make Profits in Commodities*. Lambert Publishing Company, 2003.

———. *45 Years in Wall Street*. Lambert Publishing Company, 2002.

———. *Truth of the Stock Tape and Wall Street Stock Selector*. Lambert Publishing Company, 2003.

Hobbs, Derrik S. *Fibonacci for the Active Trader*. Trading Markets, 2003.

Johnson, Jaime S. *No BS Forex Trading*. No BS Traders Publishing, 2008.

Kelly, Fred. *Why You Win or Lose: The Psychology of Speculation*. Fraser Publishing Co., 1962.

LeFèvre, Edwin. *Reminiscences of a Stock Operator*. John Wiley & Sons, 1994.

Longstreet, Roy W. *Viewpoints of a Commodity Trader*. Traders Press, 1978 (reprint).

Merrill, Arthur A. *Behavior of Prices on Wall Street*. Analysis Press, 1984.

———. *Filtered Waves*. Analysis Press, 1977.

Miner, Robert. *Dynamic Trading*. Traders Press, 1997.

Paul, Jim, and Brendan Moynihan. *What I Learned Losing a Million Dollars*. Infrared Press, 1994.

Pesavento, Larry, and Leslie Jouflas. *Trade What You See*. John Wiley & Sons, 2007.

Plummer, Tony. *The Psychology of Technical Analysis*. Kogan McGraw-Hill, 1993.

Prechter, Robert R. Jr., ed. *The Major Works of R. N. Elliott*. New Classics Library, 1980.

———. *Pioneering Studies in Socionomics*. New Classics Library, 2003.

———. *The Wave Principle of Human Social Behavior*. New Classics Library, 1999.

————. *R. N. Elliott's Market Letters (1938–1946)*. New Classics Library, 1993.

Rogers, Jim. *Investment Biker*. Random House, 1994.

Shiller, Robert J. *Irrational Exuberance*, 2nd ed. Princeton University Press, 2005.

Sklarew, Arthur. *Techniques of a Professional Commodity Chart Analyst*. Commodity Research Bureau, Inc.,

Williams, Bill. *New Trading Dimensions*. John Wiley & Sons, 1998.

About the Author

Since 1986, Robert Miner has been one of the leading educators for practical trade strategies for the financial, futures, forex and stock markets. Through his live, online, and recorded workshops and home study educational programs, he has taught traders and investors in over 30 countries his unique approach to technical analysis and trading strategies.

Robert is a first-place winner of the annual real-time trading contest sponsored by one of the leading U.S. brokerage firms and has been named Guru of the Year by the *Supertraders Almanac*. His DT Daily Stock/ETF Report has been rated number one for S&P timing of all published advisers tracked by *Timers Digest*. His first book, *Dynamic Trading* (Dynamic Traders Group, Inc., 1999), was named the 1999 Trading Book of the Year.

In 1989, Robert published *The W. D. Gann Home Study Trading Course* (no longer available), one of the first complete self-study trading courses in contemporary times. In recent years, Robert has produced several multimedia, home-study trading courses, including the *Dynamic Trading E-Learning Workshop*, incorporating multimedia interactive and accelerated learning techniques.

Robert Miner's company, Dynamic Traders Group, Inc., publishes the DT Daily and Just-In-Time Reports for the futures, forex, and stock/ETF markets. He developed the Dynamic Trader Software trading program to more quickly and accurately produce the analysis necessary for his unique momentum, time, price, and pattern trade strategies.

In the past 20 years, Robert has become one of the world's leading trading and investing analysts, educators, and technical analysis software developers. His products and services are often praised by traders and investors as the key to their success.

To learn more, go to www.HighProbabilityTradingStrategies.com.

Index